Adventures of

Alistair McAlpine

ALLEN&UNWIN

To Athena
With all my love

First published in 2002

Allen & Unwin
83 Alexander Street
Crows Nest NSW 2065
Australia
Phone: (61 2) 8425 0100
Fax: (61 2) 9906 2218
Email: info@allenandunwin.com
Web: www.allenandunwin.com

National Library of Australia
Cataloguing-in-Publication entry:

McAlpine of West Green, Alistair, Lord, 1942–.
Adventures of a collector.

ISBN 1 86508 786 6.

1. McAlpine of West Green, Alistair, Lord, 1942–. 2. Art—Collectors and collecting—Great Britain—Biography. 3. Antiques—Great Britain—Biography. 4. Collectors and collecting—Great Britain—Biography. I. Title.

709.2

Set in 11.5/13.5 pt Goudy by Midland Typesetters
Printed and bound by Griffin Press, South Australia

10 9 8 7 6 5 4 3 2

Contents

Foreword

Stephen Fay

I left the great collector a couple of months ago among his bead collection in Venice. In shallow troughs in each of the trays on the table in his study he was assembling necklaces. As he threaded them, Alistair talked of opening a bead museum in Venice. Beads sound more like a room in a museum—until you see the quantity he has collected already. There are thousands of beads in four broad and deep drawers, as well as in the trays. Some specimens from West Africa are so heavy that the chiefs who wore them as necklaces had collars made especially to support their weight.

The news on the Rialto the previous day was that Alistair's bead merchant had received a new consignment. The merchant has a shop in the Frezzeria, which lies between the Piazza San Marco and La Fenice theatre. The beads, many of which were originally made in the glass factories on the neighbouring island of Murano, come in parcels. These are random packages, and Alistair sifted through them looking for individual beads that he could add to a necklace he had begun to thread together.

He made his selection and, as he was about to leave the shop, spied a heavy Indian silver bracelet, and decided he would have that too. The proprietor was simultaneously familiar and respectful. In turn, Alistair was purposeful and fond. Good dealers know him as a rewarding customer, willing to exchange gossip as well as spend. He prefers them to be honest, as this merchant is; though if there is something he covets he can be as wily as any artful antique dealer. Though Alistair is in his late fifties, he has been collecting for almost half a century, since he was entranced by the Pitt Rivers Museum in Oxford—not far from Henley, where he grew up.

The bead collection is part of Alistair's Venetian period; he is, of course, collecting the city. This period coincided with the Australian period. There he collected Aboriginal art, early Australian furniture and the work of Sir Sidney Nolan, publishing books about the furniture and Nolan. When he recovers from the irritating heart condition that has confined him to a hospital in Harley Street for a few weeks, the Venetian period will resume. Unfortunately, collecting Australiana seems to have come to an end. He has sold the pearl farm and the pearl masters' houses in Broome in Western Australia. His absence will subtract from the gaiety of a whole continent.

Alistair is an instinctive teacher; one of his shrewdest lessons was learned in Australia. His interest in pearls developed when he became a partner in a pearl farm manufacturing brilliant South Sea pearls north of Broome. He became a friend of Nick Paspaley, Australia's leading pearling master, and one day Paspaley asked if he would like to see a few pearls he had put on one side. Alistair told the story in his column:

> He drew a bag from the safe and spilled the pearls on a velvet tray . . . The quality was truly incredible. One specimen brought to mind the parable of the pearl of great price (*St Matthew*, Chapter 13, you will recall). I have always known that feeling; finding something for which I would sell everything. It is the symptom by which a true collector can be recognised. This pearl was pear-shaped, 15 millimetres in diameter and Nick Paspaley called its colour strawberry, but to me it appeared at first to be coloured pure gold, and then changed before my eyes to pale pink. Every time I moved it between my fingers, the colour changed. I asked if I could buy it.
>
> Paspaley took it, looked it over and slipped it back into its bag before returning it to his safe.
>
> 'How can you price a pearl like this? This pearl has no price,' he said.
>
> 'No price; no deal.'

For myself, I am a dedicated collector of Alistair McAlpine. This wise story of unfulfilled yearning is one of my favourites.

Introduction

Near the edge of Plympton, a small town in Devon, stood a row of Victorian cottages. That was in the late 1950s when I last visited Plympton. Perhaps Plympton is a large town now and these cottages have been torn down to make way for a concrete town hall or some other municipal building. I do not know, and it does not matter a lot, for the most interesting features of these buildings were their inhabitants.

The Andrade family has, I am certain, long since died. I arrived at their home one day just before lunch. I was shown into their kitchen and offered refreshments. I cannot recall what the younger member of that family, or indeed his wife, looked like, but I do recall their old uncle, who sat wrapped in a rug. I was introduced to him as a young man interested in arms and armour, and he to me as a great scholar on the subject of armour. The Andrades were general dealers in the old sense, and supplied most of the antique trade in the west of England from their row of cottages called Borgia Villas. These cottages were filled with every conceivable type of antique and there was one room that I remember as if I stood there today, a room filled with Staffordshire pottery. Most of it dated from the mid-nineteenth century, and there was in this room a large quantity of dross, but among it great rarities. You purchased the first pieces that came to hand (you could not choose only the good or reject the bad). There was no other way, as the pottery was packed so tightly that only the pieces at the front were accessible. There was no place to stand the pieces that you pulled out in order to be able to compare them, one with the other. You bought the pottery as it came or not at all.

My life has been a little like that room. I have had a mass of experiences—some pleasant, some sad and many downright inconvenient at the time. In the spring of 1987 I began to write about them. Slowly one memory jogged another, and pieces from my past were uncovered, like the pottery from the Andrade's cottage. Some experiences were only fragments, some complete, and some commonplace, some rare—to me at least. So this book began. I had intended to start this introduction with the words 'I am a collector'. Then, as I thought about that statement, I realised how misleading it would be. True, I have collected items as diverse as snowdrops and chickens, police truncheons and paintings by the American abstract impressionists. I collect, I suppose, to learn; for I have never collected to possess. When a collection passes from my hands it goes in total—nothing remains, no momento. No object or painting has such beauty that I could not bear to part with it. Wander around my home and you will find little evidence of past enthusiasms. My true collection is in my mind, helped by a notebook, phrases spoken to me, a description of a room, a meal, a rare plant, a journey, the tales of travellers and travel. Slowly, over many years, this collection has accumulated.

It began in early childhood, for my mother was strongly of the view that the only proper form of education was that gained by travel. We travelled extensively, mostly by boat, in the last days of the great ocean liners, or by train—when railway trains offered a real service and air travel was still a primitive affair. I recall the amazement of my family (we always travelled as a family) when the steward on board a Viscount belonging to British European Airways explained to us that the plane was so stable that you could stand a half-crown on its edge—minutes later the aircraft hit an air pocket and coffee cups were thrown up to the ceiling and showered down their contents on all the passengers. I loved the railway stations and docks, the bustle and departure—it is in my blood, and I have no doubt that that desire to travel accounted for my wanderings in Britain searching for a particular painting or book. Barely a weekend passed that I did not scour the flea markets or travel to discover what goods the country dealers had bought that week. In the same way that I sat in the Andrades' kitchen and listened to their old uncle as he spoke about armour, so I have listened to the tales of a thousand dealers over the years—from Bond Street in London to Perth in Western Australia. And now these memories have become my stock-in-trade.

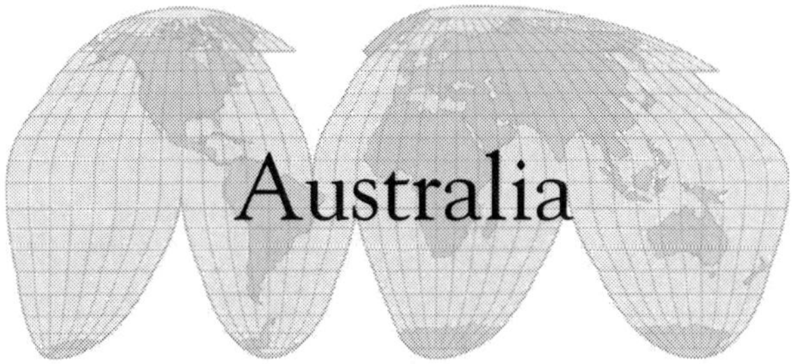

Australia

Down but not under

For Perth in Western Australia, once a boom city, the ball is temporarily over—but in 1992 antipodean optimism and sheer hard work can surely set the band playing again.

Towards the end of the 1950s I arrived on the SS *Oriana* at the port of Fremantle. Since then I have returned with great regularity to Australia, during which time I have conducted a love affair with that continent. We have flirted with each other: outrageously flirted with constancy found in few marriages; married, however, we never were. Always there was a reason for my pulling back and returning to my roots in England. Deserting my love, but never forgetting. Perth, the city where I spent most of my time, has many names, including the boom city and the most isolated city in the world. The state of Western Australia also has many names: the state of excitement, the wild flower state, the Cinderella state and the state that turned corruption into an art form. When I look back at Perth as I first found it, the history of the following years is hard to believe. At first times were good for Western Australia and Perth, and then as times changed, so also did they.

Perth in Western Australia, a state the size of Western Europe, is one of the most isolated cities in the world. There is little but desert between it and most of Australia's population in the south-east. It is nearly 35 years since I first visited the city, arriving by ship at the port of Fremantle. The great liner's decks were crowded with migrants:

migrants who had left so little and arrived to expect so much, their white skins burned red by the Indian Ocean's sun. They walked towards the immigration officers, who were seated behind desks. The migrants dragged their children by the arm as they looked around, and carried their world in a basket. A lone piper stood and played as the passengers came ashore. This was Australia, the lucky country, where now the luck has run out. The 'Golden West': that is what these people had been told by those paid to persuade them to travel there. The Cinderella state, that is what those who lived and worked there called Western Australia. But Cinderella did go to the ball, and what a ball those 35 years has been.

In those days Perth was barely a city; it was more like a big farming town. You expected to see cattle and drovers in the main street, an elegant street, with buildings of the 1930s, seldom more than three or four storeys high, built in the soft yellow Doneybrook stone not unlike that of Bath in England. At the end of Perth's elegant and comfortable main street stood a fortress known as the Barracks, a fortress that looked for all the world like a child's toy castle. In those days you never saw a police officer; crime was, as a citizen of Perth might say, 'rare as hen's teeth'. If you saw a girl standing on a street corner late at night (and you often did), she was there waiting for a bus, and at night the buses ran at long intervals.

The best restaurant was called Luis, and it is still there. In those days it was decorated with printed colour reproductions of the great paintings by Degas, Monet and Renoir—'I am told that these pictures,' said my host, 'are extremely valuable.' The food was awful and the pictures imitation—the proprietor of Luis knew little about French art or cooking. The citizens in those days all seemed to be big men, well over six feet tall, with heads like shopping baskets and faces burned brown. They wore grey suits and brown fedoras, looking at you from under wide brims that made no attempt to hide their eyes. Then things began to change in the 1980s. The movers and shakers took over from the tall men; they were short and fat, with bald heads, and if they wore a hat, it was a yachting cap. Their suits were blue, too bright a blue, with too much silken thread in the weave—shiny men. The America's Cup came and Perth became a party; the state changed the slogan on its car plates from 'The Wild Flower State' to 'The State of Excitement'. It was a small city, but the whole world now knew about Perth. This was where the tycoons came from; this was where the deals were done.

In the old days, the Swan River flowed along the very edge of the town, but the planners soon fixed that. They filled in its peaceful bays and built a motorway that curls like a tortured snake. To ease the pain of this motorway they planted gardens in between its coils, with little bridges and little ponds, and then a grateful government gave the planner who did all this the Order of Australia. Where once the architects of Western Australia benefited from their isolation and built small new buildings in scale with their town, they now started to read the glossy architectural magazines and build glossy buildings and, like the proprietor of Luis restaurant, they could not get it quite right. Now in the depths of recession the emptiness of these buildings stares through shiny glass that once reflected the greed of those who owned them. Their piazzas, empty of people, have concrete pots and windswept trees; the main street, once-beautiful St Georges Terrace, is a wind-filled canyon and the toy castle has gone.

The luck seems to have gone as well, but Australia is built on bankruptcy. There is an endless supply of optimistic Australians waiting to take over where others failed, and nowhere more than in Western Australia, for the west is a hard country and her people hardened by her; as fast as a shop fails, a restaurant or café opens. The whole population seems to have given up shopping and taken up eating. There can be nowhere with so few people and so many restaurants. Not adorned with the plush paint and velour of the past, these new places are decorated with whatever comes to hand, and all the better for it. This city, for all its changes, again has the feel of the 1960s; the citizens still play bowls dressed in their whites, and the peppermint trees still stand in the suburb of Peppermint Grove. The lucky country? Oscar Wilde said, 'Success is entirely due to luck, ask any failure.' The people of Western Australia are learning that the ball is over—Cinderella is back in the kitchen and luck comes only with effort.

The wisdom of Oz

Pearls of wisdom from a walkabout with a sizzling ending.

In the last year of the 1970s I travelled to Broome—a journey that changed my life. A man born in the year of the horse can be expected to undertake many differing forms of employment at the same time, but not in my wildest dreams did I ever expect to be a pearl farmer or, for that matter, a zoo keeper. In Broome I met and became the friend of a variety of people, none so unusual, however, as Snowy County.

The momentous events in Eastern Europe in the late 1980s and the black comedy of people collecting lumps of the Berlin Wall seemed very remote to me as I walked down Cable Beach in Broome, the most north-westerly point of Australia, where people collect old bottles and very remarkable seashells instead. The first overland telegraph reached the coast at Broome. The only bank robbery in the town's history was carried out by a man on a bicycle, and the fire station burned to the ground because the firemen could not get into the station to get out the fire engine. The smell is of frangipanis and tropical blooms in the town, and the sea and the bush along the 15-mile (24-kilometre) beach. The main tourist attraction is the Japanese graveyard where generations of pearl divers are buried, most of them killed in the course of their work. Pearls, diamonds and cattle are found here, and it is one of the world's last great unexplored wildernesses.

Early most mornings, I walked down the beach with a man who, in the vernacular, would be described as 'my mate Snowy'. He is a pearling master, or rather the owner of a farm that produces the very large and beautiful pearls that are sometimes seen around the necks of the world's most beautiful women (for that is how they seem when they are wearing them); these are round pearls of gem quality. But for every thousand pearls produced, there are only two or three that the pearling master will describe as 'super', whether they be baroque, grey, pink, golden or white with a deep, deep lustre, and no super pearl is smaller than ten millimetres in diameter, with the largest the size of a damson plum.

Snowy makes Crocodile Dundee look like a West End car salesman. Some years ago when he was starting his pearl farm, he regularly drove the three hours down the track for supplies. On one occasion the back of the truck was full of cardboard boxes containing plastic baskets, used in pearl culture, and sitting beside him was a young Japanese diver who was chain smoking and casting the cigarette butts out of the window.

'It's hot today,' Snowy remarked.

'Very hot,' replied the diver taking off his shirt.

'Bloody hot,' said Snowy taking off his shirt as well.

'Very, very hot,' replied the Japanese, taking off his trousers.

Now Snowy is used to hot weather but, before long, both he and the diver were bumping along in their underpants.

It was a rough track (in fact it would be flattery to describe it as a track). Snowy slowed as he approached a particularly deep ditch, and the cab was engulfed in a sheet of flame. The pair of them jumped out and ran into the bush, or rather what was left of the bush after a fire the previous week. Shortly, after Snowy had explained to the diver in language that tended towards the crude that it is not a good idea to throw lighted cigarettes out of a moving vehicle, the truck exploded.

Having got that off his chest, Snowy addressed their problem, which was that they were 15 miles from their camp on a road that only they used, with no water, no hats, no shoes and only two pairs of underpants between them. Snowy took off his pants, tore them into strips and tied them to his feet. The diver did the same and they began to trudge through the bush. The temperature was 46°C, and after 5 miles the diver lay down in a saltpan to die—Snowy's best efforts couldn't move him. So Snowy walked on, sometimes over rocks that were so hot that you could fry eggs on them and then grill the bacon in their reflected heat.

Eventually, Snowy reached the camp, put his head in a water trough and then called for help: 'There's a bloke out there on his back in a saltpan. Throw some water on him and bring him in.' Nothing could make the price of a Van Gogh seem more irrelevant.

Charmed by the snakes

In the north-west there are supposed to be snakes, lots of them they tell you in Perth. For myself I met only one snake in all the time that I spent on Australia's northern coastline. Crocodiles, I saw dozens of them, but snakes kept out of my way and I for my part out of theirs.

When in the world of zoos and zoo keeping, always expect the unexpected. As I designed my zoo, I made the enclosures far larger than necessary—not for the sake of the animals but rather to make people feel better about visiting these animals. The downside of this was that, although the number and variety of my mammals steadily increased,

I used to get complaints from people who had walked around the whole place without seeing any animals.

At first, I was occupied in setting up cages and creating landscapes with rocks and trees. I enjoyed the physical work and was delighted with my small collection of animals and birds. Each evening at sunset, I would walk around the enclosures looking at all the creatures, many of whom were hand-tame. I fed many of the birds with the bird food from a bag that I carried. Soon, however, the collecting instinct took over. More cages were built to house a growing collection. The feral donkeys went and scimitar-horned oryx came. In time, we had snakes too. Not just the occasional trespasser, such as the python which slipped through the wire of a birdcage, ate the occupant, and then found its bloated body prevented it getting out and so became a prisoner. Such snakes were either released in the wild about 10 miles away from potential dinners in my zoo, or consigned to the zoo's collection.

It's easy enough to catch a python. They bite but their bite does not kill. In the roof of my house at the corner of Louis and Herbert Streets on Broome's Pearlers Hill, I had a python. This snake served a useful purpose, keeping the building clear of rats. Once a week or so, the python would catch a rat, usually in the early hours of the morning, and a struggle would ensue. The snake would wrap itself around the hapless rat and would crash and bang against the corrugated iron roof as it twisted and turned in its attempts to consume the rat. After a quarter of an hour's racket, all would go quiet. Visitors were frightened out of their wits by the disturbance above their beds. It is hard to tell which was the more shocking—falling coconuts that hit the tin roof with an explosion or the rattle of the feeding snake.

The consequences of playing around with poisonous snakes can, however, be severe. If you are foolish enough to interfere with them, they are certainly capable of doing you a deal of harm. Swan lager, the locals believe, is a great help when bitten by a king brown. You must, of course, have two cans of it: you drink the first and if you have time to drink the second, you will probably survive. A welder working at the zoo was engaged in cutting up piping into equal lengths when he saw a king brown about 10 feet long scuttle into a pipe, having been disturbed. Hoping to catch the snake for my collection, he tied a sack over the end nearest the snake's head, and then he warmed up the end of the pipe at its tail with a blowtorch. The snake moved into the sack, so the welder tied the sack's neck with wire and picked it up. Unfortunately, there was a hole in the bottom of the sack and a very angry snake lost no time in passing through this hole and biting the man on the ankle on the way out, In moments, his leg turned black. Luckily there was help nearby and the hospital was only five minutes away by car. He was, however, two weeks in that hospital, suffering considerable pain in both his leg and his head. Without the hospital and expert attention, the welder would not have survived.

Broome is not a place known for snakes; in fact, they are almost a rarity around the town. On the other hand, around Go Go Station, situated on the southern outskirts of Fitzroy Crossing, a hamlet on the Fitzroy River, it is a different matter. When I stayed at Go Go Station, I was told they had shot eight king browns that day around the station homestead. The daughter of the station manger told me that the day before she had killed two king browns with one shot.

'How did you do that?' I asked. Like all newcomers, I was eager for information, especially when that information involved animals as romantic and dangerous as snakes.

'They were copulating,' the girl replied.

Kept in reserve

On the plight of endangered species in the war-torn Middle Eastern desert, the reserves set up to save them and to explain the purpose of zoos.

Many people are against zoos in principle—principles that are founded in emotion rather than rational thought. The Gulf War (1991) highlighted the need for zoos to preserve the world's gene pool of rare animals at risk in a world where people tend to be both careless and thoughtless.

The Middle East is not unfamiliar with warfare. For centuries past, the human race has fought over its fertile valleys and deserts, and has built monuments and destroyed them. Towns and cities have been consumed by warfare and rebuilt in the image of the conqueror. Great cities have been destroyed by earthquakes, and peoples destroyed by famine and pestilence. In the heart of this region lies Basra, the site of the Garden of Eden, the beginning perhaps, of life on earth. What is certain, however, is that the valleys of the Euphrates and Tigris Rivers meet here: valleys that have become the flyway for millions of migrating birds, birds that journey from Europe far into Africa, birds that travel each year from Russia to northern Australia, birds as diverse as the white stork and the small warbler. While humans are ingenious enough to improve upon destroyed architecture, and their hands are supple enough to repair broken artefacts, they have no means of replacing a lost variety of bird.

This desert area of Iraq is of particular natural importance as the meeting point of the European and Arabian species: the brown bear (seldom found now in Europe), the Arabian wolf, and many other interesting and beautiful animals and birds. The irony of the destructive attack upon Kuwait by Saddam Hussein, and the disaster of the consequences of the action necessary to remove him, is that this area was one of the few places in the world making great efforts to repair some of the ravages of the twentieth century by restoring locally extinct species to their original habitat. A small group of the extremely rare Sömmering's gazelles, along with many other animals in the Old Botanical Gardens of Kuwait City, have been shot by soldiers from Iraq. It is, however, the loss of the plans of the Kuwaiti government to establish a national park along the border with Iraq that is the real tragedy—a park where they intended to reintroduce the Houbara bustard and the Arabian gazelle, a desert reserve to which many of the species now extinct in this region would return. It must be hoped that, when the rebuilding of this region begins, these plans will not be overlooked and attention paid only to the provision of motorways, hospitals and schools.

In Saudi Arabia, the government has set up a centre for the conservation and breeding of many of its endangered species, with the intention of returning them to the wild. There are, in the centre, well over a thousand of some of the world's rarest animals: the sand gazelle; the Arabian gazelle; the Saudi Dorcas gazelle, extinct in its habitat; the Saudi wolf; and the Rueppell's fox, a small and rare sand fox. Then there is the Arabian oryx, the most beautiful of these creatures, an animal thought to be the mythical unicorn, for, when seen in profile, its long sweeping horns seem as one. It was an animal hunted for 3000 years by desert warriors and it survived. But no antelope, however agile, was equipped to withstand the advent of the automatic rifle, and the early 1960s saw its demise outside captivity. The research centre in Riyadh, on the other hand, has prospered, and the number of these rare animals has increased. There are several zoos with important collections in Israel, and the Tel Aviv University Wildlife Research Centre has done much work for conservation, and cares for many rare animals. In Oman, meanwhile, repatriation of desert antelopes has started. There is now a wild population of the Arabian oryx, the descendants of captive-bred animals returned to their habitat. Another population of the elegant animal is in Jordan, and there are plans for a reserve on the Jordanian/Saudi Arabian border. All of this work goes on in the world's most volatile region.

These animals are in great danger. In the early 1960s, small groups of antelopes were caught and taken to zoos in America and Britain: the addax, which is short-legged, beige and corkscrew-horned, and now thought to be extinct in the wild; the Damna gazelle, which is long-legged and long-necked, of which less than a thousand remain; and the scimitar-horned oryx, which is another antelope extinct in its natural habitat. The subsequent civil war in Chad and the famines that sprang from it, combined with high-powered military rifles, have proved the wisdom of this action. These zoos have become a Noah's ark for these animals—places where they can be bred and studied. London Zoo is one of the organisations active in this fieldwork and research.

Zoos are no longer animal prisons. In their modern form, they can be havens of safety. The scarce resource of these rare and extremely beautiful animals, spread among zoos on a planned basis, means that neither disease nor war will ever destroy them completely. With humans being the aggressive beasts they are, it is unlikely that the war against Saddam Hussein, or for that matter any other war, will end all wars. Consequently, we had better take good care of our zoos so that our zoos at least can take care of the world's birds and animals after terrible carnage, playing an important part in rehabilitating our planet.

G'daisy

A profusion of wild flowers flourish in Western Australia's roughest terrain. I search for the blooms that are truly wild at heart.

Happily the wild flowers of Western Australia are currently in no danger. The geography of this piece, written in 1996, is a little unusual; no tourist should follow the instructions for they will surely get lost. That my friends say of me 'he is seldom accurate but never wrong' is given verification here. The impression, however, of a drive between Broome and Perth by the inland road is as accurate today as it was then.

A mid-September walk through Kings Park, Perth, is a delight. Western Australia's wild flowers are at their best, and fill the acres of wilderness that make up this urban park. So, for the amateur who wishes to study each plant and also have access to a delicious lunch in one of Perth's restaurants, Kings Park is just the place.

For the serious enthusiast, however, Western Australia's profusion of wild flowers can be seen in a truly savage setting. Alongside the inland track between Broome and Perth, the varieties of flowers are almost without number. At first, travelling along the tarmac-surfaced highway is easy, but for the journey along the track, take food, water, tyres and petrol.

Soon after the filling station at Sandfire Roadhouse is the turn-off into the wilderness. It is just before the De Grey River. Turn left to follow the track through rocky country. Vast patches of Sturt's desert pea grow there—a red flower of prostrate habit not unlike a parrot's beak. The landscape is breathtaking, but you won't see any humans unless you happen upon a group of drovers mustering cattle on horseback.

By early evening you arrive at Marble Bar—a small town that was the administrative centre for a once-prosperous region. Now all it boasts are large red-brick barracks, built in the form of a decorative castle, and the Iron Clad Hotel, made of corrugated iron. The Iron Clad is just a pub; the guest rooms are transportable buildings parked nearby. The town's name does not refer to the material used to make the pub's bar—this is solid jarrah, not local marble. The story goes that the 'Bar' is an outbreak of spar across a nearby stream, believed by early settlers to be marble. Around the stream are trees. There is usually a great flock of white cockatoos in their branches, like large white blossoms on slender bows.

After your disturbed night in Marble Bar, the reason the Iron Clad has so few bedrooms becomes apparent: visitors drink most of the night and sleep where they drop. September is the perfect time to stay in Marble Bar, for the temperature is pleasant in a place where its range is enormous. In winter, the drunks try to share your cabin if the door is not locked. In summer, if you lock the door, you suffocate.

Drive on to Nullagine and remember to turn right or you will end up lost in the desert. On to Newman, a most unlikely town. Just as Kings Park is a chunk of wilderness in the city, so Newman is a chunk of suburbia in the wilderness, almost the same size. They could be exchanged and nobody would suspect a thing. And now to the purpose of your trip. Entering the Collier Range National Park to the south, you will see acres of wild flowers of a dozen different colours and a thousand different varieties.

Spend the night at Meekatharra, and your next stop should be Cue, a mining town caught in a time warp, its mines and buildings left almost as they were during the last century, and its wrought-iron bandstand still waiting for the band.

After Cue, the weather changes: green trees, lush grass and running streams, white arum lilies along their banks. It is far easier to see Western Australia's wild flowers in Kings Park, but not half as much fun.

No barrier to progress

Ten years after first visiting sleepy Port Douglas, the Australian town nearest the Great Barrier Reef, I returned to find tourism has turned it into a bustling metropolis.

Incidentally, the Iron Clad Hotel is so called not because it is made largely of corrugated iron; rather it is named for the first steel-hulled battleships. In the outback of Australia little is as it seems. Often I travelled in the outback of Australia visiting desert, empty coastlines, deserted towns and mountain ranges: swimming in quiet billabongs fringed with palms, the waters covered with lilies whose blooms are the most subtle of colours; driving down endless miles of track and emerging from the truck at the end of the day caked in bulldust; cooking at camp fires; and lying at night watching the canopy of stars for flashes of light that sped from one horizon to another, shooting stars. Sleepless with excitement, each day was a new adventure in a life of a myriad of changing events. Sometimes I returned, and so it was with Port Douglas.

When I first visited Port Douglas in Queensland in the mid-1980s, Port Douglas was not there. At least not there in the sense that it is today, ten years later. There was a church and a graveyard filled with the names of British pioneers—names ranging from Cornwall to Scotland. The Central Hotel, a fine Queensland building, stood on Macrossan Street, notable in those days only for two monuments, one to the pioneers who settled Port Douglas and another to the local men who died in the First World War. It took a minute to see all that was worth seeing and I drove on, excited by the prospect of the Daintree rainforest and Cape York.

I had not been back to Port Douglas since, until my visit in 1995. It has changed out of all recognition. Even the church has left the graveyard and it now sits on the foreshore beside the marina and the shopping centre that boasts such names as Louis Vuitton, Ralph Lauren and Loewe. The Mirage Hotel has been built with vast blue lagoons that double as swimming pools. A small railway runs past the town's resorts to a station complete with turntable at the marina. The marina is the *raison d'être* for the commercial explosion that has taken place, for it is from here that thousands of tourists are transported by high-speed catamarans to the platforms on the Great Barrier Reef. Here they putter around in plastic-bottomed boats, snorkel or dive on the extraordinary natural phenomenon which makes up the Great Barrier Reef, alive with fish of all sizes and coloured corals.

The place is a spectacle. Port Douglas's passport to fame and prosperity is almost entirely due to the fact that it is the closest Australian town to the Barrier Reef. Great palm trees line the roads around the town, palm trees with massed ferns growing up their trunks, manicured golf courses abound, and lawns and hedgerows are neatly clipped. The whole effect is of a model town, but a town that could be anywhere where the weather is hot and water plentiful. A Japanese restaurant seems to have been removed from Japan, a Chinese restaurant from China. The Nautilus restaurant in Murphy Street, where the food is delicious and the atmosphere seductive (coal braziers warm you as you dine in the open air), could have been taken from the Bahamas or Florida or, for that matter, Los Angeles.

In Macrossan Street near the Pioneer Memorial is Club Tropical, a modern building disguised as a cave whose bar offers a drink called a 'Comfortable Numb'. Club Tropical also serves a 'Bushman's Breakfast' which is a very large plate of bacon, scrambled eggs and snags, as they call sausages in this part of the world. I felt quite numb after working my way through this confection. I am afraid that, judged by the standards of Club Tropical breakfasts, I am a pretty pathetic bushman. Opposite Club Tropical and its exotic decor is the Iron Bar Restaurant, a bush restaurant conveniently placed for those who might otherwise travel the bush for years without finding such a place. Their specialities include 'Bob and Dolly Dyer's Seafood Platter', 'Pig Iron Bob's Steak Royal', 'Squiggy Taylor's Bank Rolled Chuck' and the 'Bradman Steak'. I asked what form the 'Bradman Steak' took, only to be told that it was very large. 'Skase's Crab Bounty' is also on the menu; it appears to be a reference to the fact that Mr Skase built the Mirage Hotel and then departed in a hurry, leaving large debts behind. The 'C' of 'Crab' is perhaps meant to be a 'G'.

Far more delightful than all the other attractions of Port Douglas is the Sunday market. Like all the weekend markets that abound in Australia, this one sells the same goods as the tourist shops of Australia on weekdays. But, hidden among the dross of tourist clutter and handicrafts, are a few real gems. The stalls that sold orchids, for instance. These rare and wonderful plants were there in plentiful supply. Many on offer were species from the forests of northern Queensland. The fruit stalls sold exotic fruit such as sapota or chocolate pudding fruit, which really does taste just like chocolate pudding. The governor's plum was for sale too—a bitter fruit with the highest content of vitamin C known to humankind, while the most exotic item was wattle seed ice-cream.

As I left I watched an Aboriginal playing a didgeridoo the size of an Alpine horn. Didgeridoos are now sold all over Australia; even the Aboriginals of Western Australian descent who have no culture of playing these instruments sell them, only they don't bother to hollow them out. However, the aspect of this demi-paradise built by an Australian man and Japanese money that interested me the most was the proliferation of government agencies offering counselling.

Darwin's evolution

Life in Australia's Northern Territory is changing, but this metamorphosis is only skin deep. Darwin is still the natural choice if you're looking for pearls or Aboriginal art.

Darwin has not changed a lot in the last fifteen years. The place *seems* to have changed: there is a grand new parliament building, a large new courthouse and a marina development that could lately have been removed from Miami. Tourists flock to Darwin in droves these days—but the essential Darwin has not changed. Let me explain. Aeroplanes leave, for reasons known only to the airlines, in a cluster around lunchtime; this information has not filtered through to the management of Darwin's hotels, and lunchtime, from 12 until 2, is when porters and receptionists disappear, leaving tourists separated from their luggage, remote from the possibility of paying a hotel bill in time for the ten-minute ride to the airport.

It's rather charming really: the way life goes on in northern Australia much as it always has. The place still has the romantic feel of the outback. There have been changes, but attitudes remain untouched by the modern world. The wife of a former chief minister in the Northern Territory has expressed surprise that no one knew her husband in Rome—'I don't care for that place,' she added. Of Athens she said, 'I expected the Acropolis to be a bit worn with age, but I really had thought those Greeks would have repaired it.' A final dismissal of Europe: 'It's all ruins.'

Surly waitresses are still to be found in the North, although not quite as surly as the waitress who, when I asked her which was the best night at the restaurant where she was working, replied, 'Monday; no one comes here on Monday.' Christo's restaurant—despite a hiccup with a surly waitress, though in all fairness I have to admit that she was a mere amateur by comparison with many in her genre—provided a barramundi cooked to perfection; I have never eaten fish like it. Restaurants, largely due to an influx of immigrants, now serve a great variety of ethnic cuisines and, what is more, the ingredients are good, the cooks brilliant and the service generally pleasant.

All of these new benefits to Darwin are far more significant than vast parliaments and marinas. Among the best of the little changes to Darwin is the Karen Brown Gallery. Karen Brown sells Aboriginal art.

One of the great changes in Australia as a whole is the art world's attitude to Aboriginal painting and sculpture—people love it, where once they ignored it entirely. Aboriginal paintings now fetch hundreds of thousands of dollars. There was recently one small hitch when one Aboriginal artist won a $50 000 art prize. 'Now I can afford to give up painting,' she announced to the assembled press—she was, however, quickly corrected, and the statement adjusted to 'Now I have the freedom to paint.' Not everyone, it seems, sees art as a way of making dealers rich; it's all very reassuring. Karen Brown represents Aboriginal artists whose paintings reflect their country, but they are not in any way instantly recognisable as the work of Aboriginal Australians, any more than Van Gogh's pictures are recognisably Dutch—often painted in France, often about France, but by a Dutchman. Adeline, one of a body of painters all represented by Karen Brown, was to my eye among the best painters of Aboriginal descent that I came across recently when visiting Australia. She paints landscapes of great vigour, and then moves her focus to a small part of those landscapes and blows that small part up in scale to, for example, a 4 foot by 3 foot painting of bush flowers. The thought process is fascinating, the effect of the vastly overscale wild flowers dramatic. Karen Brown handles her artists with great sensitivity; that too is new in northern Australia.

Across the street from Karen Brown is an old business, Paspaley Pearling, now in its third generation. The mainstays of this business, however, Nick, Ros and Marilyn Paspaley, are doing more for Darwin and Australia than just producing the North's most exciting pearls. They have systematically set about raising the quality of life of many Australians through their diverse activities that range from a boutique hotel in the pearling town of Broome to Australia's smartest jewellery shops. With publications and publicity they are raising awareness of the pearling industry in a way that the pearling industry of a decade ago could not even conceive. All of this is good for Australia, its vast northern lands and in particular Darwin.

Once upon a time in Alice

Back to the outback and I find the airport at Alice Springs teeming with tourists. But nearby is an unusual, authentic school of painters' flowers among the red earth and tin huts.

Alice Springs is at the heart of Australia; from Uluru (Ayers Rock) it is only a short aeroplane ride or a long day in a bus. Many times I have been to Alice over a period of many years. Travelling there by truck or aeroplane, an arrival at Alice is always an excitement whether it be from the urbane atmosphere of Sydney or part of the Tanami Track.

The land around Alice Springs had the green tinge about it that a rainy season brings. I watched as the Ansett flight made a long, low approach to the airport. It is May 1994 and I had not been to Alice for nearly five years. Nothing much had changed; there were no new houses to be seen as we flew towards the airport, no new roads—it seemed much as before: the low hills that hide the town, the satellite tracking station with its white domes and discs bright in the sunshine. Only when I climbed down the airport steps did I begin to think I had come to the wrong place. A sign said 'International Airport' and that is what I saw.

Gone were the collection of buildings stitched together that had passed for a terminal. In front of me was a modern airport building—there was no longer a grubby bar with grubby customers where sweat and stubble mixed with ice-cold beer; the flies had gone too. The cafeteria could seat a hundred and needed to, for planes arrived every few minutes instead of once or twice a day. Like most modern airports the terminal at Alice Springs has become a shopping mall. Gone are all those men with jaws like set squares and hands like shovels, with floppy hats and a pocket knife at their belts. Gone are the women in their ill-fitting dresses and straw hats. The days when the population of 'The Alice' came to the airport for a beer and to wonder at the miracle of flight are long gone.

Today, the airport population at Alice Springs consists of pushy German tourists and excited Japanese on a quick flip around Australia. The Germans study maps of the outback and straighten the creases in their canvas shorts and bush jackets, sending ordinary mortals reeling as they turn and strike them with their backpacks.

These Germans are well equipped for a day in Alice on the way (by plane) to Uluru (Ayers Rock), and far better equipped for the outback than men and women who have spent their lives in it. The Japanese at Alice's airport spend their time and their money buying clothes with Aboriginal designs, didgeridoos as long as themselves and paintings by the desert artists. As for the Aboriginals, apart from those who sell their products, they seem to have disappeared, blending in with the other denizens of the outback who all wear ties and suits.

The airport at Alice is not the only aspect of Australia that has changed. Up the Tanami Track that runs from Alice Springs across the Tanami Desert past Rabbit Flat Roadhouse on the way to Halls Creek, you will, if you make a detour, come to Turkey Creek. It is not much of a place compared to the standard set by the terminal at Alice Springs—just red earth and tin huts. But Turkey Creek, for all its lack of modern facilities, is the home of one of Australia's most exciting schools of painting. It first came to fame when Rover Thomas, one of its citizens, represented Australia at the Venice Biennale. His friend Paddy Tjamati was another of Turkey Creek's painters who broke away from the idea of simply reproducing tribal patterns on canvas. These two artists painted the landscapes of their country on dismembered tea-chests. These works were used in the Krilkrill, an open ceremony, and were carried on the dancers' shoulders. A television crew filming the ceremony was somewhat perplexed, for when they had set up their cameras the dancers turned their backs on them, and the same thing happened when they rearranged the cameras at the other end of the dance arena—these corroborees are complex affairs and the dancers are not prepared to alter their traditional form just to please a television crew.

Since the days of Paddy Tjamati and Rover Thomas's early efforts a great deal of interest has been paid to the work of the painters from Turkey Creek. As a result these painters have taken a great deal of interest in painting. A few weeks ago a group of them exhibited their work in a Perth gallery, artists with such wonderful names as Stumpy Brown and Jimmy Bent, Butcher Cheval and Peanut Ford. They paint their country, its myths and its reality: they paint it with great passion and perfect simplicity. In the words of Honey Pulikati as she describes one of her paintings: 'This is the river behind the station at Yungngora in the rain time—after the rain the water lies around in *purra* (billabongs); we catch fish in these small waterholes—they get caught—they cannot get back to the river.' It's all a bit like that for her people.

High among them

Sydney is full of surprising delights; for example, the camaraderie among seashell collectors in a shell shop under Sydney Harbour Bridge.

Possibly the only advantage of jet lag is that you are fully awake at times of the night when you would otherwise be unaware there was anything worth waking to see: the last hours of full moon, for instance, as it hovers over Sydney Harbour; the first hours of light before the sun comes over the horizon; and the sunrise that paints each ripple on the surface of the harbour's water and gleams on the shiny arcs of Sydney Opera House. Then there is the freshness as you walk in the Botanical Gardens, a freshness that comes with dawn, a few moments caught between the stifling heat of antipodean night and the blazing sun of day, moments when the birds sing just for the joy of singing.

None of this has changed since I first set foot in Australia in the late 1950s. None, that is, except that Opera House. In those days, it was just a building site jutting into Sydney Harbour. Work had stopped while those charged with its construction discovered how on earth they were to build the cluster of giant shells that are both roof and buildings. How could Utzon's vision sketched in the sand of a beach the other side of the world become a reality? The reality of human life however is cruel, just as is the reality of nature. The solution was arrived at, Utzon was dismissed and the engineers Ove Arup adapted his designs to ease the task of construction. The Opera House today stands heavy, solid and dominant, whereas Utzon's opera house would have seemed likely to fly away with the wind.

Not far from the Opera House in The Rocks district, under almost the first archway of the Harbour Bridge, lived Lance Moore, a man who sold seashells in a thousand shapes and colours. I say a thousand, but he may well have had ten thousand varieties in his shop. All I know is that there were shells everywhere. Great baskets of common shells, rare varieties carefully wrapped in cotton wool and pulled from a drawer filled with unpaid bills and unanswered letters, and scraps of paper each with a telephone number or an address on them. A filing system from hell. A bundle of addresses with no names, and names with telephone numbers that were no longer connected, would be pulled from a drawer with a shell he was showing a collector. One such collector was Paul Jones, a painter of flowers and sometimes shells, a man who can catch a moment of nature and commit it to paper with pencil, brush and colour.

I know little of the background of Lance Moore. He seemed once to have been a sailor or at least to have spent time on ships. Clearly he was a diver and collector of live shells. I write 'clearly' when in fact I do not know, for Lance Moore was to me quite as mysterious as the sponges and corals that decorated his walls. Giant crayfish and crabs of vast proportions hung there too, among the rows of sharks' jaws and turtle shells. Lance Moore's back office was a salon, not of writers or painters—other than Jonesy, as he called Paul Jones. No, his was a salon of fishermen, divers and collectors of shells, a salon in which your intellect was judged not by the sparkle of your wit or the depth of your education, but by whether you could put a name to an obscure mollusc. Shells were taken from cases, laid in raffia baskets, lifted and examined, occasionally compared to examples in reference books, but more often name-tagged and put away. Paul Jones sat with a discriminating eye, looking for the perfect example, for Jones only collects the most perfect of shells which he keeps in a single cabinet, each tray a work of gleaming beauty. Cowries are the shells that attract him—not exclusively, for his collection is wide-ranging, but a rare and perfect cowrie visibly excites Paul Jones. Shells have that effect on those who love them, like gold, diamonds and pearls. Men do not kill for shells as far as I know, but they come close to it.

Lance Moore held court at these gatherings, generous with his knowledge, careful with his friendships. He hopped among those gathered in his back room distributing tea and often cake. He had one leg and when tired would sleep under the table with his dogs. Today, Lance Moore is dead and he holds court no longer. Australia has lost an epicentre of real culture.

Paul Jones introduced me to Lance. Paul Jones introduced me to the joys of collecting shells. Paul and I were as different as chalk and cheese. Paul would spend days over baskets of worthless shells searching for the shell of perfection: the shell perfect in every respect, not a mark or a blemish, every curve and turn of its undulating form a thing of beauty. Never easily satisfied, he had a natural patience when it came to shells. With me it was different. I could spot a good shell, not perfect, not regular or exact to a textbook definition, but beautiful for its faults rather than its perfections. Having found this shell I needed dozens complementary to its beauty and, collectively, they became even more beautiful. Paul Jones' collection, a collection far better than mine, was kept in a small cabinet; my collection overflowed from a room. Paul Jones was a painter of shells and flowers, and each stamen needed to be exact; I am a writer with my descriptions overflowing from a page filled with a wild untutored enthusiasm, delighting in the chase, describing extravagantly the kill. My energy is an impatient energy; Paul Jones was disciplined to the extreme. He was a critic of people whom he judged and he judged harshly. He fired my enthusiasm for an area of the natural world of whose existence I was unaware. He was an amazing companion, and was also socially alert. He must have passed at least the greater part of his life without the appearance of his wallet coinciding with the arrival of a bill. It is, I suppose, a tribute to his character that this fact did not deter other people from spending time with him. Tight with money, Paul Jones was free with a far more important commodity—his knowledge. He was a painter of beautiful flowers, and his pictures were fine, controlled masterpieces, devoid of emotion and filled to the brim with information. He has left behind him a legacy of some of the world's most important botanical paintings—painting with no romance, no soul, no nonsense. Paintings as close to perfection in their description of the subject as paintings are ever likely to get. So it was, I suppose, no surprise that Paul Jones, when his eyes began to fail, put down his paint brushes, picked up a camera and soon was expert in the genre.

It is not possible to find an artist more different from Paul Jones than Sidney Nolan, a man generous with his time, his knowledge and his art. Sidney understood the world of fantasy in a way that few others really have. For many painters fantasy becomes surrealism; for Sidney fantasy became his painting: the duck that stands in the sky above the Dog and Duck Hotel, and the Mask of Ned Kelly that appears in unlikely settings. There is no softness, no theatrical devices about Sidney Nolan's painting. His landscape is the hard landscape of Australia, not the Sunday bush of the colloquial painter. His people are the men and women of adversity and the Aboriginals of desolate bush and haunting ceremonies. There is a toughness and a directness in these paintings, often rushed out from a night of frenzied painting. Sidney Nolan did not paint every day or every month. For months on end he sucked up the culture of the Western world: its myths, its folklore and its modern atrocity. Then in a few short hours he discharged this accumulated knowledge with all the savagery of Australia's heartland. Savage though his landscapes and his images may be, Sidney was a man of immense sensitivity, a man who needed paraphernalia around him, a man who could take a fragment of sculpture and bring it back to life in a dozen paintings.

It was at my home that Sidney first saw the exotic chickens that became the mainstay of his *Oedipus* paintings, believed by some who know about these things to be his most important work. Sidney was an Australian painter, not a European painter. Claimed by the officials of the Tate Gallery as a member of the School of London, he was no such thing. Living in London, he painted Australia even when the subject was Greece or Italy. There was no aesthetic that Sidney Nolan was not prepared to prey upon in aid of his Australian paintings. He was one of the few Australian artists with an international reputation; yet Sidney Nolan is the most Australian in an ethnic sense of all Australian painters.

Sadly both of these artists, so different in their approach to painting, died some years ago. I miss them greatly.

Oliver Ford: A farewell

My tribute to the late Oliver Ford, master decorator, old friend and a marvellous travelling companion—whether confronted by transvestites in Singapore or getting lost in the Australian outback.

Oliver Ford, decorator to Her Majesty Queen Elizabeth, died on 17 October 1992. He died suddenly while standing in the Great Hall of his home at Lacock in Wiltshire—in his later years he was hard to entice from there. Virtually retired from his business, he devoted his time to his garden, and a remarkable garden it was. His reluctance to travel may well have misled those who knew him only latterly, for he was in fact a great traveller, not by any means a tourist, but a real traveller who undertook long journeys. He was the most congenial of travelling companions too, filled with humour, seldom grumbling although he in fact disliked foreign food, preferring steak and chips to curry and the other concoctions of the Orient.

In Singapore, after four days of Chinese food—I am myself addicted to Chinese cooking—I asked him where he wished to dine. He chose a Japanese restaurant, one specialising in *teppan yaki.* I was a bit surprised at this, but he ordered only chopped steak and quietly bemoaned the missing chips. One night we visited Bugis Street, which is a traffic-free street. It was traffic free in those days not by city ordinance, but because the restaurateurs whose establishments were cheek by jowl along the street had started putting chairs and tables where traffic might otherwise have been. The street was filled with tourists, who in their turn became part of the spectacle that tourists came to watch. These were the days of the Vietnam War. This street was pure theatre. There were soldiers and sailors who, as the evening grew late, drank and sang; local musicians and vendors came, as the audience, lubricated by Singapore beer, became generous with money. Then began the parade of the transvestites—soon they were all muddled up. Sailors, tourists and transvestites, all on the most friendly of terms. Oliver Ford and I watched all this, we laughed and I suppose we may have sung. Then, unexpectedly, a transvestite sat on Oliver's lap. 'I am a pretend Mary Poppins,' this exotic creature announced, though how she came to that conclusion eludes me, for a more far-fetched version of that demure creature would be hard to find. Oliver protested; the transvestite kissed him on his bald head and set off for new pickings. The soldiers and sailors were all drunk, the tourists began to go home, the pimps became more insistent, fights broke out, and bottles and glasses were smashed. We headed for our hotel, and as we climbed from the trishaw Oliver, offering to pay, found his wallet had gone. Pretend Mary Poppins had not been quite as innocent as she wished us to believe.

Oliver Ford was direct about his life: 'camp as a row of tents' he often used to say; and to a female client who boasted of her dining-room chairs he said: 'My dear, I have more chance of being Queen Anne than those chairs.' But this was the stuff of London. I also knew him in the Australian outback where there is red dust and bogged vehicles. We drove the 1500 miles from Perth to Broome by the inland route through Meekatharra, Nullagine and Marble Bar, stopping in the near ghost town of Cue, with its wonderful Victorian buildings, the gold all gone and most of the people with it. The bandstand in the main street has long been without musicians. On that trip we were novices. My ex-wife Romilly, Oliver and I nearly perished.

It is a strange fact about travelling in the north-west of Australia, a land of low scrub that comes right to the edge of the track: you see no animal life, or rather you rarely see animals and birds. We had travelled for two days and had not seen a kangaroo. Oliver began to doubt their existence. I felt I had let him down badly in this matter, for I had told him that the whole place was stuffed with kangaroos; then a group of emus crossed the track and on an impulse I turned off into the bush after them. We chased for a few minutes and could not find them. Returning to the track we could not find that either. Oliver was the tallest among us by some measure, so he climbed on top of the vehicle, but he could see nothing, just bush. The path we had made through the bush, a wide track it had seemed, was now invisible, the saplings back in place, the ground rock hard. No tracks could be found: we were truly lost. We searched and searched and eventually we discovered that we were by chance only a few yards from the track.

When I remember Oliver Ford it is not fine curtains and grand houses I think of, but the Tanami Track, the banks of the Diamantina River and the Simpson Desert, sleeping on the sand in a swag under the stars, more stars than in all heavens put together. He was to my ex-wife Romilly and me a good friend.

Four politicians

Few politicians whom I knew well in Australia were among the people that I collected there. By far the grandest people, the politicians were not the most interesting or worthwhile.

Malcolm Fraser, for example, I always regarded as a stretched version of British Prime Minister Edward Heath.

I did not care for Heath either both were failures. It was not their failure that dismisses them from my hall of fame, but rather their approach to success. It was the success of others, who for the reasons of luck, or so it seems, flourished where they failed. Malcolm Fraser, I first saw in Perth. The transport system of Australia was near paralysis. No aeroplanes were flying, and it was almost impossible to leave that continent. No aeroplanes were flying, that is, apart from Prime Minister Malcolm

Frasers' aeroplane. When the prime minister arrived at the Parmelia Hotel, its foyer was filled with frustrated tourists; we sat, literally, on our luggage. We were frustrated and angry and had little sympathy for a prime minister who arrived by private jet. It seemed for one moment that this great man would speak to us poor travellers. That, however, was not to be the case; he stood in the crammed foyer for several minutes surrounded by minions and uttered not a word. We were I suppose, most of us anyway, not voters in Australia. We were, however, angry customers of the Australian tourist industry. It was one of those moments when a man's reputation hangs in the balance with the audience: a few words of consolation and forever more a hero; silence and dismissed from the rank of human being to the substrata of pompous ass. Fraser chose the latter course. I write 'chose' when in fact he made no choice at all. It was the man's instinct to remain aloof, distant, superior and cold. It was the instinct of myself, and I suppose a number at least of my companions, to hold this man forever in our contempt.

By such small and acutely unimportant criteria are politicians judged. Politics is like a pond where a stone is thrown into the middle—at first one small ring, then another and another till rings become waves pushing at the pond's banks.

A politician who understood just this is Bob Hawke—a politician who likes fishing and people. On one occasion when I went fishing with Bob Hawke at Exmouth he caught most of the fish. That was Bob's role. The King family found the fish, Bob caught them and Peter Doyle, the doyen of the Sydney fish-and-chip business, cooked them. We, myself and a couple of others were the audience. Impressed as I was by the efforts of King, Doyle and Hawke at bringing superb cooked fish to our dinner table, it was as nothing to my admiration for Bob Hawke's performance in the pub before we sat down to eat. Now the hotel or pub, as it was called, was of the genre of country hotels with all the faults of that genre. As for me, I could find no advantage other than geography—it happened to be one of the two places to stay in Exmouth. Exmouth is on a bleak peninsula of land halfway up the western Australian coast. I say 'bleak' because not many people live there and certainly no Aboriginals for they believe the land to be cursed. They may be right for when the volcano Krakatoa exploded over a century ago, Exmouth was submerged by the resulting tidal wave. Regenerated by the need for an American Air Force base and its contingent airfield, Exmouth acquired a number of brick homes and a reputation for having the best fishing in Australia. The Australian tourist industry ignored this place for many years, but then the Australian tourist industry had for many years ignored tourists. In time that all changed and change is afoot even in places as remote as Exmouth. Bob Hawke, however, ignored nobody that evening in the pub. It seems as if he had arrived at a private party. Complete strangers were greeted as if they were favourite aunts and uncles. Bob worked that room as if his very life depended on it. They were badly dressed and sweaty, and as an ungainly bunch as you would ever come across, but these people had votes and Bob hugged everyone of them. It was purc joy to watch this prime minister work among those who put him in his position and it was a delight to watch the joy of these people at meeting the great man. The contrast between Hawke on holiday and Fraser at work could not be more marked or for that matter more poignant.

John Howard is a man small in stature and with an outlook to match. Thrown into office by the excesses of the Labor government, he had not the first idea what to do with power. John Howard tinkered with Australia's economy, its taxation system and the nation's relationship with its indigenous people. Nothing much came of his tinkering; the status quo was neither changed nor enhanced. The man is tinkerer. The point of a consumption tax is to move the thrust of tax collecting from saving to spending. The economy has sagged ever since John Howard and his men were elected; the dollar has never been weaker against international currencies. The fudge over who owns the land in Australia has led to a racial tension that for the first time seemed, under the guidance of Paul Keating, to have a chance of resolution. Pauline Hanson in Queensland has risen like a phoenix from the flames of her ridiculous policies. John Howard should have defeated her intellectually and shown the obvious folly of her crackbrained plans. Instead he tried to seduce her voters, hoping that they would vote for his own party. Pauline Hanson has disreputable ideas that will not work, and if they did they would be thoroughly immoral. Race and the capacity of Australians to face up to the fact that they live in a multiracial country and that the Aboriginal people are one of those races is the most important issue facing the nation. Without resolving this issue all others are worthless.

Unlike John Howard, I found Paul Keating to be both cultured and a visionary: a man deeply interested in the wider stage. Brilliant in his day, Paul Keating was in no way a hack. His attitude to Indonesia, a vast reality off Australia's northern coastline, was constructive. His Aboriginal land reforms were the first giant strides towards racial harmony. Unlike Malcolm Fraser, a man of the Commonwealth pandering to dictators hoping one day to be the Commonwealth's chief executive, Paul Keating realised that there is more out there than former British colonies. Sadly, Keating's attempts to make Australia act her age were largely frustrated and in time he will probably be better known for his collection of French Empire clocks. Paul Keating could have been Australia's greatest prime minister, instead of which he was frustrated in much of what he wanted to do and rubbished for much of what he did. After he left office his achievements have been marginalised by the scribbling classes. His reforms have been neutered by John Howard, a man whose very life's work is in finding ways of not doing things or undoing those things that others have done. Paul Keating will be only a footnote in Australian history rather than the banner headline that he deserves to be. Life is like that and, in the same way, a horrible war on the opposite side of the world has put John Howard back in power. Whoever thought that there was any justice in politics anyway?

Christmas past

Christmas Island, once a rugged paradise, has now succumbed to modern tourism.

Far off the north-west coast of Australia, close to that of Java, is a lump of rock that successive Australian governments have never quite known what to do with. They cannot quite make up their minds to get rid of it and clearly they are unhappy at having to keep the place.

Discovered on Christmas Day 1643, this inhospitable place was named Christmas Island. Sheer cliffs, buffeted by the waves of the Indian Ocean, rise nearly 700 feet (200 metres) out of the sea and both goods and passengers from visiting ships have to be hauled from vessel to cliff top by cable car. The majority of the island is covered by rainforest, an exotic landscape of strange plants and uncommon birds. First colonised by the British, the island relied on phosphate mining as its only source of income, and Chinese labourers were brought in to work the mines. Unlike most areas that have suffered the ravages of open-cast mining, Christmas Island has not been ruined by it but greatly improved. Where the earth was scraped from between the rocks, strange geological shapes began to appear. Now areas of the island look for all the world like flower beds in a Chinese garden.

While the Chinese miners may have done wonders for the landscape, they were the bane of the pigeon population. Christmas Island boasts seven varieties of birds found nowhere else, one of which is a large and ungainly pigeon. Life on the island should have been easy for this stately creature: food is plentiful and it has no natural enemy, apart, that is, from the island's Chinese population. The Chinese, or at least those living on Christmas Island, love eating pigeon, and try as the authorities might to protect this bird they have had little success. Pigeons are not very intelligent and are easily captured; the Chinese are very intelligent and not easily caught capturing pigeons. Happily, the population balance between Chinese and pigeons is about right. The capacity of the pigeons for breeding has kept pace with the capacity of the Chinese cooking pot.

Aside from the blighted pigeons, Christmas Island's bird life is stunning. Rare varieties of booby rest in the tree tops overlooking a narrow-gauge railway, which runs the length of the island under cover of the rainforest. Black-and-white frigate birds swoop and glide an inch or two above the surface of the freshwater tanks on the beach, dipping to quench their thirst, and golden orioles circle in the sky, curling and diving in pairs, their tails flashing in the sunlight. The weather is warm, the sky blue and the view just endless miles of ocean—perfect conditions for an afternoon spent sitting in one of the bird-watching lookouts at the cliff's edge. Below, thousands of seabirds sit on the water, feeding their chicks, unperturbed by the strangers invading their privacy above.

The island's other animal life is just as rich and fascinating. At a certain time of year, Colonel crabs begin to migrate across the island. They are large (about the size of pudding plates), either bright red or blue, with long thin legs and small pincers. They move like an army through the rainforest, across roads and railway tracks, through gardens and even houses—a vast phalanx of crabs enjoying their holiday away from home. Like tourists to Christmas Island there seems to be no stopping them. Luckily for them, they are practically inedible—not even the Chinese bother with them.

In the late 1950s, the British, ridding themselves of their colonial past, returned control of the island to the Australians who were keen to own a strategic landmass some 900 miles off their coast. Now, however, the place has become a bit of a liability. The mines are no longer profitable and the Chinese workers all want to live in Melbourne. The Australians' solution has been, as the solution to such problems always is, to turn the island into a tourist paradise. The first step was to build a casino, and the next to introduce regular flights and build a hotel. When I last visited Christmas Island in 1996, I flew in the mining company's plane, staying but a day to see the wondrous bird life and enjoy one of the best Chinese lunches of my life. I have not returned since to see how tourism suits the island. I only hope that it has not altered the atmosphere that I found so uniquely powerful.

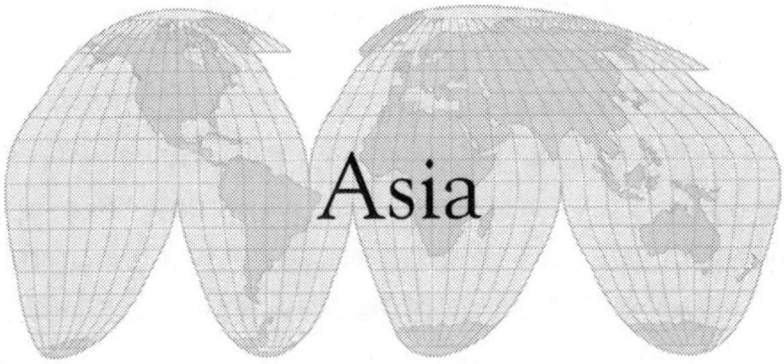

Asia

Street life in Singapore

The crowded cornucopia that Singapore once was has now vanished beneath cascading glass and overwhelming orchids.

A flight to Australia is a long and tedious affair. On a visit there in 1990, I decided to spend three days in Singapore to break the boredom. After leaving its mega-airport—a labyrinth of moving stairways, fresh-decked with fluorescent orchids, like some Eastern shrine to the modern world—the traveller encounters profuse vegetation on each side of the road into town. There are rows of hibiscus, rows of lilies and, in fact, serried ranks of tropical plants that seem at first enchanting and then monotonous—vast quantities of trees and plants, but of only half-a-dozen varieties.

Singapore is a difficult city to arrive at for there are so many trees in the city that it seems like the countryside, and so many buildings in the countryside that it seems like the city. No smell of exotic perfume there, no smell of oriental spice, just petrol. Its now expensive aroma hangs in the hot and sweaty air, kept captive by banks of cloud, washed almost daily by heavy rain. It is a good rule of thumb that if a country has a large quantity of lush greenery, it always gets a large quantity of rain. There is a monotony about Singapore found, I believe, nowhere else. The shops—Chanel, Cartier, Louis Vuitton, not one but multiple agencies of these great houses—selling their products half a season behind the rest of the world. Twelve hours by aeroplane from winter to summer, but in Singapore it is hard to tell one from the other. Seasons here become irrelevant and so the fashions in these fashionable shops trail behind, with unsold goods lingering on the shelves.

Its buildings, erected with all the advantages of blatant commerce, have failed—towers scaled down from other towns, and clippings from architectural magazines pasted into this city and then hidden with trailing bougainvillea and filled with potted palms. The high-ceilinged foyers of the early 1960s display their overgrown chandeliers of cascading glass. New buildings that were once Singapore's pride now seem like a reproach. Systematically town planners have, for nearly 25 years, destroyed everything that was old. Hotels are everywhere, snatched from any American city and built in Singapore. Everywhere there are orchids—in every foyer, in every room, on every table, tucked in napkins on trays, delivered with the morning papers; there is nowhere to go, nothing to do, that does not involve orchids, and always the same sort of orchid.

To be fair to Singapore—a city that offers no real reason to be fair to it—the mood has changed. They are now rebuilding the old buildings as quickly as they can. Chinese merchants and Malay traders are being moved back into reproductions of the shops that they occupied before they were decanted into modern blocks. Bugis Street is being rebuilt—rebuilt somewhere else, for its original site is now the headquarters of the Urban Transit Authority. The Tourist Authority feels the need to re-create some local colour and no doubt a Bugis Street Authority will be created to do just this. The days when you had to kick the pipes in Raffles Hotel to start the flow of water are long gone. The days of the old Bugis Street have passed—a street closed to traffic, and open to food and the world's greatest form of theatre: the accident of large numbers of people enjoying themselves. Tables all over the pavement, tables all over the street. Food that crosses the borders of the Far East. Nothing that you could not sell. Packed with travellers, drinking, eating, laughing and, very much later, tears and fights. The nightly parade of transvestites, quite beautiful in their way, posing for photographs with the diners, poking fun at drunks who perhaps did not realise that the beautiful girl they hugged had more to her. A visit to Bugis Street was an event. Nothing really to do with the buildings, it was about people—not special people but special I suppose because of their ordinariness. A drunken sailor standing on a table pouring beer over himself, a party of Australians, the most ungainly of travellers. How can you rebuild this? Better let it go.

To wake after the flight that night and to look down on the blue fingers of Sydney Harbour, its white Opera House and grey steel bridge, a city of clean air, a dry city with roofs poking like red pimples through its greenery, a sight that caused some great figure visiting from Europe to exclaim to the press at the airport: 'My first impression of Sydney—impetigo.'

Super sadomasochistic, sexy and ferocious

Even though the sound of it is something quite atrocious, in Singapore's toyshops I find my collector's urge aroused by their kitsch, kinky and downright bizarre stock.

If Singapore wished to be described, only two words would satisfy that thrusting place's self-esteem. Those words are 'a success'. Beauty and culture came second to the government's crusade for success. Buildings were torn down and heritage destroyed as if it were merely second-hand. Now a history museum flourishes and the ghosts of nineteenth-century buildings are converted into offices and hotels, but it is too late to recover a heritage destroyed—one now admired throughout the world. Singapore is completely in tune with our age; a new heritage of shopping fulfils an insatiable appetite for consumer products. Customised jeans, for instance—so fashionable this year and dead on their legs the next—are on offer in infinite varieties and huge quantities.

It was, however, not Singapore's clothing stores that took my interest, but the toyshops. In a shopping centre opposite my hotel I found four splendid examples of Singapore, Queen of Kitsch. The first, Lovely Land, sells such desirable items as the 'pet reading lamp'. This, sadly, is not a lamp for pets to read by—which would really be something—but a small, chubby, plastic tiger with a grotesque grin and a fluorescent shade. The Hello Kitty tracing kit was also on sale in profusion: a pink confection of almost total horror, surpassed only by the Eye Dog, a fluffy thing with large paws and larger eyes. 'Hello Kitty', it seems, is embossed on everything from portable telephones to Elastoplast.

Next door is Nick and Hanis, a shop reminiscent of the 1950s, whose contents makes the worst vulgarity of that age seem refined.

Imitation guitars are on offer, covered in (hopefully) fake Dalmatian, leopard and zebra skin. Emu-feather dusters sell like hot cakes, although the more expensive peacock-feather dusters are a bit of a drag on the market. Half-moon lamps, fully 3 feet long, hang in profusion, alongside standard lamps with mosaic stalks and painted fake oil lamps. It occurs to me that this shop contains almost everything that they did not think of in the 1950s, including violently coloured plates decorated with 3D cactuses.

Next door is World of 88—a toyshop. A 12-inch King Kong has an egg appearing out of his back, from which hatches a headless, naked man. I can only conclude that this toy's design is based on a serious misconception. Watching this absorbing event is a group of sinister, horned Batmen, all seated to get the best view. Also in the audience are three-headed, three-tailed dragons in various colours. Around the shop are displayed a tribe of robots, so fearsome that *Star Wars*' Darth Maul would look timid by comparison.

Miniature Hobby, across the way, has models of tanks, planes, ships and all the horrid implements of war. Various conflicts are immortalised in plastic: France 1942; Normandy 1944; the Lebanon war; and the Holy War—whose, I do not know. Then there is a lady in a bikini wearing nothing else except a helmet, gun belt and combat boots; whether she is there to entertain troops or customers is unclear. The purpose of her colleague in leather corset and bondage gear is unmistakable, as is that of the other PVC-clad female models carrying whips. The largest of the group has a steel tail attached to her leather suit and wears spiked sunglasses.

From here on in, it is all downhill, In Amazon Pets, a naked female pats a dinosaur. Primeval Princess pats *twin* dinosaurs. An alien eats bits of people; a lady in white stands over a bloodstained torso; and a bloke with bronze wings, long nails and a bad case of scaly skin is in a clinch with a naked woman. Both stand on a heap of understandably angry snakes; this is entitled 'Vampire Kiss'. So awful are the contents of these shops with their works in the tradition of postmodernism that I suppose they have become art. However, just this once I could resist collecting them.

Hanoi polloi

In Vietnam's capital city, Hanoi, I learn to love the terrifying hustle and bustle of the streets, and come across a haven of calm and a mythical tortoise.

This is a reflection on my return visit to Hanoi in the mid-1990s. The streets of Hanoi are jam-packed. Cycles and scooters weave their own pattern, dodging between the occasional truck or car and the 'cyclos', back-to-front tricycles with seating for a driver and one passenger. The pavements mean nothing to the citizens of Hanoi who seem to spend most of their lives cooking and eating on them. The shop-keepers' wares are spread across pavements. Cycles and scooters are parked on them, and it is not at all unusual to be confronted with a motorcycle coming straight at you.

Traffic regulations do not appear to exist in Hanoi—those who use the roads choose whichever side takes their fancy. There are traffic lights, but I doubt if many of the population know why. The whole affair has all the dash and panache of the Horse Artillery's musical ride at the Royal Tournament. And how do you manage to cross the street among this woven mass of traffic? Surprisingly easily, once you get the hang of it. The first rule is not to wait for the traffic to ease. The second rule is not to look right or left, for there is no point and in any case what you see may well cause you to lose your nerve. No, step straight into the traffic and wander slowly across the street. The traffic knows that it has to avoid you, and if you try to avoid it, it will only confuse everyone. After a week in Hanoi I had not seen a single collision, let alone an accident with a pedestrian. The sadness of it all is that five years ago there were only bicycles and in five years time there will only be cars and scooters—Hanoi is a city on the turn. Buildings are torn down apace and cranes hover over empty holes that will soon be filled with the worst offerings of Hong Kong and Singapore.

But for now it is a beautiful city—the perfect blend of the European and the Oriental. The streets have a Parisian width and are lined with trees; at their intersections the corners are cut back to give more space. Police officers stand on drums shaded by umbrellas, much as they do in Nice and Cannes. Girls sell baguettes filled with some local delight on the sidewalks. A number of Vietnamese men still wear berets as French men do, and it is not unusual to come across a French château or more often a street of suburban Parisian houses. Built at the turn of the century, the old buildings of Hanoi are wonderfully decayed. The French colonial architecture of the government offices has exotic Eastern detailing and is painted with a luminous yellow distemper.

The city jail was built by the French and used to imprison American airmen captured during the Vietnam War or, as the Vietnamese call it, 'the American War'. Nicknamed the Hanoi Hilton, ironically the jail is now to become a huge hotel. Currently the best hotel is the Metropole, a watering hole in the colonial tradition, complete with an inebriated Australian journalist in the bar.

Hanoi is a city built around lakes. Mid-afternoon, crowds stand and stare at one of the largest of these lakes: they are looking for tortoises, which sounded an unlikely story to me. However, across a red chinoiserie bridge that could have come straight from a volume of Chambers' architecture I found a pagoda, and in its back room a stuffed tortoise—almost 7 feet long and weighing 550 pounds—that is said to have lived to 500 years old. However, it is not just the size and age that makes it a remarkable beast. Indeed, this tortoise was a sort of Vietnamese King Arthur. In the fifteenth century Vietnam was invaded. The King, Le Loi, perplexed as to how he could deal with the invaders, took a boat ride on the lake and up pops this tortoise with a sword in his mouth. Le Loi beat the invaders and kept the sword until one day, when boating again, the tortoise sneaked up on him and took it back.

Hanoi is a shopper's paradise: whole streets dedicated to selling a single product and not a sniff of Gucci or Pucci anywhere. The markets are a seething mass of selling and buying almost everything from betel nuts that look like enormous carrots to crabs so small your little fingernail would look large in comparison. Then there are giant snails and large fish kept in washbasins of dirty water and stroked by young girls to keep them alive.

In contrast to all this confusion is the eleventh-century temple that was Vietnam's first university. Its gardens with brick paths, squares of lawn surrounded by stone walls and large tanks of water lilies feel quite English. In the last of these gardens stands the temple, flanked by colonnades where the steles that recorded the great and good of Vietnam are kept. In the centre of all this is one tank far larger than its fellows called the Well of Heavenly Clarity, a well that catches all the light and is the symbol of the centre of knowledge and civilisation.

Pagoda spree

The ancient city of Pagan in Burma has more temples than it knows what to do with. I was enchanted by them all.

There are few sights as wonderful as a misty dawn over the temples of Pagan in Burma, I arrived there aboard *The Road to Mandalay*, a Rhine steamer converted to travel the Irrawaddy River between Mandalay and Pagan. After breakfast I sat on the upper deck of the steamer as it gently probed its way between the Irrawaddy's sandbanks. Every once in a while the bow ran aground and we came to a sharp halt, causing the water from the upper deck's pristine swimming pool to form a tidal wave and wash along the deck.

We left our night anchorage, about three hours' sailing from Pagan, as dawn broke. The water of the Irrawaddy turned pink as the sun rose out of a distant landscape. Along the river we passed boats the shape of bananas driven by ancient diesel engines, their decks crowded with passengers and cargo. Standing at the stern and using the oars crossed like scissors, local fishermen rowed craft the size and shape of gondolas. On the shore girls washed what looked for all the world like bundles of grass, while water carts pulled by bullocks were filled at the water's edge.

The peace was perfect as we sailed along in the warm sunshine, when I noticed that the other passengers were moving towards the bow. Ever curious, I joined them. There at the top of a valley running down the river bank stood a ravishing small pagoda. It could have come from a great Anglo-Chinese garden and was in exactly the right state of disrepair to excite the interest of even the most insensitive of humans. I have always held the opinion that the possibility of improvement is almost irresistible, be it in people or places. I would have loved to have got my hands on this near-perfect building. In the two days that followed I saw literally dozens of similar pagodas (there are over two thousand in and around Pagan), some grander, shabbier, smaller and prettier, but the first pagoda that I had come across was still the one I wanted. Sadly, my hopes were dashed, for James and Shirley Sherwood had got there first and had already arranged to restore the pagoda through the auspices of the World Heritage Fund.

Leaving the river behind, we climbed from the boat and boarded the bus for town. Around the pagodas, which are still in use, you are deluged by commerce. Small boys sell postcards and brooches, older boys sell lacquer boxes and women ply flowers and all manner of religious objects, a variety of 'gemstones' (most of which are little more than glass) and Buddhas. At the airport when you leave, your luggage will be x-rayed, not for bombs but for Buddhas: the Burmese take great exception to foreigners exporting them without the proper papers.

This spirit of commercialism isn't limited to street trading. Right through the centre of this ancient city, made up of pagodas that date from the mid-ninth to the beginning of the fourteenth century, runs a road—not a bullock track but a motorway. How strange it is that when humans create something really worthwhile, sooner or later they end up wrecking it, either consciously or unconsciously.

That night the tourists lingered silently to watch a sight even more wonderful than the dawn; the sunset cutting a glowing scar in the Irrawaddy River before vanishing behind the distant mountains.

Zen and the city

There is no doubt that moving around urban Vietnam is a considerable struggle: battling the Hanoi traffic, digesting the truth about cats and dogs, and racing snails, to achieve spiritual serenity at the But Thap pagoda.

There is no such thing as an early start in Hanoi, for the streets are covered with traffic both day and night. A city that was once a crawling mass of bicyclists is now a buzzing mass of motorcyclists. Seven o'clock was the hour to depart, my guide informed me—not to beat the traffic, but rather to avoid the worst of the heat. At seven sharp we left, moving along with a large part of the population of Hanoi on their motorcycles. Happily, we travelled in a car; traffic lights, a new introduction to the city, are ignored. The traffic police who once stood on pedestals at crossroads have, with good sense, retreated to the pavements, from where they watch the traffic sort itself out, which it does in much the same way that a sluggish river finds its way around obstacles.

Parking is no problem in the city: bicycles are merely placed on the pavement, leaving the street free for pedestrians and other traffic. 'The bicyclist is king,' my guide informed me. Carried by this stream of traffic, we passed groups of Vietnamese eating their breakfast among the parked motorcycles, wing-mirror to basket with bicycles laden with flowers and fruit. To our left the guide pointed out 'dog-meat village' with its 30 restaurants serving dishes made only of dog. The meat is considered unlucky but so delicious it can't be resisted—my guide only eats dog at the end of the month; in this way he has only a day or two of misfortune.

Further on is 'snake-meat village'. It is illegal to eat snakes in Vietnam, as the meat is so popular that all the snakes began to disappear and there was nothing to eat the rats. 'Snake meat,' my guide warned, 'should not be eaten by people under 40 years old.' It has, it seems, an energising quality that makes youthful individuals unable to contain themselves. 'The more poisonous, the better the meat is,' my guide salivated. The restaurants, if asked what they are selling, tell you that they are serving dragon. In much the same way, the restaurants serving cat meat say that it is baby tiger. Snake is clearly more popular than dog, for there are some 300 restaurants in this village.

In time we turned off the road onto a cart track. We went on among paddy fields, dodging cows and chickens. You don't see many ducks, as to eat them is considered bad luck by the Vietnamese; this is good luck for the ducks, which are kept only for laying eggs. We moved along this track at a snail's pace until we came to a market, at which point the snail would have been a furlong or two ahead of us. What, however, is the point of hurrying when you pass through countryside as beautiful and exotic as that of Vietnam?

After an hour and a half we drew up at the But Thap pagoda's door. The pagoda dates from the thirteenth century, although there is little sign of the original buildings; it sits, with its stone walls, wooden building, roofs and tower, among carefully-tended gardens and sweeping paddy fields. A local poet in antiquity described the pagoda as being 'impregnated with the country's spirit'. Extraordinary as this description may be, it catches the feeling of the place. Once through the gateway, the pagoda is a magic world. Inside the buildings local people worship in the gloom, incense burns and gleams of sunlight catch the statues of Buddha and the other gods like spotlights. No museum could show these amazing works of art to such advantage. Long cloisters surround the temples, and dark streams run confined to stone rills. At the heart of it all rises the tower, the grave of the Ch'an master Chuyet Chuyet (who died in 1644); it is the sort of tower that would find a place in any grand English garden. Most remarkable of the wonders at this pagoda—surpassing even the statue of Kwan Yin with a thousand eyes and a thousand hands—are the eighteen portraits of well-known Buddhist preachers, dating from the beginning of the eighteenth to the early nineteenth centuries. Unlike most religious statuary, these are portraits of real people taken from life. Other examples can be found in the sanctuary; best of all are the portraits of the four people who paid for the rebuilding of the pagoda in the mid-seventeenth century.

Block to block

I battled bikes and cattle to reach Lang Dong Ho, home to the prince of Vietnamese woodblock printers.

An hour or so from Hanoi, depending on the motorcycle traffic, is Lang Dong Ho or that was what my guide told me. This village is not an easy place to reach. The access road or track runs along the top of the dyke that holds back the Red River (since the demise of communism now known as the Pink River) in times of flood. The dyke, some 50 feet or more above the flood plain that borders the river, is an extraordinary vantage point from which to view the surrounding countryside. Progress along the track, which is congested with cyclists, cattle and ancient vehicles, is at walking pace, giving one plenty of time to study the busy landscape; it also added an hour and a half to my journey. Strangely, some of the most beautiful sites that I came across were the brickworks that sit along the banks of the river: their kiln-like forms memories of some long-lost culture, their disused clay pits flooded with water and now home to large quantities of lotus flowers—even their bricks, stacked with Oriental precision, were things of beauty.

After a terrifying descent from the dyke involving hairpin bends and three-point turns that had grown to become 30-point turns, we arrived in Lang Dong Ho, which is home to many printers who use woodblocks made from jackfruit trees. (The jackfruit itself is spectacular to look at, but disappointing to eat; it is also cursed with a noxious smell. The wood of its tree, however, is rock hard, just right for use in colour printing.) We passed the studios of about thirty printers before we came to the home and studio of Nguyen Dang Che, a diminutive man who is the most famous printer in the whole of Vietnam—and who, if I understood my guide's interpretation of his explanation, is preserved by UNESCO.

His house has two reception rooms. In the first is a large altar, and in the second is a collection of almost five hundred different carved printing blocks, some of them 500 years old. Nguyen Dang Che explained that he used to have a great many more blocks but that they had been sent to France and had not been returned. After the formal introductions we sat down together for tea and talked. He explained that all the printer's colours come from nature. Ground river oyster shell makes a white pigment; yellow comes from flowers; the deep reds are made from ground flints; green pigment not surprisingly comes from leaves; and black from burned bamboo leaves. Other colours are achieved by mixing primaries in various proportions. The printer then kneels before a small cushion on which is placed the fine paper that he uses. The wooden block is coated in one colour and gently pressed against the paper. The same process is repeated with different blocks and different colours until the print is complete. The subject repertoire ranges from small, brightly coloured prints of animals and gods, scenes with wrestlers and parades of musicians, to a particularly exotic work showing a procession of rats wearing green waistcoats and carrying umbrellas, placards, musical instruments, flags and fish, while a cat with a distinctly hungry look in his eye watches. The larger, more sophisticated prints are about 4 feet long and printed mostly in monochrome, then touched up by hand with shades of grey; their subjects are dancers, musicians, and street and court scenes.

It all looked so terribly easy as Nguyen Dang Che set about his work. When, however, I then studied the work of other artists in the village, it became clear that he really is a master. So taken was I by his work that it was not long before I was planning a chinoiserie room in Italy, the likes of which has not been seen for a hundred years or more. The prints were just the right size and shape to use as panels of wallpaper. Then I stopped to ask their price. When my guide replied, I queried his answer:

'Are they really only a few dollars each?'

'No, that price is for a set of four.'

White Thai and tales

Fresh green tea, opium honey and Coca-Cola: I went in search of the real Vietnam.

Even though it was early in the morning the day was hot, and already the streets of Hanoi were jammed with the city's interminable traffic. After one-and-a-half hours, however, we were well on our way along the road to the north-west of Vietnam and the district of Mai Chau. This expedition was to visit the White Thai people—not a subtribe of head waiters, but rather a minority nation who live in Vietnam. There are also Black Thais, Moo and Hmong peoples and 48 other nations in the hill country.

As the road rose into the hills we passed fields of carefully clipped tea bushes; beside the road were young boys selling bags of fresh green tea. There was also honey for sale, but my guide advised against it: 'Honey from the district where the poppies grow is much better.' However, we did not come across any of this opium honey, so I cannot report on either its taste or its effect. Jars of rice wine are also sold in roadside shops, but I'm afraid I did not try this either. Ever since I had a bad experience in the home of a potter I have been extremely careful about accepting drinks in Vietnam. This gentleman kindly invited me into his home—to see his pottery, I thought, although he was of the belief that I would like an alcoholic drink. It was served in an elegant cup with no handle; I disposed of its contents in one mouthful. The potter assumed that I had enjoyed it and quickly refilled the cup—it was only then that I saw the bottle. Its contents looked, if such a thing is possible, even more horrible than they tasted. A large black snake lay curled in the liquid, and the potter watched with what was perhaps a sly grin as I finished every drop in the cup.

Passing up the chance of sampling rice wine, therefore, I went next door to a shop selling tables and chairs made from tree roots. Further along the road there were piles of tufa for sale; had I been in England I would have had the makings and furnishings of a considerable grotto. The complications of shipping the stuff home, however, were too great for me to contemplate, so it was back in the car and onwards to the White Thais and their beautiful textiles.

The village is set in a valley, with fields climbing the surrounding hillsides. Water buffalo work these fields; we were delayed on the road for a few minutes by one pulling a load of logs. Most houses have television powered by watermills set up at nearby streams. The communal house was set on stilts like the other homes. Under nearly all the houses were farm animals and looms; weaving seemed to be the main occupation. The prices of these high-quality textiles ranged from a few dollars to a maximum of US$25. Children and adults clustered around what they rightly perceived to be an eager customer. Lunch was served in the communal house: the food was wonderful, as Vietnamese food usually is. Offered a drink, I insisted on Coca-Cola—they seemed to have a considerable supply, which puzzled me as I believed (as travellers often do these days) that I had found the real country, complete with people untouched by tourism. No sooner had I begun to preen myself on finding these people lost to the rest of the world—a people still following lives of agriculture and craft—than a bus pulled up and discharged a hundred French tourists, come to visit a former colony. None of us looks our best after travelling in extreme heat—these tourists, however, were the most ungainly bunch that I have ever come across. It was then I realised that weaving and agriculture in Vietnam today are just by-products of tourism.

Trainspotting

Journeying on the Eastern & Oriental Express from Singapore to Bangkok, I spot strange sights ranging from miniature cattle to a station in the style of Brighton Pavilion.

The Eastern & Oriental Express from Singapore to Bangkok travelled all afternoon through Malaysian jungle, a jungle punctuated by rubber plantations and palm groves. As the train sped on I glimpsed long, dark alleys between the palms. Dusk came and went with equatorial speed.

Suddenly the train came to a halt. Looking out of the window I had the strong impression that we had just driven right through one of the walls of the Brighton Pavilion. I climbed down from the train to investigate and found that I was wrong, but not far off the mark: Kuala Lumpur railway station is the spitting image of Brighton Pavilion. Built almost a hundred years later, its minarets and crenellated walls, not to mention its curling staircases and chinoiserie roofs, are in such similar style that, had the station been constructed first, it would be claimed that Brighton Pavilion was a copy. It is worth taking the Eastern & Oriental Express just to see this railway station.

I scrambled back on board the train as it set off for Butterworth, the stop that connects with the ferry to Penang. I am usually an easy sleeper and this evening was no exception. My bed was comfortable beyond belief and I fell asleep as I turned out the light. The train swung from side to side, and just occasionally a swing became a jerk. Now I have, when I lie on my back a high centre of gravity. When such a jerk coincided with my moving, the bed tilted and became unfastened and I was thrown to the floor. Imagine my confusion. I did not know where I was or how I got there. I could not find a light or, for that matter, my bed.

Yet this abrupt halt to my heavy sleep was in fact a blessing. Sleep, as Ovid put it, is but death warmed up, and also I am of the view that it is generally a great waste of time. I dressed and headed for the observation car with its platform open to the early morning air.

How pleased I was to be so cruelly woken. With the dawn came a daylight veiled in mist. Monoliths of rock hundreds of feet high appeared through the haze like giants, their surfaces patterned with ancient caves and decorated with jungle foliage. Then we came to a lake, travelling its shores at a leisurely pace, and passing resting egrets and wading birds. Kingfishers overtook the train as flashes of blue that settled in the trees where monkeys took their first meal of the day.

A fisherman rowed his boat on the lake, which was edged with lotus plants. One of the most stately of the world's flowers, the lotus surprisingly also blooms in northern Italy, without the help of a greenhouse. Looking at this Malaysian lake brought to my mind a lake just outside Treviso in the Veneto where you can find these lotus plants in a large eighteenth-century garden with Chinese buildings at its edge. I wondered if the owner of that wonderful garden had constructed it from fond memories of the Orient.

Butterworth was our next stop, which was not much of a station in comparison with Kuala Lumpur. But Penang, only a few minutes away by ferry, had more to offer: a ravishing colonial church built at the beginning of the last century, followed by a hospital and colonial administrative buildings, each wonderful in their way.

On by train into Thailand, where paddy fields and villages lined the railway tracks, buffaloes wallowed in muddy waters and groups of children flew brightly coloured kites. The chickens in the farmyards were Malay fowl, a tall and muscular bird; the male is used in cockfights. I also spotted some miniature Brahman cattle—surprising since they mostly come from Sri Lanka—wandering among the palm trees on the edge of a village looking decorative. Like so many miniature animals, these cattle have a vile temper: I once kept some in England and recall several fierce encounters.

On to Bangkok, an urban disaster if ever there was one. The irony of this journey is that, while I cannot stand either Singapore or Bangkok, the journey between them is pure bliss.

Live and let Thai

Waterborne in Bangkok, I evade the snakes and crocodiles only to fall into a monstrous menagerie presided over by a very large budgerigar.

Bangkok is a name that seems to indicate that the capital of Thailand is as exotic a place as you could wish to visit. This is a reflection on my visit to that capital in 1992.

At Bangkok airport there are palm trees and orchids. Queues seem to be a speciality as well, not because there is a rush by the travellers of the world to visit the place, but rather because the young lady who deals with immigration papers takes an average of four minutes per visitor. The Thais have a reputation for friendliness, and their immigration officials excel in this respect. They laugh and talk to each other as they puzzle over the complicated forms devised by their superiors. There are at this airport nearly sixty desks all with officials who deal with such matters. But there are still queues that make the crowds at the opening of the Harrod's sale seem sparse.

Hot from waiting and from the traffic on the drive into the city, and tired of travel and dust, the hotel seemed paradise. There were green gardens touched with bougainvillea, a blue pool and the river beyond. In the foyer of this hotel stylish Italians lazed in the giant armchairs. An hour or two there, however, and this paradise changed: the stylish Italians became sluggish Germans. The pool appeared much smaller, and the river dirty. This hotel, to my mind, had become just another example of concrete and greenery decorated with elements of the Orient—elements so distorted as to lose the beauty that they once had. It had become, in fact, the sort of hotel that you find from Honolulu to Singapore.

Motorboats race up and down this dirty river: long narrow boats, their prows high in the air with bunches of plastic orchids hanging from them, and their sterns weighted down by an aircraft engine mounted about chest-height and driving a propeller at the end of a long piece of pipe. The driver lifts this propeller in or out of the water as he will. He turns it to the right or the left, spewing oil into the river and fumes into the air.

The canals have changed considerably in the last 25 years. The people who used to live there have largely moved elsewhere. Why should they live in cramped conditions over rat-infested water using only the most primitive forms of sanitation, just because it looks nice for the tourists? Anyway, tourists are there in plenty. The canals that remain have become a parade of motorboats ploughing their way through oil. The floating market seems to have moved to the land—leaving in its place a giant traffic jam of motor launches.

The houses have mostly been demolished, and only the rotting stumps that were their foundations remain. To stop the erosion great lengths of the canal banks have been piled—steel sheet piles that somehow do not really have the same feel of the Orient about them as the timber houses, although it's true that the occasional floating refreshment stall is still to be found. These dwellers of the waterways, who in their youth played in the water of the canals among the ducks and the waterlilies, are now grown and have removed themselves to flats in nearby concrete blocks built in the last few years. It is really amazing what the Orient can do to concrete. In our climate concrete seems harder than rock, but once it gets anywhere near the equator it seems to rot, crumbling away and leaving steel bars exposed which in time turn to rust, and then the concrete crumbles again.

On the banks of these canals there are occasional temples and their monks. The last part of our century seems to have attacked these temples, for lurid signs made with fluorescent tube announce whatever message was once painted on boards. These once-beautiful buildings have been crudely altered. On another canal there is the crocodile farm and, of course, the snake farm complete with a row of concrete men wrestling with concrete snakes, with men and snakes painted in frightening colour. Apart from the snakes, the crocodiles and the temples there is little to see. If you had the good fortune to travel these canals in the past, there is a great deal to mourn.

On the banks of Bangkok's main river there is a building called River City, consisting of four floors of wall-to-wall shopping. The third and fourth floors are given over to antique shops such as The Great Dragon, whose sign goes on to inform the curious that its contents are 'the ultimate expression of your good taste'. I looked inside and thought about this notice. I am bound to say it puzzled me a little. Another shop, Thai Foundry, announced that it 'casts your bronzes better'. I could see that. The bronzes for sale had indeed been very well cast but *why* they had been cast eluded me entirely.

Neither of these shops, however, had prepared me for the shock of Chieng Heng Collection Co Ltd. For a start there were the horses—horses of all periods and for that matter nearly all sizes, some far greater than life size. There were horses standing, lying, rolling and rearing—all cast in bronze. But if you are not keen on horses, they had bronze hippopotamuses, zebras, the greater kudu and leopards, not to mention grizzly bears and swans—every sort of animal in fact. The warrior department held examples of bronze warriors, both mythological and historical. These ranged from Perseus to King Richard I, and from medieval knights to the warriors of Genghis Khan and latter-day Arab warriors—one on a horse. But among all of these one piece stood out: a giant bronze budgerigar over 6 feet tall with a bright red beak.

Bangkok claims to be a city of a thousand canals—the Venice of the East? Never!

Starck staring surreal

Visiting Hong Kong I take up Philippe Starck's invitation to sit on someone's face: all this and Mao too.

The publicity blurb from the Peninsula Hotel in Hong Kong says, 'the innovative Felix Restaurant is a unique and exciting experience. Two custom-made express elevators transport customers from the lobby to the 28th floor of the Peninsula's new tower, to a world of spectacular views, a fun, friendly atmosphere and Pacific Rim cuisine'. This all sounds pretty good, in a PR sort of way, but it describes only half of Philippe Starck's masterpiece. For a start, in the most exotic lifts in which I have ever travelled, the lights begin to go out near the top floor. This gives you a bit of a shock, but nothing like the shock you get as you step into a darkened lobby where all you can see of the distant restaurant is a view of a long, glass dining table raised on a dais. The whole of this is brightly lit: customers use it as one might use the centre table in a London club. The effect of the comings and goings around this table is not unlike Veronese's vast painting *Feast in the House of Levi*; all that was missing, on the night I dined, were the parrots and the monkey.

In the restaurant proper, each chair has the face of someone known to either Starck or the hotel's proprietor printed on it. The cutlery is elegant, as is the food, which is about the only thing in the place not designed by Philippe Starck. Turn your back on the jollity taking place at the great table and you will be faced by what Starck calls the Two Snails, one each side of the entrance tunnel. These are bucket-shaped areas built around a pair of spiral staircases. At the top of one staircase is the Balcony, a small bar packed with people enjoying a drink and, most of all, a grandstand view of the diners. At the top of the other staircase is the American Bar, where I found one American reading a newspaper—a sight, in the context of this surreal place, so in tune with Starck's decor that at first I thought he was maybe a waxwork.

Under the Balcony and American Bar are the Wine Bar, decorated with a multitude of wine bottles, and the Crazy Box, a nightclub with a dozen or so small tables, each holding a silver champagne bucket with a bottle in it. These buckets and bottles are not there to provide refreshment, but rather permanent decoration—a device to stop people sitting on these tables. Travellers to Hong Kong should not miss this strange and wonderful place.

In sharp contrast (or, for that matter, in stark contrast) is David Tang's China Club. The elevator to this splendid place, however, has seen far better days, although its lighting system does not so much as flicker on reaching its destination. The decor of this club is pure 1930s Shanghai: but with a touch of taste and comfort that the smarter Londoners will know as synonymous with the name of club proprietor Mark Birley. In the Long March Bar, on the first floor of the China Club, is a collection of porcelain figures depicting Chairman Mao and his comrades. Made in the last 50 years, these are among the few manifestations of Communist art that are really interesting.

Attentive staff, excellent food and porcelain figures apart, there is another reason to visit the club. Over the last ten years or so, David Tang has put together a magnificent collection of contemporary Chinese paintings and sculpture—a genre about which I had been dubious, but these pictures look absolutely splendid and strangely at home among the 1930s decor. So impressed was I that the next morning I set out in search of their source. It was a certain Johnson Chang, whose gallery, Hanart TZ, has a fine selection of the best contemporary Chinese paintings.

Rather than sink into a slough of despond on its return to Chinese rule, Hong Kong has taken off artistically. The Felix Restaurant with its way-out decor by Philippe Starck, and the China Club with its way-out paintings by China's best artists, are both solid evidence of this.

Bali bazaar

On Bali even the fakes are faked, and everywhere is open all hours. This is a shopaholic's tropical paradise.

For a person addicted to shopping, like myself, Bali is truly a paradise. There is no object that the Balinese cannot replicate and sell at a discount. Unlike most countries where goods are copied, the fakes in Bali end up looking better than the originals. Bali is an island where antiques are made to order. Things have reached such a pitch that craftspeople are even faking fakes.

It is a place of paddy fields, where the Balinese fly giant kites in the wind. In its towns, you see patriotic statues painted cream so that they look like enlarged versions of the butter carvings which decorate the buffets of hotels, and Bali certainly has its share of hotels. I passed one heavily disguised as a Suffolk farmhouse and called the Edelweiss Hotel.

The atmosphere in Bali is pure magic. Of all the places in the Orient that I have visited, this island is by far the most exotic. It is a Far Eastern Disneyland. Village after village sells goods to tourists or to the architects furnishing hotels. Each village specialises in just one craft: a village of silversmiths, a village of stonemasons or a village of woodcarvers.

I drove from the paradise that is the Amanusa Hotel to another hotel in the same group, the Amandari. Along the way, I was seduced into stopping at a village that makes umbrellas—not the sort that keep the rain away but grand ceremonial umbrellas, straight from the Hollywood set of *The King and I*. There were umbrellas made of coloured silks; wide umbrellas on heavy poles; small umbrellas on long, thin sticks; and umbrellas three to a pole. I haggled with a village trader and bought four of these wonderful objects. The trader not only accepted American Express, but also knew how to ship the goods to Venice. He had, after all, sent a consignment there only a couple of weeks before.

I would never have made the Amandari and my lunch appointment if I had visited all the shops that caught my eye. As some nations line their country roads with trees, so the Balinese line theirs with shops. One village that I passed through made only windvanes, particularly ones that look like wooden fish. They hung in front of the shops in their dozens—strings and strings of brightly painted, wooden, tropical fish. The whole effect was extraordinary. As I drove along the main street of that village, it was as if I travelled in a submarine past some Pacific reef.

The next village seemed to contain nothing but basket makers, In fact, I saw several villages of them. In another village were fake antiques, aged hundreds of years by a few strokes of a paintbrush; and there were fake copies of the fake antiques, less skilfully done so that the genuine fakes would be thrown into favourable contrast.

Lunch at the Amandari was an absolute delight. The views from the hotel across paddy fields and gorges were stunning. The hotel has a walkway through the middle of it, because it has been built across a pathway traditionally used by monks as a route from their monastery to a nearby shrine.

Bali is still an extraordinary mixture of primitive simplicity and a demonstration of the whole population's wild urge to engage in trade. The truly horrible towns, where tourism has taken over completely and done its worst, staining the streets with fast food, multistorey buildings and sleazy nightclubs, are balanced by some of the world's most sophisticated and elegant hotels, where luxury and peace are carefully nurtured. I would go back to Bali again and again, even if it were no longer such a delightful place, for I enjoy shopping quite as much as the Balinese obviously enjoy selling.

India

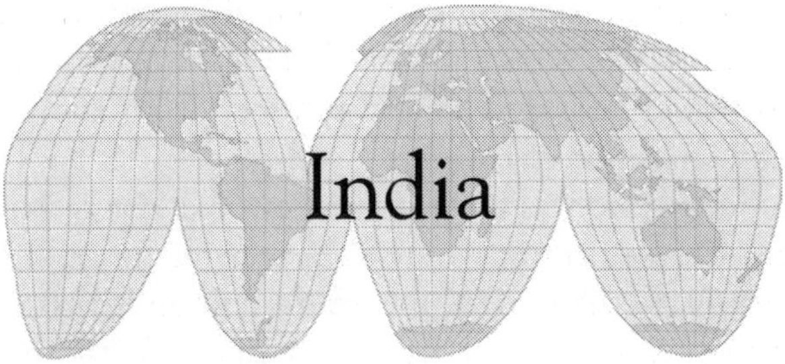

Dazzled in Rajasthan

Today the coffers of the fabled Jaigarh, the fortress guarding the pass into Jaipur, lie empty but nearby, among the burnished, pearly walls of the Amber Palace, I uncover a sparkling Rajasthani treasure.

The stalls selling crash helmets, at the beginning of the main road from Delhi to Jaipur, were ominous to say the least. Not far into my journey I wished I had bought one. The traffic in the state of Rajasthan knows no rules. Five hours later, my fingers locked to the back of the driver's seat, my teeth worn to stumps, I entered the pass that leads to Jaipur. Guarding that pass stands a sinister fortress, the Jaigarh, where the rulers of Jaipur kept their treasure.

Only the treasure's hereditary keeper and the maharajah of Jaipur were ever allowed to see this vast accumulation of wealth. The maharajah was shown it only once, on his accession, taking from it one piece that he desired. When, under the rule of Indira Gandhi, the government decided that this fabulous treasure should become the property of the state, they found that it was missing. Told that it was in any case only a myth, they were not convinced and dug holes all over the place looking for it.

Today the only treasures on display at the fort are a fine collection of weapons, including the world's largest cannon, and a splendid view of the Amber Palace. The palace cannot be reached from the fort except by a secret passage, so the traveller has to descend by a circuitous route to the village at the neck of the pass. Near rows of painted elephants, snake-charmers enchant their cobras, hawkers sell almost everything and the roads are jammed with camel-carts.

Once safely—I hoped—aboard an elephant, I was transported up the winding ramp to the Amber Palace. Below me lay the Maota Lake, with its peninsula given over to Mogul gardens. The curling marquetry of flower beds and waterways, seen from above, looks like a Persian scarf laid upon the waters.

The palace courtyard was seething with people. Foreign tourists were a rarity among the jostling mass of Indians pressing to see their heritage.

Breaking through the crowds into the private gardens of the royal family, all is peace. The water no longer runs and the pomegranate trees are past their best, but as a spur to the imagination these gardens are unequalled. The rooms off the gardens are plastered with a mixture of ground eggshells and powdered pearls, once burnished to the point where, it is said, even an ant could not crawl up them. I came across painted gateways, paved courtyards and sunken gardens with geometric pools and rills, mirrored walls and screens of stone fretwork. I felt like a midget, lost in the ornate icing of a wedding cake.

Many of the state rooms are decorated with Mogul low-relief plasterwork in the shape of bottles, stones and surrounded with curlicues. In one such room, the door was closed behind us, leaving us standing in the dark. The attendant lit a candle and turned the ceiling into a mass of stars that twinkled as the candle moved. Many centuries ago, he explained, the light mountain breezes would have made every candlelit room glisten and shine.

Back out in the sunlight of the courtyard, a trader offered me a gaudily painted puppet. 'This is John Major,' he announced in a serious tone. Seeing that I was unimpressed, he grabbed another grotesque and declared that it was Boris Yeltsin.

Indian rogue trick

Sometimes a friend in need can be an expensive business. As I found to my cost, the phrase 'guiding principles' takes on a different meaning in India.

Travelling in India has its own particular dangers—not life-threatening ones, unless you drive in a motorised vehicle—but dangers nevertheless. Take the monkey men of Jaipur, who dress up in monkey skins and are permitted to jump onto the bonnet of your car, throw nuts at you and steal your handbag with impunity. Then there are the transvestites who can be found buying their make-up in most bazaars. They ask for money and get extremely bad-tempered if you turn them down.

It is, however, the guides that you have to watch out for; they are so cunning that they take even the most careful of travellers to the cleaners. Travelling from Jaipur to Delhi, I had what might be called a 'bad guide day'. I could see the stings coming and I still fell for them.

The first occasion was at the Keoladeo National Park at Bharatpur in Rajasthan. Queuing with a mass of visitors, I waited my turn at the window where an old man was selling tickets. Patience is not a virtue in India—time after time someone pushed in front of me. Only when I was helped by a smartly dressed young man did I finally buy a ticket. 'I do not want a guide,' I insisted. 'I am not a guide,' he replied with dignity. 'I am an ornithologist.' At a barrier, my friend the ornithologist took a bundle of my rupees and bought yet another ticket. We then climbed onto a pair of trishaws. True, I spent a blessed two hours watching birds and he did show me the rare Siberian white cranes. At the end of the ride I paid and tipped the drivers. My friend then announced that the drivers expected a bigger tip to celebrate the New Year; so I paid, as indeed I paid my new friend who explained that a further tip was in order. Never again, I resolved.

The next morning at sun up, I was sitting in the garden at the Taj Mahal when a man came up to me and said quite casually, 'Move to this spot and the reflection of the rising sun will be better.' I followed his instructions and asked if he was a guide. Not a bit of it: he was a gardener but came every day to watch the sun rise before he started work. Soon I was in tow. I visited the mosque, made a donation by leaving money (taken by the gardener) and in time paid him an exorbitant fee for his services. I even gave him the tip that he asked for. It was as if I had been hypnotised.

That afternoon in Delhi I made a pledge: no more guides. I resisted fortune-tellers, hawkers and moneychangers. Even shoeshine boys I turned away with angry gestures. Soon their cries turned to what I understood as 'Your shoes look like shit'. In time, one shoeshine boy forced me to look at them and I discovered that they were indeed covered in shit. 'Perhaps you have been too near a camel,' he said. The boy cleaned one shoe. From then on, it was obvious: pay or you don't get your shoe back; pay twice if you want them both. I could have bought a new pair for the cost of having them polished!

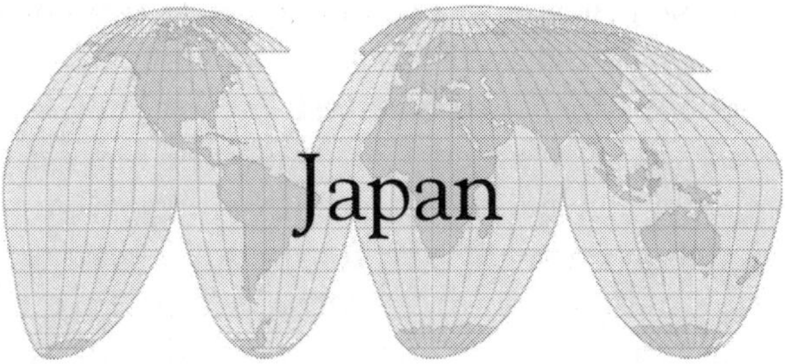

Japan

Cherry-go-round

In Japan I followed the cycle of rituals that accompany the blossoming of the cherry tree—from trunk-wrapping to merry parties beneath bountiful boughs.

There are certain places and events that seem to have become the property of The Tourist: Windsor Castle, Versailles, the Tower of London, the Changing of the Guard at Buckingham Palace and the Venice Carnivale—the list is endless. This is a shame, for each of these is remarkable in itself—well worth the struggle to see, and well worth fighting your way past the massed ranks of tourists who stand in front of a picture at Windsor Castle, or listen to a strident guide at Hampton Court. Well worth too the crowds at the Tower of London—which has the largest number of tourists visiting any site in the United Kingdom—for even a glimpse of the collection of arms and armour, a collection which is possibly the best in the world.

There are other places—for example the Louvre, the British Museum and the Metropolitan Museum in New York—which, although they have a large number of tourists, do not spring to mind in this context. Also, there are such events as the Derby and the Palio at Siena where you would expect large numbers of tourists. The Derby is basically a day out for Londoners, and the Palio an event for the Sienese which they take with great seriousness. Heaven help the hapless tourist who should pass a casual remark about the lack of flesh on any of the horses. A tourist in the wrong place is likely to be trampled by one of the several flag-waving and drum-beating phalanxes of locals. These are strictly events for the inhabitants.

The cherry blossom season, which in good weather lasts three or four days at the best, would seem to be a tourist trap thought up by some more-enterprising-than-usual government body: an event for the purpose of persuading tourists to visit Japan. The cherry blossom is taken seriously by all from emperor to doorkeeper. I do not know how the emperor celebrates Hanami (the best day for blossom viewing), but doorkeepers all over Tokyo, and I suppose Japan, are sent out early to reserve a tree. They spread a tarpaulin on the ground and surround it with tapes stretched between piles of stones. About midday they are joined by groups of workers from their offices. These groups then spend the rest of the day drinking sake and eating, pausing only to sing and dance. The same practice is carried out in the evening, despite the fact that it is dark and you cannot see the cherry blossom. The Japanese regard the cherry tree with a reverence similar perhaps to that with which the British once regarded the oak tree. There is no doubt that the blossoms of Japan are very beautiful; among the most beautiful is *Prunus* 'Shogetsu', known I believe in Japan as 'the blossom for which the emperor turned his carriage to look again'.

In Kyoto there is a temple where the cherry blossom seems to hang above the roofs of the red and green buildings, in contrast to the temple square with its white gravel reflecting the hard morning sun. Beyond the buildings is a garden, with walkways of weeping cherry, and ponds with carp and large, blue irises at their edge, with petals that tremble like exotic butterflies. There are I suppose far more cherry trees in Britain; it is just that the Japanese put them in the right places.

But for me the most wonderful sight is blossom like snow blowing from trees that grow on the banks of a canal. Even the trees themselves are worth looking at—or rather, not so much the trees but the way they are wrapped and propped, which gives them the strangest of shapes. They are propped, the Japanese say, to stop them blowing over in the typhoons. Perhaps it is really to make them look better. They are wrapped in layers of straw matting. The idea is that the boring beetles which live in Japan will drill into the matting, believing they have entered the tree, and lay their eggs between the mat and the tree, leaving the tree undamaged. I am inclined to believe that the Japanese just like wrapping things up.

The cherry blossom time is popular for weddings, with Sunday the most popular day. When I arrived at the hotel there were about twenty receptions going on at the same time. The brides were dressed in European white, the attendants wearing kimonos of the deepest plum. The bridegroom was dressed as I suppose Lieutenant Pinkerton once dressed. Attendants carried great swathes of ghost orchids—the whole effect was very beautiful. However, it seemed strange that all the grooms should dress in the same way and that all these brides should choose the same colour kimonos for the bridesmaids. Oh, how we travellers can misunderstand local customs. It was only later as I travelled in the lift that I noticed that these well-dressed grooms and bridesmaids were really the staff of the hotel in their uniforms. But then in Japan nothing is really how it seems.

Later, walking in the Ginza I saw in a shop window a painting by Yves Klein, and beside it a sculpture by the same artist—both of museum quality. Believing this to be a gallery I went inside to be confronted instead by several Japanese, stitching at gentlemen's suits of the most conservative kind.

Keeping nature in trim

I marvel at the colourful spectacle of autumn in Japan, where leaves are picked before they fall and look untidy, and even landscapes are reproduced in miniature.

The year had moved well into autumn as we know it before the leaves on the trees in Japan began to change colour, let alone fall from their trees. In the city of Kyoto the avenues of ginkgo trees had turned from green to yellow by the second week in November, but still they hung to the branches—their nuts having already fallen by this time. To pick up these much sought-after nuts, small boys dodge the early morning traffic, before they form orderly files to make their way to school. The ginkgo tree comes unchanged from prehistory, its split leaf an object of beauty used in Japanese cuisine both for decoration and also for eating. Round thin wafers are made with this leaf in the centre of them. The nuts are supposed to have a special power to increase the ability of the brain. They are quite expensive and in many Japanese households are locked away in a cupboard. Japanese men say to one another, 'Do not let the key of the cupboard where the nuts of the ginkgo tree are kept fall into the hands of women'. Having observed the attitudes of the Japanese male to his opposite sex, they are clearly frightened of anything that might change their status quo—even if it is only their wives and daughters having a surfeit of ginkgo nuts. The Japanese, being a particularly tidy race, are reluctant to let the leaves fall naturally from the trees that line their streets. Squads of them climb up ladders in November and pluck the leaves from the branches, stuffing them into large sacks supported from their waists.

There is a similar and equally extraordinary sight in Tokyo—gardeners are dangled on the ends of long ropes down the stone walls of the Imperial Palace to pull off the ivy that grows there and put it in similar bags. The leaf pluckers work like demented squirrels, and their efforts leave the trees suddenly bare. Then these men set about cutting the branches of the trees, making the whole thing into a shape pleasing to the eye. At this time of the year they do the same thing with the fir trees, cutting a branch here and a bundle of needles there. They work, several men to a tree, with certainty, never stepping back to have a look at how things are going. These arboreal hairdressers seem to know what they are about, and the result certainly is different, if not totally pleasing to the European eye.

We have a different approach to trees. For us, a tree must be large and full, the bigger the better. The trunk must be strong and have as great a diameter as possible, the branches sweeping almost to the ground. We like trees such as the oak, the beech and the horse chestnut. In evergreens, the giants among trees are the cedar and the *Wellingtonia*. We secretly despise softwood—the firs of the Forestry Commission used to fill in useless land and the cherry trees planted in the streetscape of new towns and urban gardens. The Japanese greatly admire the cherry tree for its blossom and the fir for its shape. We tend to leave trees alone until they get old and sick and then, if we cut bits off them, it is to balance and retain the shape of their youth. The Japanese like trees that look old and twisted. They artificially change the shape of the tree by tying them down or propping them up and cutting bits off them. They are forever tinkering with their trees.

I went to Japan in autumn to watch the leaves change colour; when it happens is largely dependent on how wet or how dry the summer has been. The change takes about a week and a good place to watch it from is Kyoto, a setting surrounded by heavily wooded hills. Unlike some parts of America where all the woodlands change at the same time, and to just one colour from another, the change in Japan is slow and infinitely more subtle.

The woodland in Japan is made up of many different trees whose leaves change to various colours at different times. Each morning the view is different from that of the previous evening, and each evening different from that of that morning. The light changes during the day, reversing and speeding these changes. Almost every minute of the five days I spent in Kyoto this phenomenon was different: the ginkgo trees with their yellow leaves, the cherries' shades of bronze, the green firs, patches of bamboo forest yellow and green like flashes of lightning, and the maples with their bright red leaves.

The Japanese are much taken with making things smaller. They have reproduced this grand landscape in miniature in the gardens of the Katsuura Imperial Villa. The same compositions of colour are there, and lakes, rivers and mountains have been built. It is the same landscape that surrounds the city of Kyoto. A great deal of trouble was taken over this garden 400 years ago and it has now been extremely well restored. The buildings are perfect, each in exactly the right position. But with its overhanging trees growing thick at the edge of the still and dirty water, it seemed to me very much like a Surrey garden. Humans at their best, even the Japanese, cannot compete with God: I am afraid the mistake that the creators of this garden made was not in competing with nature, but in having the natural product close at hand for comparison.

Of all the trees I saw the week I was there, the most beautiful was the red maple, and of all the gardens that of Tofuku-Ji Temple, the temple of bubbling springs. One of the best places to see these maples is the bridge between the two parts of that temple. This bridge was built, legend has it, for the convenience of the monks, who were fed up with walking down one very steep slope and up another one to reach the spot where they say their prayers. But it is my belief that they built the bridge just so they could see the trees better.

United Kingdom

Object lessons

As a schoolboy, my imagination was fired for life by the weird and wonderful objects I encountered living alongside part of the Pitt Rivers ethnographical collection.

Waterloo Station was an exciting place for a small boy in 1948. Giant engines—or at least they seemed giant to me—belched smoke, and steam occasionally erupted from between the carriages. Porters actually carried luggage and the guards tapped carriage wheels with long-handled hammers. Sadness rather than excitement was the emotion that I felt as small boys in grey suits and purple caps scuttled about. I was six years old, setting out for my first term at boarding school. The train jerked its way towards Salisbury. Small boys wept and their elders boasted of holiday feats.

We were bound for Sandroyd School, a smart prep school. I mention its name for one reason, which was that it occupied the former home of Lieutenant General Pitt Rivers at Tollard Royal. I did not realise then that Pitt Rivers was to become my great hero, as I set out for a world so different from my home: a world of discipline where there had been freedom; coldness—how terribly cold Rushmore House was—where I had enjoyed the warmth of open fires; the most evil-tasting food where at home I had eaten whatever I fancied. It was a world of mud and long wet walks, of communal baths after games, of boxing and physical training. In short, almost everything I disliked and, for that matter, still do.

In those days small boys at prep schools did not often see their parents. In the summer term parents were allowed to visit twice, arriving after lunch and leaving after tea. Usually the visit took the form of a walk in the school grounds or watching a school match. My parents hated sport quite as much as I did, and as we all had an equal enthusiasm for picnics we headed for a secluded spot.

The Rushmore estate was a lonely place with open downs and thick forests. Long rides cut in the forests led to clearings where charcoal burners and wattle makers were to be found. With little else to occupy us we often visited the Pitt Rivers Collection, at least the part of it that had not gone to Oxford, which was to be found in an old schoolhouse. I fell in love with the collection, with its shrunken heads from Amazonia, carvings from Africa and artefacts from the Orient. It was a great jumble of delight.

Most of all I loved the flints found on the Pitt Rivers estate, the pots and spearheads, the models of ancient villages and burial grounds. I suppose what made all this far more exciting for a young boy was the fact that these ancient villages and fortresses with their attendant burial mounds were all around the school. It was here that I played with my friends and fought my enemies, defending the same earth ramparts with lengths of ragwort that Romans had defended with iron spears and swords.

How I dreamt. Nothing the wretched masters tried to teach me was of any interest. I was lost to the world of Pitt Rivers, I read with a wild enthusiasm. My Latin was neglected for the adventures of the explorers who set out to find Colonel Fawcett, lost somewhere on the Amazon River. When I read of shrunken heads I knew what they looked like as I had seen one in the Pitt Rivers Collection. To teach by illustration is the point of this collection and the others that have joined it. Sadly, the collection at Tollard Royal has since been dispersed. Occasionally, you find an object from it in the salerooms, carefully inscribed 'PR' in white ink, numbered and described. These objects have a special beauty for me: they once belonged to Pitt Rivers.

To see the Pitt Rivers Collection today you must go to Oxford where the ten thousand or so objects he gave to the university are housed in the museum that bears his name. Pitt Rivers set its style, but Henry Balfour made it great. Balfour came from a wealthy family and spent his fortune on this fascinating museum. Asked at the age of 21 to set the collection in order, he stayed for the rest of his life. Balfour was not paid for this work; indeed, he paid the other staff and financed the museum's fieldwork himself. So involved with the collection did Balfour become that by 1939 he had increased the collection to over a million items, largely purchased with his own funds.

Since then the Pitt Rivers has accepted at least one new collection a week. Its exhibits extend over a vast range of periods and cultures. For me the greatest source of delight is a small silver bottle lying among a collection of magic; its label reads: 'And they do say there be a witch in it and if you let un out there'll be a peck of trouble.' If the news these days is anything to judge by, maybe that's just what some careless cleaner has done.

Permanent waves

From bright young things in the 1930s to old age pensioners today, Bexhill-on-Sea's De La Warr Pavilion has long been a swell attraction. I visit an arts centre where Henry Moore mingles with Max Bygraves.

The journey to Bexhill-on-Sea from London takes longer than that to Venice. Yet every inch of that tedious crawl through south London and suburban Sussex is worthwhile when you arrive at the De La Warr Pavilion. Unlike so much British coastal architecture which is either Regency, Victorian or Edwardian, this pavilion is unashamedly modern. It is 'modern' in the proper sense of the word: built between 1933 and 1935, in the heyday of modern art and architecture. The place is a gem—certainly among the best small buildings in Britain, arguably the best.

The pavilion's architect, one of the Modern movement's masters, was the German Erich Mendelsohn, who had arrived in Britain only three months before the competition for this building was announced by Bexhill-on-Sea Corporation. The competition attracted 230 entries, and the newly formed partnership of Mendelsohn and Chermayeff won. Sixty-five years on, this building is being returned to Mendelsohn's original vision. While approximately half has already been restored, the other half is still resplendent with tired pile carpets, flock wallpaper and municipal paint.

Caroline Collier, who presides over this arts centre on the very edge of the English Channel, has an ambitious program. Her aim is 'to take the spaces of the building back to the architect's original design.' Her brief from the Bexhill-on-Sea Corporation is 'to make the De La Warr Pavilion a centre for art and architecture of international significance'. She has fulfilled this by, in the latter case, stripping away the encrustations of architectural bad taste and hasty necessity and, in the former, by presenting a number of heavyweight exhibitions, including shows of the works of Henry Moore and Henri Gaudier-Brzeska. Strangely, this building really works, which makes it an unusual piece of modern architecture. As Caroline says, 'It's a lovely public space, with lots of sitting-about space.'

The day I visited the de La Warr Pavilion, the sun was shining and, despite being ten o'clock on a Monday morning, the place was full of life. Mostly elderly people—clean tidy people of the sort not typically associated with modern art and architecture—were walking, gossiping, reading newspapers, and drinking tea and coffee. And what is more, they were thoroughly enjoying themselves. This building is definitely people-friendly. As you stand on the staircase and look out of the window, the town of Bexhill-on-Sea and its bay lie spread out before you, the coastline stretching away out of sight on either side. You actually feel that the world is round.

On a sunny summer afternoon, the old people of Bexhill-on-Sea snooze quietly on the pavilion's long balconies. Their wicker chairs, placed side by side, face the open-air dance floor with its bandstand. Beside each chair lurks a large kitchen alarm clock, brought by the chair's occupant to wake him or her in time to hear the band strike up. This building is a wonderful example of pleasure paying for art. Most of those who come to the pavilion on a regular basis only glance at the work of Henry Moore and his fellow artists. They come to listen to Petula Clark and Max Bygraves. These pop stars of a different era are the reason this small seaside town enjoys art at its highest level, displayed in a building that is itself a masterpiece. And if you don't care for Bygraves and Clark—I was brought up on Bygrave's rendering of 'Ghost Riders in the Sky'—then you can watch demonstrations of stilt-walking, fire-eating, performance art and happenings, or engage in sequence dancing, ballroom dancing, tea dances and even go to a policeman's ball. Think about it: you can't do most of these things at the Tate Gallery without being arrested.

There is no doubt that the De La Warr Pavilion is an art resource of immense importance, but it is a small building that needs a large sum of money from a small local authority. The government should take notice of it, for it is of a genre in which Britain is all too impoverished. Failure to complete the restoration of this place should be an international scandal.

Ely does it

Confronted with a rare break in the winter deluge, I pay a visit to Ely Cathedral, where my curiosity is piqued by a variety of art both ancient and modern.

For weeks the rain had fallen like the bars of an iron fence: not like the gentle tear on a cheek that is the sort of rain one expects as November becomes December. On the CNN weather map it appeared that nowhere in the world was exempt from this great deluge. Yet this Sunday was different. There was a difference in the early morning air, a difference in the blue winter sky. Never have scrambled eggs, sausages, mushrooms and tomatoes tasted better, or a drive through north London seemed so beautiful. On the A1, normally a grind to the north, the traffic flowed with a joyful ease and, in time, I came to the Fens.

Black soil, biting wind, bright sun and clear blue sky—the land stretched flat as a billiard table for miles, and out of this flat land rose the tower of Ely Cathedral. It is a land of Anglo-Saxons, of Hereward the Wake and the last bastion of resistance to Norman invasion. The heart of Anglo-Saxon England must still beat in this place. Well, up to a point that is, for the cathedral is the work of the Normans. Ely is the better for their arrival, for what was once an Anglo-Saxon monastery became a Norman cathedral. It is a reference work of Norman architecture—a journey from the crude round arches of the eastern transepts, through the classic Norman nave, to the elegant Romanesque west tower, and the south-west transept's early English painted windows. The journey takes the best part of the twelfth century.

The marvel among many marvels at Ely Cathedral is the octagon with the high lantern above it. Designed by Alan of Walsingham, it is a masterpiece of engineering, setting Ely apart from other cathedrals and certainly from all other buildings of its age. Even today it would require extraordinary skill and technology to reproduce. This octagon is historically important, but also beautiful beyond words. It is Ely's *pièce de résistance*.

As my companion and I came in from the cold morning sunshine, the Sunday service was coming to an end—tuneless Church of England singing, consisting of sounds from throats that do not naturally make music. We quietly waited. Far from leaving, the congregation gathered around the altar, under the lantern, to enjoy a glass of sherry—a seasonable drink on a cold day. They were toasting the new bishop; a popular man, it seems.

The new bishop is not the only novelty that Ely is to enjoy, for in the Lady Chapel is a David Wynne sculpture, brand new and, at the time of my visit, shrouded in tarpaulins. 'A beautiful work,' the dean assured me. 'Quite beautiful.' Wynne's other sculpture in the cathedral, *Christ and Mary Magdalene*, sits well among the medieval architecture. The second cast of this bronze sits equally well in the small garden of what was once my Venetian home. A tribute to this work is that it can make its presence felt in a vast cathedral and yet not overpower a domestic setting.

In Ely there is a house once owned by Oliver Cromwell, that iconoclast who robbed England of so much medieval sculpture, not to dwell on the silver and gold that his men destroyed. A brief entry in the rebels' inventory of Charles I's goods says a thousand words—'Sent to ye Mint, King Alfred's CROWN'. It was melted for soldiers' pay. Happily, sculpture is back at Ely Cathedral, a building that is itself a masterpiece of sculpture.

On to lunch with friends and, as darkness closed in, back to London. The lights of an endless stream of traffic stretched away into the night like a giant Christmas decoration—a fitting end to a magical day. As I write these words in Monte Carlo the heavens have opened again. Perhaps the owners of the yachts in the harbour—people of high intelligence—know something of the weather that is lost on those of us who merely buy umbrellas.

Punting down Portobello

I take a journey down memory lane to the Portobello Road of 40 years ago, when everyone seemed to know one another and the dealers knew me as the truncheon king.

The first time I visited Portobello Road was over 40 years ago. There was not then the same general enthusiasm for anything old. Antiques were largely sold in shops and Portobello Road was just one of London's several junk markets. Goods travelled from market to market, starting in the East End and ending up in Portobello Road on a Saturday. Bargains could be had, and on Monday morning usually found their way to the antique shops of the West End and Chelsea. The stalls opened early, and bargain hunters watched as the goods were unwrapped from last week's newspapers. Everyone seemed to know each other.

In those days I collected policemen's truncheons. The dealers used to call out, 'Here comes the truncheon king.' Mine were not utilitarian objects, but rather things of beauty with the crests and arms of cities, towns and even railway companies on them. An expensive example would cost about three pounds, a masterpiece ten. More usually, however, the ones I bought cost between five shillings and a pound. The dealers, a rather sharp lot, could spot what they called a punter—and indeed, in those days I fell into that category. I would buy anything that caught my eye: as a rug dealer explained to me in New Delhi, the goods need to say 'hello' to you. He was right; if you have to think about an object or painting, it is not for you. Art is a way of expressing emotion and emotion is not something that you need to think about. Whether the goods are genuine is another matter, however, and that needs plenty of thought. ('Here,' a dealer called out, 'look at this.' He offered me a miniature French side chair. 'Some little prince sat in this.' He was wrong, of course—the chair was barely large enough to take a doll, let alone a healthy young prince.)

In those days Portobello Road was a place where the thrifty could buy Christmas presents. The New Year was a nightmare of goods being returned to the grander London shops: goods that had been placed in the stores' boxes but which in fact came from street markets. Today, goods in street markets are not dissimilar in price to those in the West End, so the practice of smart boxes and cheap goods has almost died out. An acquaintance of mine was once given a fine Ming vase for Christmas by his mother-in-law. By the end of January this vase had found its way to Sotheby's and fetched a small price. Next Christmas the acquaintance was given an identical vase by the same relative. 'I have found the pair to the one that I gave you last year,' she claimed. 'I paid much more for it in Sotheby's, but I thought you just must have it.'

Today, Portobello Road is a different place. People stream like football crowds down the side streets to the market, not a real punter among them. So many come that serious purchasing is largely out of the question. Serious dealers have now moved from the street into the comparative comfort of the arcades where specialised stalls have opened. The odd bargain that I would often find is now part of a stall offering 60 just like it. Today is the age of the collectible. Junk markets no longer exist, for we live in an age where junk no longer exists. No matter how tawdry a piece may be, it has over the last 40 years become art.

Don't look twice

If a work of art doesn't strike you at first glance, then, however well-crafted, it's not a 'masterpiece'. I muse on that most elusive of definitions.

There are many ways of collecting and few of us, let alone myself, have ever collected masterpieces; so in the event that we ever come across a masterpiece I have tried to describe the rare beast that defies description.

The summer in London is generally quiet; its inhabitants flee to distant lands in search of sun. No other season of the British year has such varied weather: you can drown, suffocate, freeze or broil on alternate days—sometimes even on the same day.

Nothing closes in London during August as it does on the Continent. On the other hand, nothing is really open either. The shops lack proprietors: left in the hands of junior attendants who know they are not really expected to sell anything, they do their best to live up to expectations. The capital's great galleries show little in August that has not already been seen in June and July. The theatres are filled with Japanese audiences to whom the plays of the western world are as intelligible as the Noh play is to us. They laugh at sadness, applaud the mediocre and ignore the truly brilliant—making an evening at the theatre with them an eerie experience.

I made my way in the summer of 1993 to Sotheby's, who were exhibiting the work of the master carpenter John Makepeace and students from his school at Parnham. It was not hard to tell the work of the master from that of his followers. For a start he had far greater space to show his efforts. Then, while the students huddled among their offerings, the master strode among his polished wood and metal chairs—which were smartly designed and beautifully executed. He also showed a cabinet that housed a model galleon, a breakfast table—its pedestal a bundle of saplings that appeared to grow from the ground—and a pair of chairs to go with it which seemed to owe more to topiary than carpentry. It was the certainty of touch that separated master from pupils: for example, a console table in blackened wood inlaid with coloured marquetry. This was an object that demanded great technical skill in its construction and was clearly a masterpiece of the cabinet-maker's art—but not by any definition a work of art, not a masterpiece as we use the word today.

The word 'masterpiece' was first used of the work an apprentice showed to his master in order to qualify in his master's trade—the best piece of work he had achieved. The word's meaning has changed, however, and a masterpiece is now considered to be a work equal to the best pieces achieved in any period.

Perhaps John Makepeace's students may feel I am unduly hard in my judgement of their efforts. 'I saw that man,' they might say. 'He only glanced at our work for a second or two.' How true these words would be; for a work of art to be a masterpiece, whether on canvas, in bronze, marble, silver or wood, it must stop you in your tracks when your eyes light on it. For myself, I do not care what the thing is made of. I have been as impressed by a prehistoric circle of stones as I have with the great medieval cathedrals, and as awed by a small painting of apples by Cézanne as by Veronese's *Feast in the House of Levi*—a painting more than a thousand times its size. They are both masterpieces. I am also as impressed with how Picasso used the handlebars of a bicycle as I am with the design of the bicycle itself, although neither of them is a masterpiece—just examples of how a good design can be used in different contexts. (Personally, I enjoy the stones laid in lines by Richard Long as much as I do the cave paintings of antiquity in northern Australia—neither is a masterpiece, but both in their ways are objects of beauty.)

Something either *is* a masterpiece or it *is not;* there is no category in between. A work of art does not improve when looked at for great lengths of time, and it certainly does not become a masterpiece simply by being stared at. Nor do you discover how it became a masterpiece that way. I had a friend, now sadly dead: Sidney Nolan, the Australian painter. At one time he spent several hours a day sitting and looking at the three painting by Piero della Francesca in the National Gallery of London. Sometimes I sat with him. Many people, I suppose, would say that during that time he learned about Piero and his painting. For myself, I feel that while I sat and stared at these masterpieces I learned about myself. Sidney Nolan just enjoyed the work of Piero della Francesca, and had the National Gallery had ten of his painting he would have divided his time between them.

No, masterpieces spring and strike the eye, grab you in the guts, and leave you breathless with excitement. That is the time to start looking, thinking, comparing and searching for answers to questions such as: Does this piece have more than originality? Does it have moods that seem to change from day to day, and qualities that transcend mere fashion? Furthermore, the qualities that make masterpieces cannot be expressed in words. They are a form of communication in themselves, with their own language, and to be true masterpieces they must defy description by those who scribble.

It's a kind of magic

Conjuring and attractive female assistants—it's a marriage made in heaven. I visit a petrifying house of horror hidden in south London.

Somewhere in darkest south London is Simon Drake's House of Magic. No address is given, only a telephone number—020 7735 4777—with an appropriate quantity of magic sevens in it. Guests are taken to the secret location in a bus with darkened windows; I went by London black cab. Secrecy was unnecessary, for the route was so complicated that I will never be able to find my way there again. The building to which I was delivered looked suitably sinister—a surprise, for it was once a public house, a place not known for its forbidding appearance.

Outside, by a doorway in a blank wall, stood a figure in black—a giant man, bald and as menacing as might be hoped. He consulted a list; I began to fear I might be consigned to some pit beneath the pavement as an intruder trying to get into this sanctum of magic by fraudulent means. Luckily, my name was there, and I passed through the door into a garden. The place was downright spooky; you could tell that without needing an advanced sense of the occult, for there was another giant standing there—a butler, I presumed, for he held a salver covered with a silver dome. The butler, feeling the cold, was moving from one foot to the other in a disconcerting manner. I thought he might topple over, so top-heavy was this freak. Then off with the silver cover—a human head wished me good evening and gave directions to the house. There is no exaggeration here; it was a genuine, talking human head, apparently severed from its body.

Inside was a crowd of guests, half of them dressed as Uncle Fester from *The Addams Family*, the rest rejects from the Rubber Ball. No matter. When you visit a House of Magic, the stranger, the better. I went down a spiral staircase into a south London hell, which was part mortician's waiting room and part torture cell. A lady, most unsuitably dressed for a funeral, got out of a coffin and tried to bite a guest's neck. Saved by a conjurer, the guest was then frightened half to death by two passing ghosts. We all laughed and then were frightened in turn. Easing my ample body into obscurity—I consider it best not be noticed on such occasions—I became enmeshed in a tangle of cobwebs.

Upstairs, a rogue did such clever things with cards that I will never gamble again. A chair whispered my future; I was quite encouraged, until I remembered the Greek general who consulted the Delphic Oracle: 'A great victory will be won,' he was told. A victory was won—by the other side. My future did not seem so rosy after that.

Then came the serious conjuring, and I *do* mean serious. I am not an expert, but I visit conjuring shops across the world at the drop of a magician's wand—the best was in Rome. Almost its equal was in Hollywood, next door to Frederick's, which is famous for its exotic ladies' underwear, but now without the least bit of magic. That Hollywood emporium, however, was filled with the stuff. I bought a paper bag from which even I can pull a vast quantity of objects, collectively far larger than the bag itself.

In Simon Drake's House of Magic there were no mere bag tricks. The magic was on a giant scale: people disappeared, had amputations, and were stabbed; everywhere there was blood, buckets of blood. More curious than all this was that Simon Drake and his assistant seemed to be having a hilarious time. The show, in settings of carefully conceived stage Gothic, was performed live—or, sometimes dead—only feet from our eyes. Even as seasoned a habitué of magic shops as myself could not divine Simon Drake's secrets. What is more, the show was beautiful as well as macabre, with floating candles and a magic wand that changed colour and danced without human assistance.

Out of this Gothic world of magic, through the garden, and into the street, and the reassuring presence of council flats. And then, for me, the greatest magic of all—I was able to catch a cab in the area devoid of traffic. I did, however, take a careful look at the cabbie before I got in.

The Mediterranean

Venetian trawl

On some of Venice's curious customs, and one place where tourists never venture.

In Venice, the gardens arrive by boat: large barges loaded with trees. This is one of the world's strangest sights. Even a couple as experienced in mobile foliage as Mr and Mrs Macbeth would have been surprised at the sight of one of these barges moving down the Venetian canals through the early morning fog with, on its decks, several fully grown *Magnolias grandiflora*, fruit trees—apples, pears, plums and damsons—and a large group of camellias, heavy with bud, ready for the first sun of spring, ready to flower.

But then Venice is a strange place and the Venetians are used to the unusual. The mosaics in St Mark's Cathedral, restored and lit so that they can now be seen, have, among all the saints and angels, a portrayal of a rhinoceros. In the year 1230, when this mosaic was carried out, this was a creature of great novelty, an animal seen only by travellers to distant lands. Perhaps the Venetians were not convinced by descriptions of this animal, for the mosaic is tucked away, high in the roof of one of the aisles, a place of little prominence for such a rare and exotic creature. In the unicorn, perversely, they had total belief. The horns of two of these mythical beasts were kept in the cathedral and a small quantity scraped daily from them and fed to the doge to give virility, health and longevity. It seems to have worked in the case of Doge Dandolo, who in 1203, aged 96, was the first crusader over the walls of Constantinople. The practice was discontinued shortly after this apparent success, as the horns were nearly all eaten away by enthusiastic successors. The horn was actually the horn of the narwhale, not as hard to obtain as that of the unicorn, but it cannot have been an easy item to lay hands on in the thirteenth century.

A few hundred yards from the great cathedral and St Mark's Square, the life of twentieth-century Venice changes dramatically. The mass of struggling tourists ends and there are no more parties of Germans and squads of Japanese. Castello is possibly the only area left today that is still truly Venetian. Past the Arsenale and its assorted Greek lions with Celtic graffiti, over an iron bridge, down the Calle del Forno—so narrow that you go in strictly single file—and out into the Via Garibaldi. This is a wide street; it was once a canal but was filled in by the Austrians in their—thankfully abortive—attempt to bring order to Venice. A street of market stalls selling vegetables and fish—just a few stalls. A street with a shop that sells freshly made pasta, a shop that sells ironmongery, and a shop that sells ribbons. This is one of the best streets in the world for one reason only: this street has exactly the right number of people in it for its size. This street only sells products that people need for their daily lives. This street has the right number of trattorias, the right number of cafés. Incidentally, one of them sells the best sandwiches in Venice—sandwiches fuller and fresher than anywhere else. The balance of this street is perfect, yet it leads nowhere. As a canal it usefully led from the lagoon on one side of Venice to the lagoon on the other. As a street it has no purpose, and so this great thoroughfare, which boarders Venice's Biennale gardens, is used only for shopping and talking.

On Sundays in the spring the people of Castello go to a restaurant called Vignoles, on an island a few minutes away in a small boat. You can only go in a small boat, usually rowed or powered by an outboard motor, for the water on the approach to this island is too shallow for larger craft. This factor dictates the kind of people who frequent the island and its restaurant. They are the working people of Castello and other parts of Venice—no tourists and no speedboats. The island is basically a scrapyard, with every sort of rotting hull imaginable beached on the mud flats around it. Through this marine graveyard, where the parts of boats no longer usable are left to die, is a landing stage of the most primitive kind and moored to it are a cluster of skiffs and *topi al terzo* (small Venetian sailboats).

The restaurant is in an orchard: unruly grass and a few old trees, areas of bare earth that have proved popular spots for families to sit on previous Sundays, and a large shed—a shed filled with grills and cookers. The food runs the full gamut of the Venetian cuisine: from *risotto* to *fritta da mare*; heaps of cooked meats; heaps of cooked flesh without the benefit of a name; and birds that would seem more appropriate to a London park than the dining table. But then at this restaurant the tables are a little primitive. Families sit on the ground or, if they arrive in time, on part of a remarkable collection of chairs at rough plank tables. They bring their own wine and some of their own food, buying what they need from the kitchen in the shed. Four or five hundred people come here on a Sunday. Mountains of food and, I dare say, a good few bottles of wine are consumed.

Families talk and argue. Lovers meet and, I suppose, on occasions part here too. It is one of the ugliest places that I have ever been to, but, with time and wine and conversation, the blossom on the trees and the rotting hulks seem just as beautiful as the grandest efforts of Sansovino and Palladio.

As a result of this piece the concierge at the Gritti Palace Hotel was deluged with requests to book tables at Vignoles, the restaurant. He was horror struck that any of his clients should contemplate visiting such a place.

News on the Rialto

The slow pattern of existence through the year in Venice, along with the pleasures of its chance companions.

For twelve years I lived in Venice, and while there I travelled in Italy. Here I record some of those travels: the people, places, and things that I came across. That period of my life was of delight and in strong contrast to my years in Australia. In Italy I saw man's art made for God, in Australia God's art made for man. The mountains, the gorges and the deserts of the latter were the most powerful experience of my life; the culture of Italy was, as it were, the icing on the cake.

When Solanio asked, 'Now, what news on the Rialto?' (*The Merchant of Venice*, Act III, Scene I), the answer was not much, for in Venice there is never much that is new—yet perversely everything is new. Venice is a town that thrives on gossip, on trivia; isolated by water, complete in itself, self-centred and self-interested, it has its own rhythms and its own scale of import. The Venetian language—still widely spoken and totally different from Italian—has no equivalent of the English word 'privacy'. The closest they can come to it is 'intimacy', a word with a very different meaning. In fact, in Venice every small intimacy is treated to a great deal of local publicity—a town where always someone watches from a window, and always someone listens from a nearby table.

The pace of Venice is modulated. Only the tourists hurry between churches and galleries: the citizens saunter, and they greet each other. There is a rhythm to life in Venice that modern convenience has destroyed almost everywhere else: the changing seasons, the colour of the salads, the different fruits and the herbs. One month *castraourie* (the smallest of artichokes), the month before the *sepie* (baby black squid), and the next month *bruscandole* (wild asparagus) made into risotto.

As the liturgical year progresses, the ringing of the bells changes, and the colours of the sacraments change. The festivals of the people are tied to the church and the availability of produce. All of this paces the life of the Venetian: the predictability of meeting a friend, or for that matter an enemy, in the street—then always gossip.

We sat in the Alla Madonna, the four of us—Paolo Zancope, a dealer in sixteenth-century Venetian glass; my wife and I; and a painter and sculptor, Ludovico de Luigi, who paints pictures of the end of Venice, a Venice overcome by industry, a Venice destroyed by tourism. A recent work, first shown in St Mark's Square, had a slightly controversial career. A deputy came from Rome to unveil it; all Venice was impressed. Unfortunately, the deputy was La Cicciolina, a former stripper elevated to parliament, a lady more used to unveiling herself than sculpture—and this is exactly what she did. Naked, she sprang astride his great bronze horse.

The sculptor was torn between fear and delight—she looked wonderful on his horse—but the authorities tend to take a stern view of nudity in the town's main square. The crowd rioted—half for Cicciolina, half against—and the horse, the artist and the deputy were all nearly destroyed in the crush. But then they were saved by as near as is possible to a miracle. Cicciolina was wearing some very large plastic pearls; the string broke, the pearls rolled all over the pavement, the crowd pursued the pearls and the police restored order.

Someone, however, had to be arrested. The deputy was immune from arrest, and so the artist found himself in court. The judge, a very attractive young woman, told him that he should have imagined that this would happen.

'How could I imagine that a deputy would take her clothing off?'

The judge replied: 'You are an artist, a man of imagination.'

'True,' said Ludovico. 'I can imagine you with no clothes on—but I cannot imagine that you will take them off.'

'If that is so,' said the judge, 'I can imagine you spending a year in jail for contempt of court.' Ludovico received, to his horror, a three-year suspended sentence.

The restaurant was packed; in the autumn there are few tourists, and the locals seem to have time to eat lunch. We gossiped on about events and people, and we watched especially what they ate. We spoke of the forthcoming Carnivale and Ludovico's plan to cast his horse in chocolate (it weighed 1100 pounds—500 kilograms—and the children ate the whole of it in seven minutes). We spoke of Venice's only bank robbery—where both the robbers and the police got lost in the maze of streets, in the end finding each other. The waiters all called Ludovico 'Maestro' and asked after his work; the artist in Venice is accorded a position in society as nowhere else. We ate *frittate*—very like a small doughnut, deep-fried, filled with crystallised fruit and pine nuts and a small quantity of grappa. What news on the Rialto? Nothing much. The boundaries all over Eastern Europe were changing as we ate, but for the Venetian, other people's boundaries always change every 50 years or so. On the Rialto they think in millennia. What news on the Rialto? Time and weather have washed Carpaccio's frescoes off its famous bridge.

Seasonal meetings

The strange rites and annual meetings—patterns of the international 'tribes' who migrate to Venice every autumn.

The whole summer Venice waited for the tourists to come, and then with the first sign of autumn they were there. Well, they weren't really tourists. They had travelled to Venice to attend four great events: the Architectural Biennale, the film festival, the annual meeting of Save Venice and the Volpi Ball. How could a ball possibly be a great event? Well this one, quite apart from being held in Count Volpi's palazzo on the Grand Canal—a palazzo whose frontage covers an entire block—had about 1100 guests. Very few people these days are able to give a party quite like the Count Volpi.

The Save Venice meeting had about 400 Americans attending it—as far as I could see they spent most of their time in the city wearing cocktail frocks and extremely high heels (the women, that is). They travelled around the canals in a vast motor launch whose wash must have done the place a deal of harm. The film festival crowd kept very much to itself, isolated on the Lido, most of their time locked in cinemas and the rest of it coming to terms with daylight. The women, in Ray-Ban dark glasses and toting Louis Vuitton bags, had blond hair and painted nails. The men—mostly balding—looked similar, but did not paint their nails. There was a touch of leather about both sexes. The architects at their biennale seemed to be everywhere and were immediately recognisable. There were thousands of them on the evidence of those two weeks in September.

The extraordinary thing about this biennale was the uniformity of dress worn by those who attended it. The men were dressed from head to foot by Giorgio Armani; their sage-green jackets had a casual but expensive look to them. White shirts buttoned right up to their Adam's apples, no ties, and on their chins a dusting of designer stubble. They all wore glasses—round with transparent frames, and I had the feeling that these did nothing to assist their eyesight one way or the other—and carried a plastic tube for drawings in much the same way as a senior military man carries a baton. The female of the species sported monks' habits in browns and blacks, or sometimes khaki; their hair was club cut, and what make-up they wore seemed to have been there some time. Their look was ecclesiastical—all wore black sandals with open toes.

For the first time in ages a new building has been erected in Venice by a foreign architect, and what is more a British one. Jim Stirling's bookshop in the gardens was the centrepiece of the 1991 biennale. It seemed to be like some *bateau-mouche* removed from its journey up and down the stretch of the River Seine that passes through Paris, and left in the middle of a Venetian park. And so here is the glass boat, complete with floodlights that illuminate the night sky—or at least for the first couple of nights. The authorities have switched them off now. Jim Stirling himself calls it the boat shop—he claims that it is inspired by the *vaporetti* that move the population of Venice from one place to another, but *vaporetti* have far less glass than this bookshop. This is definitely a *bateau-mouche*. As a bookshop, for me, it does not work: standing turning the pages of a book in a glass cylinder, however beautiful it may be, is not my idea of fun. I need ladders and shelves, benches and dust in any bookshop I am prepared to patronise.

The Swiss had an interesting pavilion. The work there by Herzog and De Meuron showed a great leap forward from the cuckoo clock. There was no sign of a Swiss Army penknife, the other great achievement of Swiss design, but instead rather large photographs of their work. It seems to me that exhibitions of architectural drawings are very limited in their use—architects make them to explain to builders how to erect their buildings. These drawings have to be read in the way a book is read. Unlike paintings they are supposed to mean something, to convey a complicated message to people trained to understand that message. One of the reasons we have so many awful buildings is because the people who hire architects can very seldom understand their drawings.

Instead of exhibiting architects' drawings you might just as well take a page of an ancient Chinese manuscript, enlarge it till the manuscript is several feet square, frame it and hang it on the wall. It would be as beautiful as many of the drawings in this biennale and just as incomprehensible. This exhibition is really only for the professional—or the totally ignorant who just like to look at shapes.

The Greeks also tried hard this year. Normally they arrive in Venice with a bundle of designs for rehousing the Elgin marbles. This year, they decided to give this improbable dream a miss. The Greeks had a competition for the rebuilding of their pavilion in the Biennale Gardens. The designs were on the whole exciting, and a definite improvement on the existing pavilion; one scheme by Christos Papoulias and Ioanna Theocharopoulou was very good. The problem, however, is that the existing Greek pavilion is a listed building and cannot be touched in any respect.

The biennale is over now; all the pavilions stand closed in their gardens, rather desolate with the leaves from the trees heaped in their doorways—and so they will remain until the next biennale comes around, or somebody thinks of another use in the meantime for this strange collection of buildings.

Murano's melting moments

On the Venetian island of Murano they huff and they puff, and they still blow liquid glass into the shapes Titian and Veronese knew.

Men in overcoats, with scarves round their necks and trilby hats pulled down over their eyes—not in disguise, but rather as protection against the chill winds that come to Venice during the last days of winter. A visitor crossing St Mark's Square will certainly be approached by one if not several of these man. They sidle up to you in the most furtive of manners. 'Murano,' they whisper. 'Murano?' the startled visitor replies. 'Murano glass—you wish to visit Murano and see our glassworks?' 'No, no,' the visitor protests; after all, the winter visitor to Venice has come to see the work of Palladio and Sansovino and the paintings by Titian, Tintoretto and Veronese. It is culture not glass that has drawn this visitor. Watching the lace making and glass-blowing is for tourists. 'No, definitely NO.' The man in the camel coat and muffler, seeing no easier customers on the face of the rain-swept square persists, and finally a compromise is arrived at. The visitor agrees to make the trip to Murano, and accepts from the glass-maker's persistent agent a free ticket on a motorboat to his factory. The agent begins to search for new customers and the visitor enters Florian's Café for a hot chocolate and a wastepaper basket to throw the ticket in.

Most serious people who visit Venice never get to see its glass—how wrong they are, for the soul of Venice is found among this glass, the truly horrible and the sublime sitting side by side on the shelf. You are taken by the company's boat to Cenedese's factory; the glass companies like to take potential customers to Murano in their own boats for fear that the visitors might end up at the factory of their competitors. Just a smile at one of these men in overcoats puts you in the category of a customer. First you are shown a maestro at work. It all seems so terribly simple: a puff here and you have a glass balloon. A flick of the wrist, and it becomes a plate. As the maestro works with the hot glass, it seems to have no colour other than that of the heat.

As the glass cools the colours come, each one in the right place. The Japanese tourists flash their cameras, the bulbs exploding in unison. (The Japanese seem to have the haziest idea of the state of Europe's climate, travelling at all the wrong times of year, spoiling completely the silence and desolation that Venice's winter visitor seeks.)

It is tempting to miss the Japanese and therefore the maestro, going instead straight to the showrooms. But resist temptation, and watch the maestro at work long after the Japanese have left to make their purchases. Stay and watch the ballet of the glassmakers, as the rods with molten glass dripping from their ends pass from hand to hand. Each furnace serves two maestros who are assisted by eight apprentices; they weave between each other as they serve their masters, who sit on wooden thrones and roll the rods on the iron arms of these great chairs, shaping the glass with tongs. The timing has to be perfect and there must be no collision on the way to and from the furnace—the glass is malleable only for seconds. The Japanese tourists have been led away to rooms for tourists. The visitor will be taken to the upper showrooms—oh horror! First thoughts are always correct. Here is room after room, shelf after shelf of coloured glass, each example more vulgar than the one before. 'Will you take a coffee?' Antonio Camarte, Cenedese's master salesman, is at work. 'This is a decanter designed by Paolo Veronese—well, we don't know whether it was designed by him, but he used it in his painting *Supper at the House of Levi*. 'Will you take a little wine?' he says as he pours from a green bottle with a spring-held cap. 'This glass is also by Veronese.' He passes the wine. 'This,' he says, 'Tintoretto used this bowl in his paintings.' Titian, Giorgione, Bellini and Carpaccio—all the names of Venice are there on the shelves. Glasses from the fourteenth, fifteenth and sixteenth centuries, glasses economic in their design, glass extravagant with twists and curls, colours subdued and colour vulgar—they are all there. Did they really use glasses like these in the Renaissance? Of course, in Venice everything was possible. The population became so extravagant in their tastes that sumptuary laws were passed to save them all from bankruptcy. Maybe it was the tales that Antonio told, but slowly the glass took on a sort of beauty as you moved from century to century; each design seemed to have its relevance.

'It's not all good,' says Antonio. 'Look at this horrible commissioned work; this is how they like it.' I must confess, I liked it too—I held it in my hand.

'How much is this?'

'Two thousand pounds.'

'I had better put it down in case I break it.'

'Why, we will make another. Glass breaks, thank goodness—how else would we earn a living.'

Infill traitor

After conquering Venice, Napoleon wanted to build an office in St Mark's Square; he wasn't going to let a church by Sansovino stand in his way.

When Napoleon came to Venice he did not come as a tourist, the way his fellow citizens do today. (The French are obsessed with Venice; few of them seem to go anywhere else.) He came as a conqueror and, in the manner of conquerors, he started to remove objects he found attractive—he had them crated up and sent back to Paris. The four Greek horses were among the treasures he sent home. These horses had already done quite a bit of travelling, as the Venetians got them when they sacked Constantinople, and the Turks had taken them from the Greeks. Wellington defeated Napoleon at Waterloo and the horses were sent back to Venice by the misguided Wellington—they would have looked wonderful in Trafalgar Square. For years they stood above the portico of St Mark's, and then they were put away in a small attic of the cathedral and replaced by fibreglass replicas.

Napoleon admired St Mark's Square as well, but it was too large and too solid to dispatch home. He stood in the great square and remarked: 'This is the grandest drawing room in Europe!' He so admired it that he decided to build his office across one end; the only problem was that on the site of his proposed office building stood a rather nice church by Sansovino, the Venetian architect, and beside it a chapel by the same hand. But this problem was not insurmountable. Napoleon just pulled them down and started building.

Not everyone knows of this act of vandalism, and St Mark's Square is often quoted by conservationists as a great example of how, if buildings are preserved, our hearts can be lifted and our lives enhanced. As a result, architectural history stands still. In fact, Napoleon was not the only vandal to have a hand in producing this marvellous square. St Mark's Square has been changing for the last thousand years, but I doubt if it will change again. Have we lost our self-confidence? Do we feel unable to produce great buildings? Do we lack the courage to improve masterpieces? Well, the answers to these questions are really of little importance. The truth is that today we ask the opinion of too many people. Few were consulted when Sansovino was commissioned to build his church and its chapel—and I doubt very much if Napoleon canvassed the citizens of Venice when he pulled them both down. In any event, the building he replaced them with is totally out of keeping with the other buildings in the square and fits in wonderfully. It has a neoclassical facade with generals from the ancient world parading along the frieze. There is an empty space in it—for which a sculpture was commissioned. But the Battle of Waterloo intervened, and Canova's statue of Napoleon never reached its appointed place—in the centre of the frieze that runs the length of what was his office block and is now the Correr Museum.

An exhibition of Canova's work has opened in the neoclassical interior of that building, but the statue of Napoleon is not included. I am told that it is hidden in a Venetian attic. Several dozen of Canova's works are exhibited, however, and very fine they are too, from great monumental works to the pair of small baskets of fruit carved in marble. The *Three Graces* are there, not the *Three Graces* lately moved from Woburn Abbey or a version of that sculpture, but a copy. There were three copies made of it, each identical. His classical figures are wonderful and the setting for them is perfect. There is a bust of Napoleon among them, looking like a classical god—no wonder Canova was his favourite sculptor. But when you see the portrait of Domenico Cimarosa, it becomes clear that Canova was more than just a sculptor who could fill an orangery or carve a frieze; he was more than just a fashionable artist of the nineteenth century. There is a model of his tomb, but the real thing is in the Frari and is at last being restored, for it has suffered for some time from marble sickness, a kind of 'flu' that causes the stone to disintegrate over a long period of time. I am very taken by his plaster casts with the nails still in them, nails that the men who carved these figures in marble used as reference points, for Canova did not carve his own work.

Sadly for Canova, down the street—or rather the Grand Canal—is another exhibition, 'Leonardo and Venice'. Sure enough, there are a number of da Vinci's drawings, small but beautiful things, coloured with a wash of the same shade as the ink in the drawing. A glaze introduced onto these drawings gives them a remarkable luminosity. What advertises itself as a show of the drawings of Leonardo has five paintings by Giorgione, including the *Three Ages of Mankind*. There are several sculptures by the Lombardo family and paintings and sculptures by other Venetian artists. It is a show worth seeing for these alone but, needless to say, Leonardo is the star. It is a testimony to him that his small drawings stand up to and knock for six the works that surround them. Leonardo could do more with a few lines on a piece of paper six inches by four than Canova could do with a ten-foot block of marble.

Something fishy

I go hunting for fraudulent mermaids on the banks of the Grand Canal.

Despite the fact that it was mid-winter, Venice was blessed with brilliant sunshine: the sort of sunlight that chisels anew each stone detail on the faces of the city's buildings. It was a glorious day, just the sort of day to hunt for mermaids—any self-respecting mermaid would surely be sunning herself on the edge of the sparkling waters of the Grand Canal.

Strange as it may seem, mermaids *are* to be found on the banks of the Grand Canal, They are, unfortunately, dead. They are preserved in Venice's Natural History Museum, which I found—after a considerable trek and much ringing of its doorbell—to be closed. It will remain so for some time; renovation and rearrangement of its collections are the reasons. In Venice such a closure can be almost indefinite.

For instance, the bridge in front of the Arsenale, made famous by Canaletto, was pulled down two years ago and replaced by a temporary one nearby. This seemed curiously efficient, but all was explained when the canal leading to the Arsenale was then closed. It has remained so ever since, with little sign of work being carried out, and certainly no work that would involve the closure of this important canal. It is yet another Venetian mystery. The customers at Paolo's Bar in the Campo Arsenale are bemused by this lack of action. Many reasons have been advanced—many as exotic as the mermaids. Indeed, perhaps this is the reason for the closure: a breeding colony of mermaids must not be disturbed.

When the Natural History Museum reopens, its mermaids will be seen by observant visitors to be frauds. They are made by fixing the top half of a small monkey to the lower half of a large fish. These fake mermaids were popular items in the fifteenth and early sixteenth centuries. It was a time when every self-respecting millionaire felt the need for a cabinet of curiosities, in much the same way that millionaires today feel the need for a collection of impressionist paintings. The cabinet of curiosities, or *Wunderkammer*, allowed its owner to possess a microcosm of the world. Impressionist paintings allow the millionaire to forget about the world and concentrate on collecting more money and more paintings. Both types of collection have, however, one thing in common. The *Wunderkammer* in the late Middle Ages gave the idea to visitors that its owner was of a superior education and perhaps had magical powers—certainly that the owner was powerful. It is the same with collectors of Impressionist paintings. A testimony to wealth, education and power hangs on every wall of their mansions.

There are, however, a few collectors and dealers who still admire the ethos of the *Wunderkammer*. One such is Peter Adler, a dealer in ethnography and African textiles, who designs, makes and sells remarkable jewellery with stones from India and beads from Africa. His home is in London's Sussex Gardens, where he deals from a modern *Wunderkammer*. It does not contain an example of every aspect of the known world as a true one should; however, it does contain immensely beautiful objects nudging other objects that most people would consider extremely ugly. The sublime sits well with the grotesque, the inconsequential with the important; the objects of considerable scale are found with objects so small that a glass is necessary to examine them. Peter Adler's establishment is a work of art, a cross between Disneyland and an important museum. Sadly, there are no mermaids in his crowded home, but it has nevertheless one of the best atmospheres of anywhere that I know to sit and drink a cup of tea.

Polishing off the past

Decay is not always a bad thing. Returning to Venice on a surge of 1970s nostalgia, I revisit an old haunt to discover that restoration can be a tragedy.

The month of August in Venice is usually extremely hot and sunny. In 1973, however, the rain came down in streams, pockmarking the sands of the Lido beach, while the waves of the Adriatic crashed against its breakwaters. Each evening the hotel staff assured me that the weather would change; each morning the rain showed no sign of abating. 'What on earth shall I do with my two small girls?' I asked.

'Take them to see the puppet theatre in the Ca' Rezzonico,' came the reply.

The seventies were bad years for Venice, or so it seemed at the time. The palazzo appeared to be closed when we arrived. Up the stairs to the piano nobile and into the entrance hall we passed. Around the walls were arranged high-backed armchairs, their legs and arms carved as blackamoors. Between them were tiered console tables, again with blackamoors, bearing blue-and-white pots. The room, despite its vast dimensions, seemed as if it were still in use. The textiles on the chairs and the walls were tired; their colours, however, were rich in the gloom of the unlit room. Alone we moved from room to room, unhindered by either tourists or guardians. It was as if we wandered unseen through the home of a Venetian nobleman: at each moment we expected to come across his family taking tea.

In our travels we met an attendant who gripped my eldest daughter by the hand and led her to a narrow window. Outside the rain beat upon the surface of the canal. The attendant slowly pulled back the faded curtain that flanked the window; I could not imagine what he was going to show us. There, behind the curtain, was a pigeon sitting in a nest. Gently the attendant eased the pigeon to one side to uncover a pair of chicks. My daughters were more taken with this sight than with any of the Venetian republic's more majestic trappings.

This March I returned to the Ca' Rezzonico to visit an exhibition of eighteenth-century Venetian porcelain. The lower hallway off the water landing has been perfectly restored and now has a cloakroom, a café, a bookshop with plenty of souvenirs for sale, and the offices of an 'Institute'. Directing you to these various joys are signs in the curious visual language of museums the world over. Upstairs, the piano nobile now has modern freestanding screens a few feet from its walls, which hide equipment controlling the humidity. Modern showcases hold the collection of porcelain, which in the event turned out to be rather dull. No matter, however, for exhibiting dull porcelain is no offence compared with the destruction of the atmosphere of what is perhaps Venice's finest baroque palazzo.

It is the spiritual subconscious of a place, the inner being that grows with time and use, that sets it apart and gives it real beauty. And this spirituality has nothing to do with being clean and tidy, nor has it anything to do with being preserved for eternity. For some years I have had my doubts about wholesale conservation, let alone restoration. Their results are pleasing enough, in a scrubbed sort of way. They are, however, less than satisfactory for those who know how these great works once were.

Sermon in stone

I sing a paean of praise for Palladio's masterpiece, San Giorgio Maggiore. *I found the Venetian church at Advent resounding with lyrical sermons and a rich history.*

The deck of the *vaporetto* was a chilly place to stand. My fellow travellers—all Venetians—were well wrapped against the cold. The occasional gondola wandered on the Lagoon near the mouth of the Grand Canal. A large speedboat with giant engines—a stray from the French Riviera—lingered off the Piazzetta. Built of shining mahogany, with a ladder for swimmers to climb up over its stern to lay in the sun on the white vinyl cushions on its decks, this boat looked ridiculous in the winter weather. Its engines spat smoke and canal water, all its power useless with nowhere to race. The *vaporetto* pulled away from this alien craft and headed for the island of San Giorgio.

Once, when Venice was young, this island was called the Isola dei Cipressi; it had vineyards, vegetable gardens, artisans' dwellings and a small church. Then in1559 all that changed: Palladio started work on what many believe to be his masterpiece—the church of San Giorgio. On its facade a pediment surmounts four columns whose bases stand many times the height of a person; its doorway is flanked by St George, a warrior, and St Stephen, a cleric. Palladio died in 1580, long before his work was finished, so he never saw the beauty of San Giorgio's tower and its pair of spires or its domes.

On this day the light in the church was cold except around the Great Altar which glowed with warmth; four priests and an abbot stood before that altar, their purple Advent vestments reflected in the golden orb that bronze angels hold high above it, the angels never so black, cold with winter light. To the side of the priests stood monks; the voices of the small choir hidden from view came and went as the responses passed from one side of the church to the other. The voices rose and fell, making their own music. Sometimes there was the feeling that they would fail, and the congregation stiffened with expectation, but they sang on, frail, soft, filled with calm, confidently aware of their own beauty. The service is extraordinarily austere, matching the church's hard, classical design.

The abbot faced the altar and God, his flock behind him. He gave a spirited sermon. I do not understand a word of Italian but I loved hearing him speak, for like a bricklayer who mixes the cement that will hold his bricks together, he separated his words as with a trowel, then mixed them again, smoothed them off, divided them up, and mixed them yet again.

What a church this is: on each side of its altar is a great masterpiece by Tintoretto. Tintoretto's last work is in the chapel behind the altar called the Death Chapel. Past the heavily carved choir stalls up a winding stair is another chapel, and over its altar Carpaccio's *St George Slaying His Dragon*. However, this chapel is not famous for that wonderful painting, but rather as the only room outside the Vatican where a conclave has been held. On the death of Pope Pius VI in 1799 (he had been Napoleon's prisoner in Venice for many years and that emperor took a lively interest in who was going to be elected as his successor) the cardinals met in that upstairs room. Meanwhile, Napoleon sat in the apartments he had constructed across the end of St Mark's Square, a square he called the grandest drawing room in Europe. It took them from December 1799 until March 1800 to decide on Pius's successor.

This church and its monastery have seen much history. One of its abbots was Henry Stuart, Cardinal Duke of York, the last of the Stuart line, and his name is written on parchment framed and hung on the wall of the room where the cardinals met, along with the names of all the monastery's abbots. Now his body lies at St Peter's in Rome with others of his royal race. Unsuccessful in their attempts to reclaim their thrones, they lie in a foreign tomb paid for by George III, the heir of their usurper.

As the congregation took the sacrament, the organ on its balcony high above the altar was playing for the first time during the service, the organist choosing strong, swift music by Vivaldi and his contemporaries. The congregation slowly returned to their seats and the abbot sat for a moment in silent prayer; then he rose and blessed them, finally saying, *La messa è finita*. At his words the organ broke into wild baroque music and the priests, followed by the abbot, swept from the church like warriors, their purple robes flowing behind them. The organist played on; I could hear his music long after I left. Stepping down San Giorgio's steps to the piazza in front I halted. I could see all Venice before me, cold and proud, more beautiful than ever before.

The venerable bead

The centuries-old history of Venetian glass beads—exported all over the world—deserves to be revered. I am an obsessive bead-stringer.

On the face of it 'new beads for old' might seem a pretty good deal, but not if those beads happened to be Venetian. Old Venetian glass beads have now become rare and valuable, a fact which is surprising, for at the end of the nineteenth century one in ten Venetians was engaged in making them—16 000 tons in 600 different shapes and colours were produced each year. The beads of Venice were sent literally all over the world—to China, to Indonesia, to the Naga tribes of India and the Indian tribes of North America—and were exchanged for the goods that these people acquired mining or hunting. But by far the greatest quantity were sent to Africa.

This trade in beads had been carried on by the Venetians since the fifteenth century—their earliest beads were small cubes of transparent glass, pink-tinged or deep blue like uncut diamonds or sapphires. Then a century later the fashion changed and chevron beads were made. Oval-shaped, their layers of coloured glass were faceted at the ends to form the V-shape chevron patterns that give them their name. The blue chevrons with red and white lines were sent to Africa where even today they can be dug from the sand dunes, giving some East Africans the idea that these beautiful beads grow in their continent's soil. The chevrons are the most valuable of the beads from Africa, and vary in size from that of a green pea to a large goose's egg, although only three of these large beads are known still to exist. Red chevrons were sent to North America—red with black and white striped ends—and are perhaps the rarest and most valuable of all.

Now many of these antique beads have started to return to Venice where they are sold by Michael Pociello at his shop in Prezzeria, which is filled with beads of different colours and shape. I asked Michael how he became a bead merchant. 'By accident,' he replied. I wondered what sort of accident could make a man take up such an exotic occupation, for Michael sells beads from all lands and all eras, and it is no exaggeration to say that he has trunkfuls. They come strung together fresh from the necks of tribal people. Michael sorts and then sells them to make necklaces for European women.

It all started when he was running a silver shop. 'I was in my shop when an African came in, and asked if I would buy some old beads that he had brought with him from Kenya.' Michael resold them the same day. 'I searched Venice till I found him and he gave me his address.' Michael then went to Africa and bought more beads from the man. In fact, to begin with he swapped new Venetian ones. As the trade in beads grew Michael contacted other dealers. His expeditions to Africa increased and he then started to go to India too. When the Indians saw the sorts of beads that Michael bought, they set about making brand new ones which Michael bought and then sold to those who could not afford the old ones. These beads sit in his shop, cauldrons of them, like so many brightly coloured and wonderfully shaped sweets.

Three years ago I started buying strings of beads that came from Africa from Michael. Every night I would sit at home and cut the strings, sorting each shape of bead into a pile. Then I sorted the contents of that pile into colours, putting each colour into a small white box. Within days my house was filled with small white boxes, each with its own colour and shape of bead. I found the work obsessive—you can't imagine my delight when I found a particular bead that I had not expected in a necklace. For three years I sorted and strung beads. I told my friends that I did this in order to be better able to contain my fury at the Chancellor of the Exchequer's handling of the British economy. The threading of tiny beads onto a string takes considerable concentration, and all other thoughts go from your mind except, I suppose, the seductive beauty of all these many coloured beads, and thoughts of the necklace in a multitude of colours and shapes that you can make with them.

Schnabel saves the day

For some, Venice abounds with art-world shocks and horrors during the Biennale, but I was heartened by Julian Schnabel's sheer virtuosity, marooned among the many bizarre installations.

The Venice Biennale of 1997 was much like that of any other year. In 1995, a work of art involving ants had to be removed because the ants were of an endangered species. This year one work of art made from old bones had to go because in the hot weather the bones stank. Undaunted by this offering in the Giardini di Castello, I decided to visit the arsenal and its Corderie where the works provided by commercial galleries are shown. Seldom open to the public, the Corderie is a wonderful building, with columns of rendered brick supporting parallel balconies that run its entire length of several hundred feet. Above these balconies is a pitched roof, its clay tiles seen through bare timbers, the whole held together by heavy beams. This building is truly one of the wonders of Venice, although its contents during my visit were objects to wonder about rather than wonder at.

Standing almost astride the entrance was a very large flat chrome sculpture entitled *Elephant*. A work by Jeff Koons, it looked more like *Popeye after an Encounter with a Steamroller*. Inside the building an earth mover, decorated with tinsel and coloured shiny glass balls, played the part of a Christmas tree. Two vast inflated white beach balls by Maurizio Mochetti filled even the grand space of the Corderie floor to ceiling. Seven brown human skulls of fibreglass, by Dinos and Jake Chapman, each the size of a family sofa, lay littered about. Bones seemed to be the fashion this year. Then I spotted a brilliantly executed, life-size model of a man, with a camcorder held to his eye, standing in front of an extremely long, super-realist painting of people of a beach. As I searched for a sign indicating who had made this sculpture, the man walked away. Jason Rhoades had on display a Ferrari in various stages of undress. This was a complicated work, and the artist had kindly provided a written description of what it was about. A great mistake, because if you have to explain your own work it merely means that there is something missing in the wretched thing. I loved the Ferrari, but hated the rest of Mr Rhoades's effort. At the very end of the Corderie hung four large paintings by Julian Schnabel. I cannot express what a relief it was to find them—they were truly brilliant, thoroughbreds among a bunch of dray horses, and had the quality that for centuries has set the greatest painter apart from the rest. I should, however, have quit while I was ahead. Hearing the sound of children shouting from a small room, I entered, curious as ever. Before me were a rack of small spiderman outfits, toys scattered all over the floor and televisions showing noisy children at play. As I left I looked to see who had created this work and found that it was by Elin Wikstrom and called *Oh Hell*—my sentiments exactly.

Fanaletto

Blown away by modern art's mediocrity, I tell a hair-raising tale of a Venetian painter and his moneymaking breeze.

Some years ago in the early autumn, when the sunshine in Venice was bright but the air had a slight chill, I sat on the terrace of the Monaco Hotel with the Venetian artist Ludovico de Luigi. He drank wine and I a large Macallan single malt whisky, heavily diluted with water. As we sat looking at Venice's buildings polished by the sunlight and listened to the shouts of the gondoliers as they loaded nervous tourists into their pitching gondolas, Ludovico and I reflected on the matter of art.

The work shown in that year's Biennale was, we thought, unbelievably bad—little did we know that in the next one it would be even worse. Who on earth, other than a museum, could buy these awful paintings and sculptures? Few were on a domestic scale. Ludovico countered that it would make little difference if they were masterpieces in a more conventional sense, for masterpieces were not what people wanted to buy these days.

Take my friend, Ludovico continued. He paints appalling pictures of Venetian gondolas and buildings. At one stage he used to paint a gondola in the morning and a building in the afternoon. However, business has been so good that now he paints two gondola pictures each morning and two building pictures in the afternoon, and if he stays up late he can fit one more of each into an evening. 'The man is making a fortune', said Ludovico, 'and his paintings are cheap and terrible—just as awful as those wretched works at the Biennale.'

Ludovico took a long draught of his wine and then wiped his mouth with a red spotted handkerchief previously tied around his neck. He said that this painter did, however, have a problem. What problem was that? Not one of money, I supposed. It turned out that painting these pictures quickly was one thing, but getting them to dry in time to sell quite another. As a solution the painter had acquired the most enormous fan, which blew cold air around both paintings and painter, speeding drying time but leaving the painter with a permanent cold in his head. Still, at least he was very rich, observed Ludovico, who went on to comment that he too had once had the chance to be rich—very rich.

It seemed churlish not to ask about this chance. It was in the winter, and a good client of his was staying in the Gritti Palace Hotel, an old lady who had with her a minuscule Frenchman—perhaps he was her boyfriend, who knows. This old lady had bought many of Ludovico's paintings and he hoped that in time she would buy many more. The day came for her to leave and he set out for the Gritti to say goodbye. When he arrived, he found the hallway filled with about three feet (a metre) of water. The lady stood on the staircase looking at the water, which was far higher than the wooden walkways to the Gritti's front door, where the boat stopped. The tiny Frenchman danced attendance on the old lady but claimed he was too small to carry her. This task fell to Ludovico who put her on his shoulders, her legs around his neck and set off for the boat. Soon Ludovico felt a tug at his jacket and looking round listened as the Frenchman spoke to him in frenzied Italian, a language that the old lady did not understand. 'I am her heir, don't you understand. Drop her in the water. She'll die of a chill and no one will blame you.' And as Ludovico started walking again to the boat he insisted, 'Drop her quickly and I will give you twenty per cent of the inheritance.' Ludovico took no notice. 'Thirty per cent then, but do it quickly. It's a wonderful chance, too good to miss.' As Ludovico moved forward the price rose in stages to sixty per cent.

As Ludovico put the old lady safely on the boat the Frenchman burst into tears and the old lady turned to thank Ludovico, remarking 'My friend, how he hates to leave Venice, see how sad he is.' I asked Ludovico about the old lady. 'Oh, she was one of the most tiresome women that I've ever met, but very rich.'

The day we sat on the terrace of the Monaco Hotel enjoying the October sunshine was in 1990 and the crash in the art market had just begun. No one could possibly have foreseen how far that market would fall, in exactly the same way that no one can truly see when it will again rise to its former heights. The world of art is very uncertain and clearly filled with hazards, not only for the dealer but also for the artist and the collector as well.

Models of excellence

In Venice I praise the Palazzo Grassi's spring show on architecture during the Renaissance and find the architectural models particularly appealing.

The sun sparkles on the lagoon. The tourists begin to arrive in Venice—the waterways to the airport lined with tripods to mark the channels are filled with a pack of racing water taxis. These motor boats, their bows high out of the water and pennants fluttering, charge each other like the war horses of medieval knights. The taxi-driver knights engage in a passage of arms as they pass, shouting and waving greetings to their colleagues. Their passengers sit nervously as their taxis rear and plunge in the wake of a boat just passed. The increased activity and not the weather is the sign that spring is here.

The Venetian does not truly accept that the season has arrived, however, until the official opening of the Palazzo Grassi's latest blockbuster, this year 'Rinascimento de Brunelleschi e Michelangelo'—two great figures of the Renaissance. The painting used in the posters and on the cover of the catalogue is of Michelangelo showing his model of St Peter's to the Pope—and a very fine painting it is. The exhibition contains very much more than the work of these gentlemen, however. Do not be misled by its title, which is rather grand and follows the Italian habit of putting the best goods in the shop window where exhibitions are concerned. In addition to a parade of well-known paintings and drawings of buildings by these two masters, this show ranges across all aspects of Renaissance architecture: its patrons, its builders, its architects and other examples of Renaissance design. Any one who aspires to be an architect should visit the Palazzo Grassi this summer, and I do not mind taking a sizeable bet that many who visit it who are not architects will wish that they were.

I think that it is the models that make the exhibition so exciting. I love architectural models of any age, but those of the Renaissance have a quality about them that cannot be described in words. That, I suppose, is why Michelangelo is showing the Pope a model of his new cathedral instead of trying to explain a drawing of it to him or writing a report. The model has a power that words or pictures do not. The model is the distillation of the architect's art, the perfect building unspoilt by the client, who perhaps will say: 'I hate these—take them off.' The model is how the architect first intended the building, and over the years it stays that way untouched by subsequent generations who believe that they can make improvements, undamaged by people living and working in it, empty, pure, a work of art no more or less, untested as to whether it works or not, unaltered by builders who subtly change as they construct or engineers who swear that the structure is unbuildable in this form. The model is the architect's own interpretation of his inspiration. I must say that I was enormously taken with the models on show at the Palazzo Grassi. I have for years attended their summer exhibition and I am convinced that this one is by far the best I have ever seen, with its impedimenta of builders and architects, portraits of patrons, books on architecture and narrative paintings that make a point.

One painting that is truly a masterpiece—by whom no one knows or even why it was painted—is *La Citta Ideale*, which normally hangs in the Ducal Palace at Urbino. Painted at the end of the fifteenth century, it shows a city square, in the centre of which stands a circular building, one that is probably owned by the state. In our age it would be used as a post office or an office for paying social security. In Venice, even today, the finest buildings are used for such purposes. In Britain we have no buildings as beautiful as the one in the painting. Indeed, most of our municipal and state architecture is built of concrete. It is not that twentieth-century British architecture is awful—far from it. We have produced some of the world's best architects who can compete on equal terms with their colleagues in that profession in any age. It is just that the state unerringly chooses the worst of them to carry out most of its buildings, and they design buildings that they don't have the budget to construct. The painting that I write of is a capriccio, its buildings unchanged by owners who would redecorate them. It has the purity of architectural thought removed from real life. Perhaps that is what makes it so terribly appealing.

Leave this architectural paradise created at the Palazzo Grassi, leave Venice and its water taxis behind and drive across northern Italy. Drive along the motorways or take the back roads, it matters not. Beside the orchards of fruit blossom, the rivers and the fresh leaved woodlands with their flowers, you will find the most horrendous modern factories, shopping centres, houses and buildings with no apparent purpose.

Pissoir artist

Jest in time: at the Marcel Duchamp exhibition in Venice, I find that the (lavatorial) humour of his Dadaist urinal still appeals.

It is not the change in the weather that heralds spring in Venice, but rather the pack of motor boats that prowl the Grand Canal in the vicinity of the Palazzo Grassi. The reason for their presence at this time of year is the opening of the annual Palazzo Grassi blockbuster—this year (1993) the work of Marcel Duchamp. The cargo that the motor boats carry are guests on their way to the official opening. These boats push and shove to land their important passengers on the palazzo's private landing stage. Those less pushy or not so well practised in the art of shoving have to spend some time prowling that stretch of canal waiting their turn. In any country other than Italy, in any town other than Venice, the passengers would have been dropped at the *vaporetto* (water-bus) stop, a place from which it is just as convenient to enter the palazzo as it is by its own landing. But not here. This is the land of *bella figura* (good face), and it must be the official entrance with its line of civic officials doing the greeting or nothing. To enter from a bus stop would definitely be *brutta figura* (bad face), and such behaviour might take years to live down. Indeed, a person's social standing could be entirely destroyed by how that person arrived at an exhibition of the work of Marcel Duchamp.

There is an extraordinary irony about all this, for Duchamp was tackling exactly this aspect of life when he first exhibited a urinal. 'It is art,' he said. 'I chose it'—or words to that effect. The argument has raged ever since but, sure enough, Duchamp's urinal is hung in the Palazzo Grassi—not at eye-level as a picture is hung, not on a pedestal on the ground as a sculpture is shown; no, the lavatory basin is hung about right for a fully grown man—too high for small boys. The day I went to the show there was a group of large men behaving like small boys around the urinal. I was left wondering whether Duchamp always intended the audience who looked at this piece to be the work of art rather than the pan itself.

Duchamp is perhaps best known for the objects he used to provoke: the bottle rack, which is a box full of measuring implements; a stool with a bicycle wheel mounted on the top of it. (I suppose the latter may have been used in a garage to ease the repair of punctured tyres.) Chosen by Duchamp, all these objects provoked an argument about the nature of art. Then there are the casts of intimate parts of the human anatomy and the defacing of Leonardo da Vinci's *Mona Lisa*—she looks very well in a moustache painted by Duchamp. These are all about Duchamp the thinker. The exhibition is light on the work of Duchamp the painter, inevitably I suppose, for his paintings of real consequence came only during a very few years when he worked in a style that was truly his own.

Marcel Duchamp came from a family of artists—himself and his two brothers, Raymond Duchamp-Villon and Jacques Villon. The exhibition, as always at the Palazzo Grassi, is better studied in the catalogue than the palazzo (half a dozen of their catalogues and you barely need buy a book on art ever again).

In his early years Duchamp gambled through work in many styles—impressionistic, fauvist and cubist. The cubist paintings are clearly important, possibly brilliant. Then there are the works with glass. For many years a freestanding one of these, called *A Bride Stripped Bare by Her Bachelors, Even*, stood in the Tate Gallery. The label with its name was fixed to the wall nearby; unfortunately, next to the label was a painting of a naked lady with a couple of fully dressed men looking at her. Who this was by I cannot remember—but its association with the Duchamp label became the source of much misunderstanding and frequent complaints from those who take the trouble to complain about what they regard as pornography. There can be no confusion at the Palazzo Grassi, however, for a similar glass piece is clearly labelled—and not in the slightest erotic.

When you look at Duchamp's work you get the feeling that he had thought of everything that was to happen for the rest of the century, tried it and then tired of it. In 1918 he painted one last major picture, *Tu m'*, and then gave up painting and took up chess. After this he only made objects. William Rubin, writing in his great book, *Dada and Surrealism*, said of this last oil: 'The elements splay out over the surface yet appear to hang together like a Duchampesque mobile'. It was Duchamp who later named Calder's sculptures 'mobiles'. After this work Duchamp thought that painting had had it—perhaps he was right.

Celtic crossover

At the Celtic exhibition in Venice in 1991, I find the superb—and small-scale—craftsmanship of a culture that embraced all Europe, over pagan and Christian eras, a shining example for our times.

The Palazzo Grassi is a very large palazzo indeed. It is not one of the most distinguished buildings on Venice's Grand Canal; indeed, it is a somewhat cumbersome building, but it was recently converted to hold exhibitions and it has improved. Gae Aulenti, the architect responsible for Le Quai d'Orsay in Paris, also carried out this conversion, and I must say that she has done a remarkable job on both these unpromising buildings.

The exhibitions at the Palazzo Grassi are financed by the Fiat company and appear annually. At first they seem to be exhibitions of the blockbuster kind, but on close scrutiny—or perhaps not such close scrutiny—they are something else. Long on information and short on objects is the formula that they follow. There is always a catalogue several inches thick and very heavy; you need strong arms to carry it home in the handy see-through plastic bag provided.

The exhibitions are always political. They promote one ideology or another: 'Italian Art' or 'The Origins of Venice' (the Phoenicians) are two of the recent ones. The current exhibition, 'I Celti', is about

Europe, one Europe. We were all European first and we will all be European last. It sets out to prove that the Celts were the first Europeans. It records the parameters of that culture as it stretched from Hungary to the northernmost point of Scotland, from the late-Bronze Age to the third century AD—truly the first time that Europe had a common culture, and happily it will be the last. However, much as one may admire Celtic art, it is the very variety of Europe that makes the place interesting. The Celtic culture extended over this remarkable area and period of time because of the migration of peoples carrying a distinctive culture with them as they followed the mineral deposits in Europe that could be made into bronze—bronze they needed to make the art and artefacts of their daily lives. The Palazzo Grassi comprehensively records in its catalogue the progress of that migration.

The exhibition is different. Finding the Lindisfarne Gospels illustrated in the catalogue I rushed to see them. They were not there at all, but still safely in the British Museum. The famous bronze jugs are similarly still at home. There are in the British Museum alone perhaps a dozen Celtic masterpieces not included in the Palazzo Grassi. The exhibition is only a starting point for a pilgrimage around Europe en route to the many museums that house this culture: a trailer to whet your appetite.

A very large room in this palace is entirely filled with sinister fibreglass trees; a small golden craft sails among them. The trees are as black as the boat is gold. Gold, tiny and very, very beautiful. This large room devoted to this tiny object with its theatrical presentation gives the feeling of some ancient and unrevealed religion. It has all the mystery and impact its designers intended. Unfortunately, in the small print there is a footnote. This gold boat is not *the* gold boat at all—*the* gold boat is still in its museum in Dublin. Among the other absent objects is the Aesica Brooch found in 1884 at Great Chesters in Northumberland and now in the Newcastle upon Tyne Museum. Sir Arthur Evans, the great archaeologist who had himself dug up a great many works from antiquity, said of this brooch: 'It is probably the most fantastically beautiful creation that has come down to us from antiquity.'

Also not in this exhibition are any of the group of carved stone heads from Yorkshire, some two feet high, some only a few inches. These heads are to be found not in museums but still in the countryside, built into stone walls or the piers of gateways, owned by farmers who, out of superstition, kept them on their land.

The Celts were remarkable people, and their culture must surely be among the world's greatest. The Celtic world spans many changes in Europe. It extends from pagan times to that of the early Christians, and some of its best examples date from the early Christian period and are found in Ireland and northern Scotland. They include bell shrines and book shrines with intricate line patterns that show a sophistication seldom achieved since. These people were migratory people and they carried their art and artefacts with them, so of necessity—as with other migratory cultures—their objects tended to be small. The strange thing about the Celtic culture is that, unlike most works of art that are distorted and often destroyed by magnification, the proportion and workmanship of these often tiny objects is so perfect they are improved by increasing their size. The poster for this exhibition shows the face of a goat in bronze. In reality it is less than an inch and a half high; in the poster it becomes two feet high and still looks wonderful.

This exhibition may lack many of the great masterpieces, but as I wandered through this vast palazzo, I saw no object that was bad or crude or poorly made. These people, the Celts, were truly the first Europeans showing a common culture, but, unlike Europe's current small club, they stood for something grander.

For richer, for poorer

Visiting Sicily I find that the island is paying a price for its growing prosperity.

The car ferry swung in a great curve as it made its way from Reggio di Calabria to Messina. It pitched gently in the light breeze, the sun shone and I listened to the shouts of schoolchildren. There were no towers or minarets in Messina, no grand hotels overlooking golden beaches, no Norman castles or Moorish mosques. Beneath the grey layer of pollution was a town about which it would be best to say as little as possible for fear of causing offence. In a few words, the best aspect of Messina is the motorway and the speed at which the place can be left.

Half an hour away perches the town of Taormina, a place for which my guidebook promised great things. The things were not that great. The Greek theatre overlooking the sea lacked the presence and the acoustics of Epidaurus. Sitting high in the auditorium of the latter, I could hear the guide, standing on stage a hundred or more feet away, tear a piece of paper as if he had torn it in front of my face. Sadly, the Greek theatre of Taormina is a poor affair, the Norman church likewise. The town is tourist-ridden, its only delights a cake shop in the main street whose ancient proprietor knows the art of working with marzipan and a garden built by an English lady. Whether her planting has survived is hard to tell, but the garden's layout is English, as are its plants.

I walked in the garden that evening and the scent of the plants was overwhelming: large bushes of *Philadelphus* that the Italians call *seni d'angeli*, breasts of angels. Among the borders and shrubberies this English gardener had built the most extraordinary follies: cottages and towers, grottoes and pavilions; just as if some giant magpie had built its nest from fragments of Greek masonry, Norman columns, medieval tiles and nineteenth-century terracotta. They gave the rambler the strangest of feelings: exotic as the buildings by Gaudi in Guell Park, Barcelona, and as futuristic as the Watts Tower in Los Angeles. In their midst, the town council of Taormina had built municipal tennis courts for the entertainment of the town's citizens.

I walked in these gardens as the scent-filled dusk turned to a darkness of royal purple, and then I returned to my hotel by way of the main street. The shops were still brightly lit; what they sold were tourist goods of little use to the population or so I believed. Loud music came from the square that lay halfway along the main street. Crowds had gathered in front of the Café Wunderbar to watch a fashion show in which mannequins strode a catwalk clad in Versace's gilded excesses and Moschino's fashionable jokes.

As I looked around me I realised that these spectators were not tourists but natives of Taormina—the young men in expensive jackets, the girls dressed as if they were strolling in Rome. Sicily is no longer the land of peasants and donkeys, nor are its citizens sad women in black and sturdy men in tweed caps with shotguns slung across their shoulders. The shops of Taormina don't sell peasants' dresses and workmen's clothes any more either, for people have grown rich on subsidies from Brussels and tourists from Germany. Shops offering high fashion and flashy jewellery are of far more use to them than those that sell peasant pots and pans. Sicily is an island of six million inhabitants and they are now rich.

Early the next day I set out for Enna. I drove across golden plains watered by aqueducts and cultivated by tractors. In the distance I could see farmers' mansions and Norman castles, churches with domes shaped like half an orange and painted that colour. I passed unfinished buildings left to their own devices and sections of motorway leading nowhere. High on a small mountain stands the town of Enna. Roughly at the heart of Sicily, it is a town of narrow streets obstructed by lines of expensive cars. I have never seen so many cars in such a town. The cluttered streets curl upward and at their summit a castle that once boasted twenty towers is now reduced to the ruins of six. I stood on its battlements and looked out over all of Sicily.

I strolled in Enna's streets, and watched a funeral and a wedding, but all the while I felt a sense of claustrophobia. After I left I stopped my car, wound down the windows, and waited while it filled with the scent of wild flowers that bloomed in profusion all around.

From baroque to beef

Palermo is a puzzling city where 'civilisation' and shabbiness go hand in hand. I concentrate on its baroque and Byzantine wonders—and on its beef buns.

Palermo must be the only place left in Europe where the ruins of bomb-damaged buildings from the Second World War still stand untouched. Only the minimum of effort has been spent on them: a timber joist to prop up a facade here, a scaffold to support an arch there, the occasional window bricked up to strengthen a wall. Where restoration has been undertaken, such as on the town's opera house, the work has stretched over twenty years and there have been rumours of fraud.

For all Palermo's shabby appearance, the city is wealthy. The streets are filled with traffic of the most expensive kind. The market district is horrendously busy, and the produce fresh and seldom long on display. The restaurant where I dined was decorated in the art-nouveau style of a peculiar late-twentieth century variety. I arrived and the place was deserted. I knew the restaurant was open for they had accepted my booking. I walked in and studied the buffet. It appeared excellent. Each fish was curled into a lifelike shape, a piece of catgut pulling its tail towards its mouth. The fruit was in pyramids, the salads graded in shades of green, with roundels of cheese to their right and multicoloured desserts to their left. All this and yet not one customer, or for that matter any sign of a waiter.

I rattled the door, coughed and then gave a considerable 'view halloo'. A man appeared. I took him for a waiter although I am bound to say that there was nothing about the fellow to show I was correct. He took me to a side room and offered me a drink. I protested that I had come to dine. He insisted and pointed out that the cocktail was on the house. I chose a ten-year-old Macallan whisky. He seemed delighted. Palermo is indeed, I thought, a strange place. I sat for 30 minutes studying the horrendous decor, and then ten waiters arrived, hurried me to a table and served my first course. As I sat I could hear the strident tones of what I took to be a fascist politician addressing an audience. The waiters had all vanished. I was impressed by this Italian dedication to a politician's words and so I waited patiently until cheering indicated that he had finished, at which point the waiters appeared with the second course.

Had I known about sport, and football in particular, all would have been clear to me. Italy, it seemed, had just won the European Cup. The restaurant filled with customers, and when I left a jolly good time was being had by all. I write about this experience only to demonstrate that Palermo is its own place, with a population who live their lives as they will. All who come from outside can go hang themselves as far as Palermo's citizens are concerned.

Do not try to understand how events are ordered in Palermo—the answer will always evade you. Do not go there for shopping; the shops offer little that you want. Do not go there to loaf on Palermo's beaches: they must be among the world's worst. Go to Palermo to stay in the city's grand hotels, and to see their still-intact original decoration which dates from the end of the last century. Sit where Wagner once sat; wander in cloisters from the beginning of the millennium. Go to Palermo to wonder at the way Christianity and Islam entwine; see the totally bizarre Convento dei Cappuccini, the catacombs where the corpses of the rich were mummified from the sixteenth century to the 1920s. There are over eight thousand of them dressed for their daily life in death. Revel in the baroque, with each church vying for the greatest number of cherubs that can be fitted to a wall. One church devoted to the Battle of Lepanto has its putti carrying out the work of God and putting the Saracens to flight.

If Palermo is the home of the baroque, it is also the home of Byzantine glitter: the perfect Cappella Palatina, the Royal Chapel designed by Roger II in 1132 and indicative of the fusion between Byzantine, Norman and Sicilian civilisations; and the much grander monastery at Monreale high above the city of Palermo with its Romanesque portal by a Pisan master and bronze doors of the same period. The Arab Norman cloisters have double columns, many of them inlaid with golden mosaics. The beauty of the place is staggering.

This lazy and sullen city, Palermo, has been around so long and seen so many strangers come and go that it has learned to cope with civilisation and not to take the present too seriously. If you must eat in Palermo, give the restaurant with art-nouveau decor and football-crazy waiters a miss and visit the Antico Focacceria where they serve Palermo's greatest delicacy; beef buns, perhaps you will begin to understand the place.

Lecce's legacy

In the exuberant baroque architecture of the Apulian town of Lecce, there is a unity amid its eclecticism.

The rain came down like steel rods, but no weather, however bad, could spoil Lecce's beauty, just as no weather, however wonderful, could further enhance the pure joy of Lecce's baroque architecture. There is no doubt that Lecce, in Italy's south-eastern region of Apulia, is one of the capitals of the baroque. The stone of its buildings is yellow with a gentle pink tinge like a permanent sunset, and is so soft that it can be carved with a knife or smoothed with a carpenter's plane. Detail upon detail crowd cornices, clutter capitals and scramble up facades—figures and animals abound.

There comes a time in the history of all great towns and cities when their inhabitants start to build. So it was with Lecce in the sixteenth, seventeenth and eighteenth centuries. The amphitheatre, dating from the time of Hadrian (second century AD), was built over and the cultures of the Normans, Swabians and Angevins were subdued by the new fashion—'Lecce baroque'. Buildings shot up everywhere: churches, mansions, monuments and the castle of Charles V, but the Piazza del Duomo is a true gem. To one side of it stands a five-storey bell tower built at the end of the seventeenth century and designed by Giuseppe Zimbalo (who also designed the cathedral). This tower is like a child's toy consisting of five separate 'buildings' sitting one on top of the other, each slightly smaller than the last, with a balcony defining where each level begins and ends.

The cathedral itself was built on the site of a twelfth-century church, demonstrating that not every building can be preserved. Our forebears were far less timid about pulling down one masterpiece in order to build another, though perhaps our current timidity is justified by the poor quality of much of today's architecture. While the people of cities such as Lecce had a great urge to tear down and build again, we have a great urge to preserve, restore and build nothing.

On the other side of the Piazza del Duomo is the Bishop's Palace, built in the early part of the fifteenth century and then rebuilt halfway through the sixteenth, with its outstanding first floor loggia. Next door is the Palazzo del Seminario, designed by Giuseppe Cino and built at the beginning of the eighteenth century. These buildings, constructed over a period of 300 years by different architects, sit together as if they had been designed by one man on one particular day.

Leave the cathedral by the back door, pass along a maze of small alleys and you come across the most perfect of Roman theatres—the contrast between the delight of the baroque piazza and the bold efficiency of the Roman theatre is dramatic. Lecce is undoubtedly a town to walk in, slowly, with your eyes towards the heavens, feasting on the details of the city's complicated facades. The Basilica di Santa Croce, generally regarded as the most perfect example of Lecce baroque, has nowhere near the charm of the Piazza del Duomo. Built from plans by Gabriel Riccardi, its construction began in 1549 and was continued by Francesco Antonio Zimbalo, Cesare Penna and Giuseppe Zimbalo. I was not surprised to learn that this church had been worked on by four different architects as it has without doubt the most complicated facade that I have ever come across. Like a great wedding cake, it rises with tier after tier of embellishments fashioned by workmen who carved the soft Lecce stone with the ease of great pastry chefs applying icing-sugar decorations. You can like Lecce baroque, indeed love or loathe it, but in the end you have to admit that the citizens of fifteenth-century Lecce, when they set about building, were gripped with a wild enthusiasm for their task.

Chaos theory

In the heel of Italy there is a disorderly museum collection to fire every boy's imagination. I rediscover my childhood among its birds and bones, crocks and cannons.

The old town of Gallipoli, on the heel of Italy, is reached by a long causeway which leads you into its narrow streets, crowded with grand, provincial baroque buildings. A road follows what were once the ramparts, and inexperienced visitors will have the joy of circling it several times while trying to park their cars. But having overcome this initiative test they will find the town a true delight. You can't just walk down Gallipoli's narrow streets staring at a map. You have to work in this place, crane your neck upwards, peer through open doorways and poke your nose into courtyards. In the town centre sits the Museo e Biblioteca Communale. Once a library, most of the books are now long gone and the building has become a museum. This museum, a relic from a different age, was made in the days when collections were put together to enchant. Architecturally, the building's lack of proportion and ungainliness make it a real joy. On the ground floor are the exhibits. Great arches support a balcony which runs around the building and carries a collection of books. Above this the walls of the third storey are pierced with windows that illuminate the whole interior.

The collection is of the sort guaranteed to fire the imagination of a small boy. I can appreciate a Titian or a Tintoretto in a great museum but it is collections such as this one in Gallipoli that really excite me: stones, bones, birds and Greek pots—not Greek pots of British Museum quality but ones with barnacles and coral still clinging to them. Everything in this eclectic collection has been found locally, from the rusty cannon to land mines from the Second World War, and from fossilised and stuffed fish to obsolete bank notes in denominations which include literally dozens of zeros. Portraits of local worthies and local views have a wonderful provincial quality that city dealers like to call primitive. Cabinets contain a mixture of coins, corals, shells and stones. There is no order about this place, no attempt to educate the public. The museum is a true cabinet of curiosities.

The strange thing about a place like this is that it excites the curiosity in a way that carefully curated museums can never do. If your eye lights on an object there is precious little chance of finding out exactly what it is. But at least here you feel the need to try. Modern museum design tells you what to look at and everything about the object. With his imagination untroubled, the small boy leaves feeling it was all rather boring. In a museum such as the one in Gallipoli, he leaves with a burning desire to collect, to discover and to learn. I left Gallipoli with a notebook filled with architectural details and ideas for a new garden. I also left with a desperate hope that no idiot will ever tidy up the museum.

A little night music

Opera, brass-band style, rings out over town squares in southern Italy, which sparkle with fairy lights during a string of summer festivals.

The town of Spongano in southern Italy has little to recommend it: no great church, no castle, no fine palaces with painted ceilings. Spongano is, for most of the year, a town for driving through, stopping perhaps only to buy fruit from the mobile greengrocer's van parked in the square. For a week in August, however, the town comes to life. The town becomes a fantasy of coloured lights under which local bands on decorated bandstands play popular operas on glittering horns and trombones.

On my visit, the evening began with a church service and parade, followed by fireworks. After this, the citizens of Spongano got down to the serious business of opera. The elderly population sat in the serried ranks facing the bandstand, while the youths of the town milled around the edge of the square eating and drinking. The conductor, a slim man in a bright-green suit, gripped his baton like a dagger as the band broke into the overture of *Turandot*. Stabbing the air in front of him, he became more and more excited. His audience, on the other hand, sat silent staring ahead as if in a deep trance. Then with a great crash of symbols, banging of drums and blowing of trumpets it was all over. The square shook with applause.

So much did I enjoy this experience that instead of turning in at midnight, I set out for a neighbouring town which had its own outdoor performance—it seems that during August all the small towns of the Salentine Peninsula are *en fête*. As I walked into the town's square only the hard core of the audience were left. Sleepily they sat in the hot night air as the band struck up a splendid rendering of *Cavalleria Rusticana*. In that small southern town, in the blackness of night, lit by bright fairy lights, no opera could have been more magical.

The next day I was longing for more, so I set out for Tricase, a large town with a fine church and many good baroque buildings. Tricase's festival was much larger and grander than those in the surrounding towns. There was dancing in one square and pop singers in another, but the *pièce de résistance* was performed in front of the church in a square packed with people. On a stage were four performers and a considerable sound system. The performers strike up the *pizziche*, the ancient folk music of the Salentine Peninsula. This strange music comes from an ancient tradition of driving out madness, a condition often induced by a bite from a spider, seen as the force of evil. When these ceremonies are performed, the 'mad' person is first taken to a church in Galatina where they pray to St Paul. Later they dance and dance to the music of the *pizziche* until after many hours they drop from total exhaustion and the madness is cast out. Seldom have I listened to such a contagious rhythm.

Strength in numbers

Sunhat and slide rule at the ready, I escape to Apulia to wax metaphysical in the harmonious interiors of the Castel del Monte.

Loreto Aprutino—a few kilometres from Pescara on the road to southern Italy—was desiccated. The old town lay baking in the sunshine with not a sign of an inhabitant. The Castello Chiola, the hotel where I was staying, was huge and empty. 'The restaurant is closed,' I was told. 'Try across the street.' As dusk fell I crossed the street and learned two things. First, the restaurant was empty; second, it was excellent. When travelling in rural Italy, the rule that operates in cities—avoid an empty restaurant like the plague—is reversed. The empty restaurant is the one in which the mother of the household cooks for you alone.

Early the next morning, I set out for Apulia. The motorway that runs beside the Adriatic Sea was edged with oleanders in full flower; butterflies flew in groups across the road. Traffic was sparse, and every so often there was a break in the vineyards that sloped towards the sea. That gap was filled with a field of sunflowers: dark-green foliage, large yellow petals and barren faces, each plant identical to the next. At Andria I left the motorway and headed up a road between olive groves.

The Castel del Monte is truly the world's most beautiful castle. Its majestic flat top emerges out of a rise in the road, on a distant hill covered in Roman pines. For kilometre after kilometre it maintains its distance until, with a final burst, the model castle becomes full-grown, dwarfing its mount and the pines around it. Walking up the winding path through the cool shade of the pines, one is ill-prepared for the sun and wind, both red hot, that surround the keep and beat against the final flights of stone steps. Once inside the castle's door, however, solid stone walls and high ceilings ensure an ice-cold interior.

The Castel del Monte was built in the mid-thirteenth century by order of the Emperor Frederick II. It was used for the diverse activities of impressing rebellious citizens and celebrating the wedding of the emperor's natural daughter with Richard, Count of Caserta. When, in the eighteenth century, it was abandoned, the castle became a shelter for shepherds, brigands and political refugees, until at last the Italian government bought the place for 25 000 lire. Since then conservation work has been carried out from time to time.

The debate about the design of this castle seems never-ending. It is built to a meticulous geometric design, in accordance with a series of mathematical formulas. For instance, the musical consonances of Boethius's sound numbers (2, 3, 4, 6, 8, 9 and 12), the Fibonacci sequence, in which each number is equal to the sum of the two preceding numbers (1, 1, 2, 3, 5, 8 etc), and the golden section (1:1.618) are all here. The octagonal keep is edged with eight octagonal towers. The symbolism of these octagons seems to have played an important part in the castle's history and is responsible for its beautiful appearance. The octagon is the shape of a font, as well as a symbol of the resurrection. Eight is the number of the wind rose on mariners' charts, showing the directions of the principal winds; it is also the number of the spokes in a wheel. These symbols, associating the castle's structure with the earth and sky, suggest a link to the metaphysical world.

There can be no doubt, however, that this structure owes its beauty to its strictly ordered form, stripped of all extraneous decoration. Inside this cool, beautiful place you can hear the hot wind thundering against its walls. The atmosphere is wonderfully romantic.

Pot luck

Things were looking bleak: 'industrial' was how the guidebooks described the southern Italian town of Grottaglie. Little did I suspect that it would prove to be home to the most wonderful pottery . . .

It was with some delight that I received the news from friends that they would take me to Grottaglie. The time of departure was to be 6 a.m., the earliness of the hour only serving to heighten my anticipation. No sooner had my friends left for the night than I set about my collection of guidebooks. Grottaglie has the heaviest density of population in this region. Its Romanesque church has been rebuilt, declared one guidebook; an industrial town in an industrial area, declared another. What on earth had I let myself in for?

As 5 a.m. drew close after a restless night, I became more and more depressed. Up and ready at 6 a.m., I was prepared to live with my mistake—by 8 a.m. everybody else was ready to depart. Time in Italy often plays but a small part in life. We eventually set out in a two-car convoy. The sun was shining, and the countryside sparkled with the first taste of autumn. Grottaglie, a few miles short of Taranto, took under two hours to reach. Barely a sniff of industry was to be found—unless you call the making of handcrafted pottery 'industry'—for Grottaglie is a town of potteries. There are 50 or more in this small place, their shops stuffed to the portals with pots of all sizes and shapes: straight-sided jugs that were pure white and nearly two feet tall, simple bowls in bright colours, traditional pottery, innovative pottery, useful pottery and useless pottery.

The dinner service that caught my eye was simple, coloured a citrus yellow and with a thin stripe of green at its edges. I came across this dinner service in the pottery of Nicola Fasano. (It seemed that almost every pottery in the place was owned by a Fasano.) All of a sudden I realised I had found the source for the pottery I had admired the world over. Wonderful pots in which to keep bread, in two colours—dark and light brown—with a stripe where the glazes blend. Mugs with spots and stripes, plates with simple designs, and plates with designs of the utmost complexity. Among this proliferation of potteries is La Ceramica Vincenzo del Monaco. This, I was told, was where the Agnelli family take their custom. Fine as it is, the work lacks the vigour of the less grand potteries. In one such sat a potter of vast dimensions making figurines of a humorous nature. It was in this shop that I came across a fruit bowl the likes of which I have never seen before. At first I thought it was a pottery colander raised on a pedestal—I could not understand it at all. Then it was explained to me that the holes were there so that freshly washed fruit could drain.

Many of the potteries are in caves hollowed out of the steep slopes of the hill on which the town was built. Grottaglie is a town of low, terraced houses with wrought-iron balconies, each balcony rail with brightly coloured pottery finials at its corners. Occasionally, the traditional vaulted construction of these homes escapes into the street to form the support for a balcony.

As for the rebuilt church, it has one of the most beautiful portals: two columns supported on the backs of cantilevered lions, topped with a further pair of lions from which an arch of leaves springs. Sadly, the inside does not live up to this promise. The dome of the church, on the other hand, is wonderful, coloured in stripes and geometric patterns with tiles made in the old town. Taken as a whole, the old town of Grottaglie is an engaging place—old houses, narrow streets and occasional flashes of brilliant architecture. Definitely a place worth getting up early to visit.

Gurgling most gloriously

Visiting the palatial headquarters of a southern Italian water company, I found the glamour of the good old days when industry celebrated itself in style.

At the turn of the century much of southern Italy was an arid place. Water was its rarest treasure and those who controlled that water its princes. It is therefore no surprise that L'Acquedotto Pugliese, the water company formed to irrigate the land around Bari, built a palace to house its offices. This palace, called 'il Palazzo dell'Acquedotto Pugliese di Bari', is the most extraordinary of places.

The building stands foursquare on a full city block, its facade rough-hewn blocks of local stone embellished with wrought-iron candelabras, and its drainpipes decorated with wrought-iron snakes. The imposing entrance has the feel of a medieval castle, all in coloured marble and stone. Ahead of you on entering is the large gateway to an internal courtyard, whose central fountain demonstrates that the company has water to spare and plenty more besides. The fountain's wonderful imagery shows a pollarded tree supporting a carved stone city in miniature—wealth through growth made possible by water.

As befits a palace to the gods of water, there is water symbolism everywhere. The massive staircase is built of polished stone blocks, as is the finish of the walls around it. Its skirting is remarkable: almost two feet high in a mottled brown polished marble. Before each landing, a large brown marble pitcher pouring brown marble water onto the skirting of the step below appears in bas-relief.

Upstairs, on the first floor, water dominates everything: there are floors inlaid with coloured marble that show horses drinking from a river and kneeling women pouring water from vases carried on their heads, and stone columns of women who seem to have come from Egypt, each pouring quantities of stone water onto a basin that houses an uplighter.

And as for the murals, they are to water what the paintings of Titian and Tintoretto are to God. A room that I take to be the company's boardroom is a veritable shrine to water. The walls are painted with murals showing agriculturists wasting water as if the resource were inexhaustible, while from their workplace an aqueduct flows through olive fields to a prosperous city beyond. In the surrounding panels animals feed off lush pastures and women wash clothes. Everywhere is prosperity brought by water.

The carefully designed furniture is a masterpiece of restraint but carries on the water theme. Severe modern lines battle with a baroque exuberance of water, streams, rivers, waterfalls and bathing figures. Usually the water is represented by mother-of-pearl. Where there is no marble or stone, there are wallpapers printed or painted with the theme of water. Painted pots pour streams of blue and white water around the architraves of beautifully crafted doorways; even the carpets—almost Vorticist designs—represent wealth through water. Small female faces with mother-of-pearl hair appear in the woodwork, again representing water. As the Ancient Mariner put it, 'Water, water, everywhere,/ Nor any drop to drink.'

This place, recently restored by the directors of the water board, is a masterpiece. For commercial premises to be so exuberant and unashamed is extraordinary; I doubt the likes of it will ever be built again. It is a fine example of the patronage so common in its era—wealth getting together with art and artists. A natural production that works, while the offerings of today in the same genre seem so desperately artificial.

Going to pottery

I break bread with the locals in the Italian town of Ostuni, and blow the whistle on other unexpected delights.

Brindisi Airport is not the most exciting place in the world, despite having a most beautiful Romanesque church standing at the end of its main runway. The church is well worth allowing an extra half an hour to visit, either before take-off or after arrival. The road from the airport is almost rustic, and in the first days of March the fields that flank it were covered in wild flowers. Beyond the fields, low hills rise and slowly approach you as you speed along an almost empty road. And then there is Ostuni, a town nestling near the top of those hills. The buildings shine bright white in the sunlight; the cathedral stands out a dark brown.

The town's buildings were clustered high in the hills as a defence against the Saracens. It did well to be fortified, for through the centuries it has known the rule of Messapians, Romans, Lombards, Byzantines, Normans, Swabians, Angevins and Aragonese. It has known the tyranny of the Spanish family of Zevallos, the Bourbons and finally the liberation of the Risorgimento. Scattered among the olive groves surrounding Ostuni is a wealth of material from prehistory—grottoes, large heaps of stone called *specchie*, the crypts where some of the earliest Christian churches are found, and, most amazing of all, dolmens in which the arrangement of rock leaves one wondering how they were built without the assistance of cranes or complicated winches and scaffolding.

The town itself has an indefinable charm that sets it apart from other white-painted towns with narrow streets. Restaurants abound, so I suppose tourists must come here in the summer, but the closest I could find to a tourist shop was a local pottery—or so I thought until the proprietor explained that the strange figures of birds and people were, in fact, whistles. It seems that Ostuni has a tradition of making whistles in pottery. Owls, fully two feet tall, are pottery whistles. The most intimate parts of the male body, both in miniature and life-size, are pottery whistles. Cows, houses, carabinieri, characters from Italian history, snorting bulls, cars and motorbikes are all reproduced as pottery whistles.

In the town square, I sat and drank the juice of blood oranges and ate focaccia baked with herbs and tomatoes, a bread peculiar to this part of Italy. Led by the aroma, I found the baker of this remarkable bread a street or two away. In Mr Farina's *panificio*, I bought focaccia in a dozen different forms, with combinations of olives, nuts, artichokes and tomatoes, along with other herbs and vegetables that I did not recognise.

A few doors down I found a maker of tambourines, a serious artist who makes them for folk musicians. He demonstrated the local rhythms on his instruments: these rhythms, he claimed, are inspired by the calls of local birds. 'It is just my idea,' he said, with considerable modesty. Up the narrow streets I wandered, past the eighteenth-century church of San Vito Martire, now a museum filled with stones, broken pots and bits of bones. Sometimes as I walked I caught a glimpse along a street of the plain below and the Adriatic.

At last I came to the town's fifteenth-century cathedral, a fine example of late Gothic architecture. It has a wonderful circular window in the middle of its facade, with glazing bars as heavy as the spokes of a cartwheel. Either side of this window, the roof-line of the cathedral's wings curved upwards, echoing the downward curve of the roofing either side of the apex. Standing back, I waited as I caught my breath—not from the long climb on a warm day, but rather from the beauty of the place.

Happily Napoli

The fiery Italian city of Naples can be heaven or hell.

Naples does not make much of a first impression on the visitor. In common with other Italian industrial cities, it has never quite worked out where the countryside ends and the city truly begins. As you approach from the airport the views are of uninspiring ranks of tatty concrete flats and rows of washing.

At my hotel, a fine old building on the esplanade, I was shown to my room by the junior manager. Waiting until he had my full attention, he opened the shutters with a flourish. The view was stunning. There is a magic to the bay of Naples that has managed to survive centuries of warfare, crime and general deterioration. Naples is a city where you must look for beauty. It offers the most wonderful treasure hunt, where nothing is easy to find. But each wonder found after a hard search is all the more satisfactory.

I set out to hunt for a masterpiece, starting at the Piazza Plebiscito, the most important piece of nineteenth-century town planning in a city where the majority of buildings seem to have been dropped into place at random. This large square is edged on one side with the Palazzo Reale and on another by curving colonnades which meet at the Church of San Francesco da Paola. Commissioned by Napoleon's General Murat, then King of Naples, and finished by Ferdinand I, the piazza is all very impressive but I found no masterpiece there.

The day was hot and I succumbed to the allure of Café Gambrinus's cool interior. This famous café was long the haunt of the city's cultural and political elite. But it was not their company that I sought but an ice-cream from the café's vast array. Then I walked up the fashionable Via Toledo, and passed through alleys lined with bookshops.

Off the Piazza del Gesù Nuovo is the church of Santa Chiara. Approached through a long arcade is a faïence-tiled cloister. Beautiful as they were, neither the cloister nor the church was the masterpiece that I sought. Nor was it the sweet-scented cloister garden.

I returned to my hotel tired and hot. The next day was the same but on the third day I was strolling on Via Monteoliveto when to my right, at the end of an alley, I spotted an unusual building. Curiosity led me on and I was well rewarded. The Church of Sant' Anna dei Lombardi, built in the fifteenth century, is truly a masterpiece. Constructed by Lombard emigrants it could have been transported with them from northern Italy. The first of a series of chapels along either side of the nave holds the funeral monument of Maria of Aragon and an altar by Girolamo da Santa Croce, built in 1524. Each chapel along the nave is linked with a simple doorway and each is more exciting than the one before.

The chapels and the jigsaw of broken sculpture alone would have made Sant' Anna worth a visit, but struggle past scaffolding and rubbish and you will find a chapel with a life-size terracotta pietà by Guido Mazzoni. The casual visitor might well depart after finding this extraordinary work, but there is more to discover. Down a narrow passage is the old refectory, converted into a chapel. Its vaulted ceiling was painted by Giorgio da Verona in a work of incredible quality. I had found my masterpiece at last.

Charterhouse of Padula

Travelling through Italy, I came across a little-known gem—the empty monastery at Padula—and was bowled over by the grandeur of its architecture.

Long after you have left Rome and are well on your way down the spine of Italy, driving past Monte Cassino and on past Naples, you come to a motorway sign with a dozen names on it. One of them points the way to Padula. Never in your wildest dreams could you expect the remarkable building you will find there. Some miles from the motorway, across a hot plain, you see in the distance a group of hillocks. Halfway up the first of them is a dusty car park and an unprepossessing café; beyond is the modern village of Padula. None of this is encouraging. Opposite the café is a wall with a substantial gateway. Beside the gateway is a modest chapel.

Travellers could be forgiven for wondering why they have come here. To drive on seems the only solution; the café sells a poor selection of ice-creams, its cold drinks are warm, and there is no remarkable restaurant nearby, while the building across the road is, to put it mildly, uninteresting. But what a mistake that would be, for behind that simple wall stands the Charterhouse of Padula. Once through the wooden gate and into a large courtyard, the facade of a palace, complete with niches and statues, confronts you.

This is, however, no palace but a monastery, although it seems a palace when you walk around it—and as grand as any in Europe. In 1732 Gatte declared: 'Among the monasteries belonging to this (Carthusian) order, the one at Padula is regarded as superior to all others.' Which was no mean feat, for the Carthusians were at that time by far the wealthiest among many wealthy orders.

The main cloister is 340 feet wide and 490 feet long, has a perimeter of 1660 feet and an area of 166 600 square feet. Everything about Padula is immense, not least the great elliptical staircase at the end of the main cloister. It rises several storeys and has great windows, open to the elements, that look out towards the mountains across the lands of the Charterhouse. The staircase cost 64 000 ducats in the sixteenth century, which by any standards was a vast amount of money. Contemporary comment is that the monks didn't know what to do with the accumulation of treasure.

Despite its baroque twists and turns this staircase is not the most beautiful in the monastery. There is a simpler staircase of far greater beauty: a curling snake of stone with no visible means of support that leads to the library. The library itself has a vaulted ceiling painted to contrast with the simple walnut bookcases, and mirrored in the tiled floor. It is a stunning room.

Padula is not just one great cloister, however. It has many other cloisters, some large and some small, all with gardens and fountains at their centres. There are brick pavements edged in stone, tanks filled with dark silent water, and a profusion of chapels, one leading to another, with scagliola panels on the fronts of the altars, their coloured foliage twisting and turning, cherubs frolicking and flowers blooming. There are intricate patterns on the tiled floors and heavy baroque ceilings decorated in a gold leaf discovered by Fra

Bartolommeo, who had learned the new technique of laying dark gold on stucco, which he described as 'something very beautiful and of long durability that they cannot believe in Naples'.

Who on earth was the architect for this great masterpiece lost in the countryside? No one seems to know for sure. However, the name of Michelangelo keeps cropping up. Despite the evidence of the great ciborium—sketches by Michelangelo depict a similar object—it is unlikely that he worked at Padula. The idea for the ciborium was most certainly Michelangelo's, the realisation of it most certainly not. I like to think that the architects were the monks themselves; that educated, well-read and travelled, they took a little from here, a little from there, and created a recipe for a masterpiece.

More importantly, they had the funds to employ the greatest craftsmen and the space to build as they liked. Among the many wonders of Padula, most are of the soul. Two, however, are strictly temporal. The wine cellar is perhaps rather larger than the modest lifestyle enjoyed by monks might call for. Contemporary comment was pragmatic and accurate: 'We say that wine is not suitable for monks, but since in our time it is difficult to convince them we assent to this on the condition that it is not drunk to satiation, but with moderation.'

But what is good wine without good food? Padula's kitchens are vast; its chefs once purchased 242 eggs a day. During a visit by Charles V they made an omelette from 1000 eggs. The good life came to an end with the arrival of Napoleon and republicanism. The monks, stripped of their wealth, their books and, I suppose, their wine, struggled on until 1882 when the monastery became the property of the state.

Now all that remains are shadows of past glory, fine but empty architecture, romantic gardens, a maze of floors and ceilings and the most staggering scagliola panels.

Sold on Milan

After a disappointing morning in Milan, my faith in the city was restored by the discovery of a very desirable chest of drawers, a candle shop and a couturier.

Each spring I travel by train to Milan. I enjoy the ride, except when I am robbed. That, however, is usually on the return trip while the train stands in Milan station. And what a station Milan has: a masterpiece of fascist architecture. I never cease to wonder at its grandness.

This particular spring the sun shone as I strode towards the centre of Milan and the famous shopping streets of Via Monte Napoleone and Via della Spiga. The air was fresh, the flower shops filled with blossom, the street stalls laden with bunches of wild flowers, and the vegetables in the greengrocers fresh and small just as vegetables ought to be. I had set out to enjoy myself and that was exactly what I was doing.

Then I came to the shops. The fashions in Milan are always exciting—well, nearly always. This time they were extremely dull, with the same designs in a dozen colours. The market has changed in the last year. The rich Milanese now keep a low profile with so many of their husbands having been arrested. Now is not the time for shopping. The parties of Japanese tourists surge forward as if some great river were in flood and its waters flowing down Milan's shopping streets—hitting you about chest height as you walk along. What is more, the clothes in the most fashionable of shops seem all to be made in small sizes. I have always thought of Milan as a city of tall women and now I found the place full of midgets. It was all most disconcerting.

I took my mid-morning coffee at Café Goya. The place was not busy. The sandwiches did not seem quite the same either. My mood was darkening. Lunch at Bici was excellent but the restaurant, normally packed, was quiet. I walked the streets and searched the shops that sell modern furniture in the hope of lifting my spirits. My mood became black.

So great was my despair at Milan's apparent lack of style that I visited a furniture showroom I would never normally have bothered with and there it was, the most beautiful of chest of drawers, in pale wood, slim as can be and with drawers that swing open so that you can see clothes that are normally lost at the back. Elegantly designed, a truly magnificent piece by a young designer. Other examples of his work were a stylish desk and a chair to go with it, not to mention a pair of corner cupboards.

I left that showroom and, as often happens in spring, the sun had gone but that made no difference as I felt so pleased. I strode again all the way to the Brera and at a whim turned down Via Fiori Chiari and stopped at a shop selling candles. I hate candle shops; they usually have a disgusting smell about them, a scent that you find in The Body Shop, which I suppose is meant to be indicative of health and nature. How I hate that wretched smell. This candle shop, Candele Murn, was different. Its smell was the mildest mixture of pure wax and lemon, and its candles were round and the size of parmesan cheese, each with a dozen wicks that burn at the same time. These candles can sit all year in a garden; they have a solid beauty about them.

I knew a lady once who gave a party in Turkey. She decided to have candles in her garden, rather small ones which she fixed to the back of tortoises. The idea was that the tortoises would roam in the dark unobserved, taking the candle flames with them. The candles were fixed to the tortoises, the darkness came, and with their candles alight the animals were released. At first the idea worked. The garden looked truly beautiful as the tortoises moved hither and thither. However, soon the tortoises all headed for the shrubbery and before long the whole place was on fire.

My wife had been given the name of a young and talented dress designer in Milan, and bored with the contents of the fashionable Milanese shops made an appointment for us to visit him at 5 o'clock. Stephan Jansen's studio was remote from the fashionable shopping streets. He designs brilliant, clean-cut clothes in sensuous fabrics mixed with garments that are just pure fun—clothes made from emu feathers, dyed brilliant colours.

My trip to Milan was not in the end the disaster it had seemed at lunchtime. The town does have objects and clothes to offer that are rare and beautiful. The only problem with the whole day was that the dress designer was a Frenchman, the candles came from Turkey and the stunning chest of drawers was designed by Chi Wing Lo, a Chinaman living in Athens.

A cut above in Milan

The world's finest grocer and handcrafted knives to cut its produce: a slice of Milanese life.

Milan is not one of the world's most beautiful cities. The Milanese have not had, over the centuries, a great interest in architecture in the same way that the Florentines or, for that matter, the Romans have had—rather the reverse. In fact, it took them over four hundred years to complete their cathedral. If it had not been for Napoleon who said, 'For the sake of God, finish this work now', I imagine they would still be building it. Milan, however, has grown its own beauty, a beauty of spirit, a beauty of enterprise, a beauty that comes from the natural exuberance of the Milanese. You can see it in their great manes of hair, and in the heavy gold jewellery and diamonds that they wear. Milan is, by and large, a city of wealthy people and they show it. While the women of the rest of the world are afraid to be seen in even the skins of rabbits, the Milanese wear sable at the first sign of a cold spell. They are unashamed in their pursuit of luxury, so their city has some of Italy's finest restaurants and certainly the word's finest grocer: Peck's. This is a shop of such beauty that it seems a crime to buy anything and to spoil the patterns: patterns of glazed meats, patterns of mushrooms, patterns of pastas—food that has been treated with as much artistic care as culinary. In the same street is the Café Goya, an old-fashioned teashop with straight-backed chairs, ancient waiters and bridge rolls filled with ham or egg. A strange survivor from past years packed, however, with the Milanese.

This is not a tourist city filled with bemused foreigners; it is a working city used to its limits by its citizens who revel in the wonder of their own town. In this age of tourists packaged here and packaged there, it is a phenomenon well worth observing. Milan must be one of the greatest shopping towns in the world: jewels, fashion, food and Lorenzi, the seller of knives. Lorenzi sells only the greatest of knives, not knives like the Swiss Army Penknife—a knife with a hundred uses and useful for none of them. Its very name should give a hint of its value as a penknife: the Swiss Army cannot have been in action for many centuries. The penknife, similarly, with its bright red colour, small white cross and multitude of blades, is only useful for small boys to show to their friends; under no circumstances would I use it for any serious purpose. Lorenzi's knives, on the other hand, are very serious, made by master cutlers, the doyens of their trade: Tommy Lee, Jim Kelso, Howard Hitchmouth and Christian Wimpff. These men produce knives of great beauty, with blades made from several hundred strips of metal pounded together, ivory carved handles, grips made from rare woods and semiprecious stone, and steel engraved by the most talented of engravers. One knife by James A. Schmidt of New York with a handle made from stag's horn carved with the face of a goblin, his eyes small opals, sells for £5000. Why not? That, after all, is only a fraction of the price of a ball gown by Valentino. Milan is that sort of city: steak knives by Deniq, £1500 each. And what about the forks that go with them? 'Well,' said Mr Lorenzi, 'that's a problem. It's very hard to find a competent fork-maker today.' He had what seemed to be a perfectly good range of forks. 'Those forks—how could you use those forks with Mr Deniq's knives? The tines are square.' And sure enough they were.

'What on earth difference does that make?' I asked.

'The taste,' he replied. 'The taste of the meat. A square tine tears the meat; the right size of round tine just pierces the meat.' It is wonderful to find a man so steeped in his craft, but my general experience with sharp, round tines is that, although they pierce the meat well, they also tend to pierce the tongue.

It is not only knives that Mr Lorenzi sells but also cigar boxes made just to your specification, a range of strange pipes and unusual walking-sticks. Then there are the really useful items such as a bonsai pruning set; twenty or so surgical-like instruments in a smart leather roll; and, the most exotic of all, a strange contraption with an ashtray, a small clip and a rubber ball. It was explained to me that you light your cigar, place it in the ashtray, put the still burning match in the clip and press the ball to expel the air from inside it—puff, the match is out. I suppose this machine is for a man with extremely bad breath. A city of shops that sell pointless luxuries.

The Milanese work hard. As for luxury, what we call luxury is never pointless, for the providing of luxury enriches the lives of all that it touches; like it or hate it, approve or disapprove, luxury is that strange fantasy without which the world would be an empty place.

Bolognese resource

Bologna, its medieval museum and a scheme whereby the town's monuments are restored in public view—a spectator sport for which funds can be collected.

Bolognaise sauce is served with spaghetti the world over, and wherever we find it outside of Italy it is one of the most repellent forms of food. The advance guard of Italian cooking, it has become universally used and abused. All this is strange since Bologna is the mecca of food in Italy and the sauce that bears its name is, when served in its home town, pure magic. The cuisine of Bologna is the best in Italy—Italians say the best cuisine in the word, and there are good grounds for this claim. The Bolognese take food, and all things connected with it, seriously.

Bologna is a serious place. A red city. It has red-painted buildings and, for that matter, is the heartland of the Communist Party in Italy. One of the few places left in the world where a genuine Marxist can still be found. The headquarters of the resistance to the recent change of name by the Communist Party of Italy. Communists they were and, despite the changes in Eastern Europe, Communists they wish to stay.

It must be something to do with the food, for in Bologna there are streets filled with food shops: fishmongers, greengrocers and butchers. What is noticeable about these shops is the quality of the produce. Not in one shop, but dozens of them. Among the most remarkable is A.F. Tamburini, where there are heaps of cheeses and rows of cooked meats—among them a dish of pork crackling fried beyond recognition and with a taste so good it is beyond description. Dishes of olives, perfect in size and shape. Piles of different sausages, wines and breads.

Travellers go to Rome and one hears them talk of Florence and Venice. But while the *cognoscenti* visit Lucca and Urbino, Bologna has an industrial ring about its name that turns the visitor away. Bologna, nevertheless, is a town of beauty with its arcaded streets—not just the main thoroughfares, but the lanes as well.

The medieval museum, for me, is a perfect one. Small enough so that the whole of it can be seen in less than an hour. The one in Bologna has the most comfortable seats I have ever found in any museum. I have never approved of people who sit on benches and stare at objects for hours on end, but in here I would happily sink into one of the sofas that are in every gallery and rest in comfort surrounded by objects of beauty. The museum begins with a cabinet of curiosities. A small cabinet, but a real one, complete with objects from exotic lands collected in the sixteenth century, including a unicorn's horn and a chastity belt, without which no such cabinet would be complete. The museum also has a small group of stone crosses from the twelfth century, crosses mounted on the remains of Byzantine columns. They used to be positioned at the intersections of all roads in the district, but when Napoleon came to Bologna he undertook a plan of urban redevelopment and the crosses were nearly all destroyed. The remaining examples (of which there are only ten or so) are strange and wonderful.

Bologna has its share of grand churches and Renaissance buildings. It is not a beautiful town in the sense that Venice is a beautiful town. It is a worker-like town where the people work hard. The people seem dull by comparison with those in Milan, but they do have heart and soul. In the main square there is a fountain with a figure of Neptune, who presides over four putti playing above the heads of mermaids, whose breasts liberally distribute water. This fountain by Giambologna was made in 1556 and has recently been restored. The restoration took place in a large wooden hut nearby. This hut, smelling inside like a Scandinavian sauna, was built for the occasion and named Neptune's House. It is now used for the restoration of other of the town's monuments. The public are admitted and they can walk along galleries at different heights to watch conservators at work with hoses and scalpels. All this to sympathetic music. As you leave, it is suggested with the utmost of tact that you might like to contribute to the activities of these conservators. There is, in my view, no better way to raise money for these purposes than to show the public how it is spent. There is nothing that the public enjoys more than to be admitted, if only for a few moments, behind the scenes. Many of our great museums, always in search of funds, might do well to study the example of the town council of Bologna. The Bolognese are a polite and precise people. They think about projects before they undertake them and they do not encourage waste. In the cafés around this town when you buy a cup of coffee you are given water as well, but here only in a small glass.

There is wealth in Bologna, real wealth—not just a few rich people. A large part of the population are wealthy and they know why. For they work extremely hard and carry a large part of Italy on their backs.

A roamer in Verona

Verona, where I find fierce opera lovers, a handsomely restored castle and a shop full of toothbrushes.

The rain had fallen for several days—hard rain. The cafés in the Piazza Brà were deserted, outside that is. The tables, where tourists normally sat eating their ice-cream and drinking *tè freddo* made from peaches (popular in Verona's hot summer), stood in pools of water. The rain had washed the dirt of the tourist season off the pink marble pavement, revealing its true colour, and had polished the marble built into the walls of the great amphitheatre where, on summer evenings, opera is performed.

The productions are often gigantic. For *Aida* or *Turandot* the cast is sometimes over a thousand strong. It rains in the summer as well, but the orchestra is quickly covered in plastic sheeting. The audience, wearing pack-away raincoats, leave the arena to sit in the bars until the downpour is over. The opera fans who visit Verona are a robust lot. I can recall a famous tenor being heckled unmercifully. He stood, during the last act of *Tosca* on the battlements of Castel Sant'Angelo, the Roman castle where Cavaradossi is taken to be shot, and he sang. The evening breeze filled his shirt and it expanded like a tent. The same breeze shrank his voice, and as he sang 'for shame for shame' the audience, almost as one man, shouted back, 'What a shame he is flat, take him off.'

In winter the chairs are taken into storage and the arena is bare, with just the remains of some set, no longer wanted, piled beneath an arch. The tourists gone, only the Veronese sit in the cafés; they read the papers, drink hot chocolate and eat brioche. Most of the trees in the piazza have lost their leaves, the water drips from the branches of the cedars, and the weather is cold.

Verona is situated in the shade of the mountains. The summers are hot, very hot, with occasional storms, and the winters are cold and wet. The people, as with all northern Italians, work hard, and have over the last few years prospered. The opera fans who come to the city in the summer are not the source of the city's wealth. The arena holds 26 000 people and a few more uncounted who climb in over the walls. The visitors are a bonus, filling hotels in the summer season when all right-minded Italians take their holidays. The city sits in an industrial area and this is how it earns its living. The shops sell good clothes, particularly shoes—the whole place is filled with shoe shops—and china and glass of quality also seem to be popular. The Piazza delle Erbe, whose wonderful name conjures up stalls of country produce and the sweet smell of freshly picked herbs, is not so at all. Rather, stalls sell large buns stuffed with roast pork or sausages, and all the smells that go with this trade. It is also a market for cheap clothes and small birds, of which there are too many to a cage—a study in cruelty that is needless and wasteful. The shops of Verona have their own eccentricities. Shops specialising in umbrellas or hats are seen in many towns; shops that boast 70 varieties of tea, as one does in Verona, are not uncommon; but where other than in Verona will you find a shop that sells only toothbrushes? Toothbrushes of all shapes and sizes, brushes for a dozen or more different purposes, and the paste to go with them—small tubes of paste, flat tubes with just enough paste for one night, coloured brushes and paste to match.

In winter the River Adige, which flows through the town, is a cold green; in the summer it looks no warmer. On one bank stands Castelvecchio (old castle), so called simply because at the end of the fourteenth century two new castles were built. Like other castles over the years, Castelvecchio was knocked about quite a bit. After the Second World War it was largely restored and used to house the city's collection of medieval paintings and sculpture. In the early 1960s the castle had the good luck to fall under the control of Carlo Scarpa, the architect commissioned to superintend its final restoration. This he completed in 1964, using the materials of the twentieth century with great style—concrete with a planked surface and iron girders left exposed. There is, in this building, no conflict between the old and new; thanks to the care with which he chose the scale of every beam or truss, the boldness of his materials allows no conflict with the work of a different age. Carlo Scarpa approached his task meticulously—nothing left to chance. For each piece of sculpture he designed a base; the grandest being the platform on which the equestrian statue of Cangrande stands. The statue of Cangrande, a lord of Verona and the man who built this castle, dates from the early fourteenth century. He sits astride his horse, his great helmet hanging on his back, both man and beast wearing armour. The platform, a slab of rough-cast concrete, is cantilevered from a wall of the castle, high up so that Cangrande looks out over the river and at his great bridge that spans it. Above his head is a roof to protect this extraordinary work—arguably amongst the world's greatest equestrian sculptures. Carlo Scarpa has done well by Cangrande and he has done well by Castelvecchio, for what was once a Renaissance castle housing a fine collection of art is now turned into a masterpiece.

Paradise in Padua

I have been inspired to return again and again to the world's oldest botanical gardens in Padua, and I still find them full of earthy delights.

Thirty-five years ago I visited Padua for the first time. It was the end of September and the weather was still warm, but there was a mist that hung about the city that day, a feel of winter in the air. I walked down a cobbled street. The leaves had just begun to drop from the willow trees that edge an adjacent canal, and ahead of me stood the gate piers of l'Orto Botanico dell'Università di Padova—the Botanical Gardens of the University of Padua—the oldest botanical gardens in the world, founded in 1545.

I have often returned to Padua, a fine city well worth the trouble of revisiting but why should my memory hold so exactly the details of that first visit? It was the gardens. Never for me have they looked more beautiful: the high gate piers, one pair on each of the four sides of this garden, with large urns atop them, urns grotesquely disproportionate to the columns, urns with wrought-iron gates between the piers. The gardens are encircled by a high wall; inside this wall is a magic world—flowerbeds laid out in symmetrical patterns, and small boxes edged in stone, each one with a different plant growing in it. The whole of this enclosed garden is not more than a hundred paces in diameter. There are beds around the inside edge of the wall and then a circular path inside which are four squares with radiating beds, and fountains at the squares' centres. The whole garden is dissected by a path running from gateway to gateway and at the point where these paths join there is a roundel, again with a fountain. The plants? On that day they had all been cut down; in each of the stone compartments stood only stalks cut off an inch or two above the ground, and a label in iron to describe what had flowered there the season before.

The mist, the stone, the gravel of the paths, the bare stalks and the fountains that did not run. I have often returned to that garden. I have seen it in flower and I have seen it coming into flower. I have seen it become more derelict and I have seen it the subject of a considerable amount of attention. The urns have fallen from the gate piers on which they sat. For some years they just lay there until a tidy-minded keeper put them together and now they stand at the feet of their columns.

The fate of this garden has always been one of ups and downs. Seven years after its founding there were 1500 species of plants. Some of these, first introduced to Europe in these gardens, have now become common: for instance, the potato in 1590; lilac in 1565; rhubarb in 1612; the sunflower in 1563; and what I suppose was a great novelty in 1642 but has since become the gardening equivalent of a cliché—*Parthenocissus quinquefolia* or Virginia creeper.

It was Francesco Bonafede who persuaded the Senate of the Venetian Republic to set up this garden, arguing that you cannot teach in the abstract alone, and that it was important for the students of medicine to see the plants that were the source of cures they could prescribe. The gardens have remained virtually untouched since that day. Their contents, however, have had good times and bad. By 1752 there were 3500 species, a hundred years later 16 000 species, but by 1945 only 3800. And then, after the Second World War, came good times and the number of different species held by the gardens had increased to 6000 by 1983.

The enclosed gardens are surrounded by an arboretum of about two acres. The trees here are not particularly exciting, though several have been planted on important occasions or by special people; one, a chestnut tree planted by the founder, unfortunately looks as though it has not much longer in this world. In an attempt, I suppose, to add to the attraction of this garden, small areas have been set aside for rock plants and cacti. Here, as almost everywhere else, it becomes clear that less is better than more—this garden will benefit only from putting a stop to improvements. Beyond the garden walls rise the towers and domes of the Church of San Antonio—a view that has remained unchanged for centuries.

My most recent visit to the gardens was in August 1991. I was very taken with the small area devoted to aquatic plants: the same geometric beds edged in stone, but with water in them instead of soil.

Two *Nymphaea* took my fancy: *Nymphaea victoria*, the giant waterlily named after Queen Victoria, its leaves several feet across, famous from the engraving of the specimen at Kew where a small child is shown standing on a leaf; and a *Nymphaea* I had not seen before—*Nymphaea euryale*, which is another large-leafed waterlily, its leaves like the skin of the crocodiles that I am certain lurk beneath it in its native waters. Beside these two exotic waterlilies is a tank with lotus plants in it. *Nelumbo speciosa* 'Williol' was then in full flower, which did not surprise me in northern Italy, for it is possible to grow and flower the lotus plant in the open here.

Climbing around the urnless gate piers were two varieties of *Campsis*, both in full flower: one red, one orange. On one of these piers is fixed a notice in stone, erected when the gardens were founded. It says, roughly translated from the Italian, 'Do not knock on this door before ten o'clock in the morning or before Saint Mark's Day. Do not in any way damage the plants or stand on them, or you will be punished by a fine, imprisonment, and exile.' It seems that Italians of the sixteenth century took their gardening rather seriously.

Arts council

In a town between Florence and Pisa, a provincial mayor holds council in the local museum—and who can blame him? There is much to covet in Pistoia.

In the first mild days of February, gardeners begin to twitch. Bulbs begin to burst through the earth, and for those who plan gardens, real or imaginary, Pisoia in Tuscany is the place to visit. On the motorway, for several kilometres between Florence and Pisa, there are garden nurseries. Mature trees and pyramidal *Magnolia grandiflora* by the hundred stand side by side with pyramidal box and holly. Weeping cedars, weeping copper beech and almost every other variety of weeping tree—in short, every form of manicured tree and bush that you could possibly need to construct an Italianate garden. It is a choice that would leave even the most adventurous gardener somewhat confused about what to buy.

The day was fresh and still bright as I left the nurseries and entered the town of Pistoia, where many of the buildings were destroyed during the Second World War and have since been rebuilt. Pistoia has that wonderful provincial atmosphere found in Italian towns which don't own enough masterpieces to draw the tourist coaches. Yet, like every other self-respecting town in Italy, Pistoia has a museum. On the day I visited it a kind woman sat selling guidebooks at the top of a steep staircase in the palazzo that housed the museum. 'It is difficult for me to let you into the museum at the moment,' she explained as I bought a few guidebooks—I love guidebooks, even when they don't really guide you. 'It's the mayor; I must ask him for permission to let you in.'

The mayor—who holds council meetings in the museum—agreed to my visit and I was let into a room hung with religious paintings of the fourteenth, fifteenth and sixteenth centuries. Some were astounding, and among the best was the *Infant Jesus with Saints* by Ghirlandaio. There was no sign of the mayor. 'But you have only seen half the museum,' the woman told me as I left. 'The mayor is upstairs with the rest of the paintings.' In a room filled with modern work from Pistoia and the surrounding district sat the mayor and councillors, deep in conclave. I enjoyed seeing the mayor, who seemed a jolly fellow, but I am afraid I had already seen the best of the painting.

Across the square, however, stands a real gem: the black and white marble baptistry. In 1975 it was restored and eighteenth-century additions removed. Only a font, signed by Lanfranco da Como and dated 1226, stands inside; it is large enough to immerse the bodies of several people at the same time.

Abbey life

Twenty years after my first visit to the ruins of Pomposa Abbey near Ravenna, I return and run the gauntlet of parking attendants and souvenir stalls in search of the past.

Among the marshes and low-lying land of the Po delta nestles the Abbey of Pomposa. When I first went there on a winter's day in 1977, the abbey, which lies off the main road to Ravenna, was a desolate place. There were few buildings around the abbey; even by mid-morning the winter mist still hovered above the creeks and ditches between the Po di Goro and the Po di Volano. I picked up the key to the abbey from the barman of a nearby trattoria and went exploring.

Both the campanile and the basilica had that wonderful crumbly feeling about them; the atmosphere of the place was one of an intense and fragile beauty. It was as if the whole of this immensely elegant church would, piece by piece, become one again with the surrounding marshes. I returned the key and stayed for one of the best pastas I've ever tasted. Each year I have intended to return to Pomposa; this summer, I finally did.

Alas, things had changed. The mood was set by an officious lady in the car park. The trattoria had expanded, and there was a new restaurant that sold fast food. I avoided both, along with the souvenir stalls that had opened nearby, and paid to get into the museum that had opened in the buildings of the abbey.

The greatest treasure of Pomposa is still there, much as I saw it when I first visited. The Romanesque marble font, supported by four archaic telamons, is without doubt a masterpiece. Elsewhere all is neatness; the gardens are clipped and trimmed and the stone carvings from different periods—once strewn about the abbey's ground—are now carefully catalogued, lit and displayed.

The brickwork of the campanile, built in the eleventh century, is now as clean as a new pin. Inside the basilica, the mosaic floor has been manicured and the frescoes retouched. The facade of the basilica has been tidied, and the frieze of stone carvings, which must have come from across the Adriatic, set into its wall and cleaned to perfection.

I have always enjoyed bits and pieces, and Pomposa has some of the best: pots and bits of pots, and iron crosses from the twelfth century—all the stuff of life in this abbey. A small fifteenth-century fountain in the shape of an upside-down Turk's cap is a thing of beauty, and a fragment of a tenth-century frieze with a griffin is exactly the sort of thing I'd love to own.

Pomposa is still beautiful, but now it has the rejuvenated beauty that has been carved by a surgeon's knife, not that which comes from the dignity of old age. Pomposa has been 'saved' by being wrenched out of time and deprived of its mystery. It has become a place to see, rather than a place to find.

Sabbioneta: curtain raiser

I am amazed by the Renaissance town of Sabbioneta and its trompe-l'oeil *theatre*.

On the road between Mantua and Parma there is a stone gateway. This is no ordinary gateway but the Porta Imperiale, and behind it and its wall is a town to remember. The day I came to Sabbioneta the rain fell from the sky; I so nearly passed that most beautiful of places without another thought, ignorant of its existence. Curiosity, however, got the better of me—an open door of any sort is a temptation I cannot pass.

Built on the site of earlier fortification, Sabbioneta was the inspiration of Vespasian Gonzaga, the head of a junior branch of the Gonzagas. He created a fortress greatly in advance of its age, and inside it a tiny but carefully considered and complete city. Why he built it in this particular part of Italy is something of a mystery.

Vespasian Gonzaga was a military man fascinated by artillery; perhaps he just indulged his interest in fortifications and talent for town planning or, like so many who are responsible for so much of the world's great architecture, just enjoyed building. Vespasian died in 1591, and the estate passed to his daughter who lived with her husband elsewhere. Sabbioneta fell asleep. The soldiers left and then the people—there was no reason for them to remain. Sabbioneta's walls crumbled, trees grew and everywhere briars flourished.

In the mid-eighteenth century the Hapsburgs occupied the town, then the French, and then Hapsburg troops again. In the nineteenth century wandering scholars visited, and soon this secret and forgotten town became known as 'the little Athens'. Its buildings, much damaged by the soldiers of successive occupations were by now used as storehouses for grain and farm equipment.

In the 1960s the Italian government started restoration, and slowly a masterpiece has been uncovered. Sabbioneta is the most wonderful example of a provincial city. Where in Florence, Rome or Venice architects would have worked with grand materials, here they used paint, the most skilful of *trompe-l'oeil*. This town is a great city in miniature, with a castle, churches, Winter and Summer Palaces, squares, statuary, parks, houses for nobles and dwellings for those who served them, shops, hostelries and, most wonderful of all, a theatre.

When Shakespeare produced his plays at the Globe Theatre, his actors competed for attention with rowdy crowds on an open stage. The citizens of Sabbioneta sat in their court theatre surrounded by frescoes in the style of Paolo Veronese. The actors played beneath a proscenium arch. Behind the audience is a great colonnade topped with statues in the antique style; between its arches paintings of more statues, each standing in its own portal. Along the walls, noblemen and their ladies look down from balustraded balconies in the style of Veronese's work at the Villa Maser. Supporting these balconies are classical arches through which the landscapes of northern Italy can be seen, and nestling in these landscapes are spires, columns, domes, ruins and the fortifications of hill towns—all the work of a painter.

The grandest church stands in the Piazza Ducale, its facade dramatically styled in zigzag patterns of white and pink Verona marble. The Ducal Palace is across the square. Luckily, damage to it seems to have taken place only as high as a person can reach. There is room after room of the most exotic painted ceilings. Behind the palace is the church of the incarnation of the Blessed Virgin, an octagonal building. As you look up you see a great dome, the trick of a craftsman's brush. Over the altar is the statue of Vespasian by Leone Leoni, a work of great quality, comparing this Gonzaga duke with the Roman emperor whose name he took. Leoni was a pupil of Michelangelo and this portrait owes much to his master.

A short walk away is a splendid building perhaps 300 feet (90 metres) long, a colonnade underneath and a gallery above, with its walls painted with busts of Roman generals and trophies of arms. Nearby is the Summer Palace, an enchanted place, with room after room filled with the vitality of its paintwork. As I stood in a painted room I looked out at a garden everywhere. I knew why I loved this place. The strongest human instinct is to improve—if this place could be improved, restored, put back to just how it had been 400 years ago. For myself I hope it stays much as it is, for the joy here is of what might have been, and to dream of what it all might be again.

Barterhouse of Parma

On my first trip to Parma, I enjoyed the fair, perusing stalls and miles of the new 'antiques' such as cookie jars, sunglasses and jukeboxes.

Prowling through the pages of a magazine, I came across an announcement of the twelfth annual 'Mercante in fiera' to be held in Parma the following weekend. This great gathering of dealers in antiques and objects one day destined to be antiques boasted 600 exhibitors. Its theme this year, for reasons that escape me entirely, was 'Return to the future'. However, accompanying this announcement was a colour illustration of a most splendid jukebox. I had never been to Parma before, and my friends had told me that it was a fine town—the birthplace of Verdi they said.

They were right about Parma. It is indeed a fine town, even in Italy, a country stuffed with fine towns. Parma has good food and good buildings; its baptistry is perhaps the best Romanesque building in the whole of Italy; its cathedral dates from the twelfth century. Hidden in a monolith of a building, constructed in the sixteenth century to house soldiers, their supplies and the men who administered the state, is the most wonderful court theatre. Destroyed during the Second World War, the theatre has been faithfully rebuilt—if the guidebook had not confessed to this I would never have guessed. My friends were wrong in the matter of Verdi's birthplace, for he was born at Roncole, near Busseto, north-west of Parma. It is, however, in Parma that Verdi is revered—his works are performed to perfection in Parma's Opera House. Its audience is perhaps the most knowledgeable anywhere and so also the most critical.

The rain on the day I arrived in Parma came down continuously and as solidly as palings in a fence. I was soaked on my way from the taxi to the entrance of the 'Mercante in fiera', a dash of fifty yards. I then set out to walk around the great gathering of 'antique' dealers. I measured my morning's walk; it was four-and-a-half miles (slightly more than seven kilometres) in total—the stalls cheek by jowl and piled high with goods. I do not know how many paintings, prints and objects were offered for sale there, but the number must have run to several million. I have spent most of my life visiting fairs like this and I have never seen the like.

There were, of course, many stands that sold brown furniture, and even more of pictures of varying quality, but never before have I come across a man who deals exclusively in cookie jars. Some were in the shape of the characters from *The Muppet Show* and *Sesame Street*, some from the last century and even, I suppose, the century before—though those jars probably contained biscuits. My favourite was a monk whose head lifts off to allow you to get at the cookies. This monk had written across his chest in bold letters: 'Thou shalt not steal'. I have come across dealers in gramophones before, but never dealers in scent bottles; I have seen second-hand sunglasses for sale—on occasion I have bought a particularly snazzy pair—but never before have I found a shop where they sell nothing but sunglasses; and so it went on all through my perambulation around the sheds that held this fair. I found four stalls that sold only second-hand telephones, stalls selling medals and stalls selling make-up and, unlike the dealers in tables and chairs of dubious age that purport to come from the seventeenth and eighteenth centuries, these dealers were all doing splendid business.

What fascinated me was that even when they were not selling their scent bottles, make-up or second-hand telephones, these stalls were crowded with people looking at what they offered. The truth of the matter is that the urge to collect spreads far wider than is generally realised. The brown furniture and paintings judged useful by most people furnishing a home are not regarded as items they have any real desire to collect. It was the dealers selling fountain pens and watches who were doing the business; the market these days is in the second hand. Strangely, I came across only one or two stalls offering second-hand clothes—I had expected rather more—but then America is the mecca of second-hand clothes and perhaps that fad has not yet reached Italy. One stall sold only black lace and jet jewellery; it was, I must say quite beautiful.

This fair was the home of the specialist dealer, and specialist collectors seemed to be there in profusion. The dealer in jukeboxes was the one who caught my fancy—including the jukebox whose picture had drawn me to Parma in the first place. I had an idea: I would own this wonderful machine with its flashing lights and stained-glass facade; I would fill it with recordings of Verdi's great arias, and at the insertion of a coin and the press of a button they could blast across my sitting room.

'How much is this machine?' I asked.

'Sixty million lire,' came the reply. I protested at this price, and the dealer looked at me with contempt.

'It has all its original plastic,' he pointed out. Such are the antiques of the future.

The artful loggia

Among the Caesars in the galleries of the Palazzo Altemps in Rome.

In Rome just fifty yards from the Piazza Navona, in the Piazza Sant'Apollinaire, stands the Palazzo Altemps. It is not a building that is easy to find and, finding it, one at first wonders whether it was worth the bother. The only aspect of the facade that is of any interest is the red banner announcing that this is a 'Musea Nazionale Romano', and then, in much smaller letters, that it is the 'Museo Ludovisi-Boncompagni in Palazzo Altemps'.

In past centuries the Ludovisi Collection at the Palazzo Altemps was a pilgrimage site for artists, students and scholars. Housed in 75 acres of gardens, the collection contained 339 sculptures. Then in 1883 Prince Rodolfo Ludovisi sold his estate to property developers, much to the annoyance of those scholars who had enjoyed their visits. (In all these tales of the nineteenth century, there is always an impoverished prince or count who spoils everyone else's fun by disposing of his own property.) The destruction of the important gardens proved to be not all bad, for in the course of the work the developers discovered the Ludovisi Throne. This throne—it is called a throne for want of a better word—dates from the fifth century BC. It is believed to have been part of the furnishings of a sanctuary of Aphrodite on the Ionian coast of Calabria, but whatever its origins it is undoubtedly one of the world's great works of art and worth a hundred Roman gardens.

The Palazzo Altemps now contains sculpture from three great collections: the Altemps, the Mattei and of course the Ludovisi. Small by the standards of today's great archaeological museums, the Palazzo Altemps and its contents can be viewed in an hour. It is not size that really matters, however, but quality; and here at the Altemps is quality of the highest order. I came across one masterpiece after another, all beautifully presented on simple stone plinths. The

Brancaccio Bull is a spectacular example. For many years, this almost life-size Egyptian bull of black diorite was missing its hindquarters—that is, until someone spotted them in the Museo Barroacco, where they had been made into an ashtray, complete with bronze legs.

Nothing, however, prepares you for the experience of walking into the sixteenth-century loggia. It is the most exotic and opulent of places; once stuffed with sculpture, it still has the twelve portraits of the Caesars from the original collection, some retaining their inscribed bases. Fine as these sculptures are, however, it is the loggia itself that takes your breath away. The ceiling is a painted arbour, decorated with flowers and fruits, including new discoveries for the time such as the pineapple. Peacocks and turkeys (the turkey was then considered an exotic bird) stand alongside pheasants, cockerels, storks and even an ostrich. At the end of the loggia is a shallow grotto or fountain from 1594.

The Palazzo Altemps really needs two visits: the first to look at the sculpture, and the second to examine the frescoes and the building. It all seems so casual that you miss so much the first time. Take the cupboard room, for instance; this is a large space used for entertaining in the fifteenth century and called 'the room of the notables' in contemporary documents. On the west wall a fragment of fresco illustrates a buffet loaded with jars, plates, bowls, flagons and tazzas.

In Italy there is always a part of any museum you cannot see. On the Saturday I was in Rome, that part of the Palazzo Altemps was the Teatro Goldoni, one of the oldest private theatres in Rome, rebuilt after it collapsed in 1575. In 1905 it became the venue for magic-lantern shows and then a cinema. My companions at lunch that day had seen it and said that it should not be missed. It will not be; for who needs even the bait of an unseen ancient theatre to draw them back to such a wonderful museum? Not me.

A religious day in Rome

The city of Rome lays before its admirers the grandest of architectural glories, but it also shelters stunning surprises. Here are some of its lesser known delights.

Few would argue that Rome is a grand city. Its buildings outshine the masterpieces of Florence and Venice, and its churches are among the grandest in the world. But away from the Colosseum, Forum and stately churches of St Peter's, St John Lateran and Santa Maria Maggiore there is another side to this city. Wander the streets, leave the traffic behind and you find secret corners where wild flowers grow; and if you are sharp-eyed you can still spot broken fragments of stone and marble from past ages which hint at vanished glory.

In the back streets of Rome the worlds of art and agriculture begin to merge. I suspect this is no accident, for the Romans were ever conscious of the links between the two, agriculture providing not just food but also the beauty of cultivated land. In ancient times Romans used the columns of ruined buildings and turned them into rollers. Pulled by men or horses, they covered over the seeds in the furrows. Thus art returns to agriculture, helping to feed the next generation of artists and architects who will build future monuments to the ingenuity of humankind and the glory of God.

This interest in agriculture is wonderfully displayed in the fourth-century mosaics that decorate the ceiling of Santa Constanza. This church, tucked away behind Sant' Agnese, contains the tomb of Constantine's sister. It is one of four of Rome's most beautiful churches, each one Byzantine, each one dramatically different. A simple, quiet, small church, Santa Constanza has ceilings composed of an intricate design of pheasants, jays, peacocks and thrushes. These birds pick at branches clipped from trees still laden with fruit. Among the birds and vines, the peaches and the pomegranates, are bacchanalian figures treading the grapes in rustic huts. Farmers tend the fields and drive ox carts, and wild deer drink at streams, watched by squirrels. There is a brightness and a peace about these simple colours and images that refreshes the mind.

Not far away is the Basilica di Santa Prassede, which stands in the shadow of Santa Maria Maggiore. Santa Prassede's Byzantine mosaics are more magnificent and more involved with the image of God than those of Santa Constanza and are a good deal later in date. Christianity by this time had begun to move away from the pagan idea of rustic life. The mosaics here are beautiful nonetheless.

Walk a further twenty minutes and you will come to the Basilica di San Clemente, high above the Colosseum on the road to St John Lateran. The Basilica is twelfth century and rich in mosaics on the ceiling, walls, columns and floor. The church is small, the stonework is pure, and the whole effect is a delight. In a cloistered courtyard where the columns support a lean-to shelter you could for all the world be in a country stable yard, yet the mosaics in this church are perhaps some of the grandest in Rome and certainly the equal of any to be found in Ravenna. Underneath San Clemente are the remains of a temple to Mithras which is also interesting but hardly as spectacular as the Byzantine mosaics.

The last church I visited that day was tucked away in a back street which was not filled with flowers but clogged with traffic. Santo Stefano Rotondo is but a few yards from San Clemente but there isn't a hint of a mosaic in the whole place. The only decoration is the remains of some frescoes by an unknown hand, happily slowly disappearing for they depict the grisly ends met by many of the church's saints. The building of Santo Stefano Rotondo has been restored and is quite the most beautiful of the four churches. The dome is supported by a ring of columns set midway across the floor and braced by a beam that spans the church, supported by four giant columns. The effect is wonderful. No paintings to speak of, no mosaics, no gold or coloured glass, just whitewash and architecture. Santo Stefano Rotondo is the best of the lot.

The buying game

Distressed by the transformation of a favourite bar in Rome, I warn against the strange habit of buying up a business you like only to change it utterly.

Rome in the early summer is always extremely hot. This was one of those hot days; the Spanish Steps were crowded with young tourists and the sellers of cheap paintings and grotesque caricatures of girlfriends and family. Among them was a new trade I had not seen on the steps before—men and women who braid coloured beads into the hair of other men and women. I scrambled through the seated ranks of buyers and vendors and those there to watch or just to rest. I clambered past the flower sellers at the foot of the steps, past the tourists who bathe their feet in the fountains, and out into the streets of Rome, into a world of squealing brakes and snorting scooters.

These are not the sort that as a young man I used to ride—decorous, upright Lambrettas or Vespas transported me, and Rome used to be populated with them: young men at the handlebars with their girlfriends perched side-saddle behind, clinging to their male friends with more than the enthusiasm of companionship, for these young men and women risked their lives in the city streets of Rome. Now the men drive a Piagio, a Spacey, a City Express or a Suzuki. The women sit astride and it is the pedestrian who is at risk. One vehicle I came across rejoiced in the name of the Nippomoto Urban Kid—a truly remarkable means of transport. I wandered in the side streets, walking cautiously along the crowded pavements of Rome's main thoroughfares, always wary of those modern scooters and the midge motor cars that creep up on you, and then knock you down. For Rome's traffic is a legend—almost stationary when it is supposed to flow, moving with the speed of summer lightning where no traffic is supposed to be, and all the while the day seemed to become hotter.

I headed towards a bar that I recalled in the Via della Croce. I never knew its name. I did not need to—it was always there, a haven from summer heat, tourist crowds and the confusion of the abusive traffic. The bar in the Via della Croce was no ordinary bar; it seemed caught in a time warp—cool and cavernous—and around its walls racks of the world's greatest wines. The bar was of faded mahogany trimmed with zinc; it still had a brass grille and an aged cashier—just as it should be—and there were small china trays of *cherecetti* (snacks) on the bar. Behind it were cold stone sinks filled with bottles of wine—wine of several dozen different vintages by as many and more different makers—which could be bought by the glass. A barman who possibly owned the bar would discuss the merits of the different wines as you drank—a man of intelligence who knew when to speak, whom to speak to and whom to leave to their thoughts. I walked through the door and the bar was gone, or rather it had changed so much that it was as if it had never existed.

In all undertakings that pull ahead of their fellows by showing a quality and care in how they conduct their affairs, who become yardsticks of whom people say, 'I admire that', or 'I would love to own that', there comes a time when they should close. The bar on the Via della Croce was like that. How much better if I had found in its place a shop selling shoes or cheap clothing—far better death than a humiliating decline. It is a curious feature of life that those who buy a business that they and many others have greatly admired imagine that the one thing that business needs is changing. They then proceed to do just that, ruining what was in its way a masterpiece. These people have neither the originality nor the wit to spot which aspect of a business truly constitutes quality; they buy great names and strive to make them greater—in fact they destroy them utterly.

I once nearly fell into this trap. I owned a bookshop and desired to expand the business, so I sought to buy a fellow bookseller's business—Heywood Hill. I had long admired it; it was run in the way a bookshop should be run. I entered into negotiation and we arrived at a satisfactory price; the shareholder would sell, I would buy. But I did not buy. I hesitated and then I drew back, for I knew that if I owned that business I would change it and to change it would be to ruin it. I stopped—for I liked it as it was.

There is a difference between being a customer and the role of a proprietor. The bookshop that I took pleasure in as a customer would become a millstone around my neck if I had responsibility for its management—happily Heywood Hill fell into the hands of a man who owned no other bookshops and has left it unchanged. I buy my books there and take pleasure from the fact that it exists much as I knew it. Those days were long ago now, and I have learned that among life's myriad pleasures, the pleasure of ownership with all its responsibilities is the least of them.

Ambassador's reception

On my latest visit to Marrakesh, I sample the souk of the day, receive some dirty money and encounter a particularly welcoming ambassador.

The best kept secret in all Morocco is the quality of the food in the Place Jemaa el Fna, the beating heart of Marrakesh. As the sun sets, the stallholders erect their stalls, much as a general might arrange an army. In the front row, tea and cakes. Behind them, egg-sandwich stalls, and then the meat—lamb heads, hearts and livers. The rearguard are sellers of oranges, figs and dates. On the right flank, the row of snail-sellers, who stand on high benches behind their stalls that serve food chin height, or to customers perched on high stools. Most tourists avoid this food as if it were being served by the armed forces of Attila the Hun. The plague, they believe, surely lurks among these less-than-mouthwatering delicacies.

For two weeks I took my evening meal at one or other of these stalls and the food was not only hygienic but also totally delicious. My visit to Morocco was, on this occasion, truly a journey of discovery. Among the best of the discoveries was the Riyal El Cadi, a small guesthouse of a dozen rooms. Built around a series of courtyards, the Riyal is one of the most congenial hotels I have ever stayed in. The food is fresh, simple and totally wonderful. The proprietor, the former German ambassador to Morocco, is a mine of information. Already famous for his collection of Turkish kilim, he now concentrates on Berber textiles. Much of his collection hangs in the guesthouse, and as it is arguably Marrakesh's best collection in this specialised field, other collectors are drawn to his guesthouse. The politics of Moroccan textiles go well with the fresh croissants, pancakes and splendid jams at breakfast. The decoration of the Riyal is impeccable. And for comfort, the ambassador produced a new definition of that word in terms of a hotel. 'What shall I do with my dirty laundry?' I asked. 'Just drop it on the floor; it will be taken care of,' he replied.

Just down the street—which is a euphemism for a short but immensely complex journey—is the Riyal Tamsna. This place, presided over by the elegant Madame Martin, is no ordinary teashop. A selection of Moroccan lifestyle goods are available here. It is a haven for those who are tired of shopping in the souk; here they can buy Moroccan style with quality, a rare commodity indeed. Madame Martin, needless to say, knows her onions when it comes to quality, for she is the local adviser to an internet site, www.capitaltaste.com. This site is immensely useful to travellers as it highlights not only the best but also the hidden treasures of many interesting cities. Shopping in Marrakesh is the *raison d'être* of the whole place and, like much else in Morocco, seems to lack logic. Offer in payment a dirty dollar bill and it will be refused. Replace this note with a pristine dollar and, as change, you will receive a handful of the dirtiest notes you have ever seen in your life.

Walk in the Place Jemaa el Fna and you will be warned of the dangers of the souk by a dozen guides who offer their services. Marrakesh, however, is a city where crime barely exists, for the simple reason that crime does not pay as well as trade. Swindled, you will most certainly be; to be robbed, however, is a most unusual occurrence.

For the true collector this place is a paradise. Textiles, unknown a year ago, are now on the market. As prices have risen, so have tribes begun to give up their treasures. Each day dealers have new textiles, pottery, woodwork and jewellery of great age and beauty, objects whose price is the figure that the dealers can be persuaded to part with for them.

In the souk is the textiles auction market, an auction in which foreigners cannot join. A foolish Swiss couple tried to bid; outrage spread among the crowd. They were still bidding when the lot was knocked down. Since the time of the ancient Sumerians, the system for conducting auctions has been firmly established, a system copied by the cattle auctioneers of the Chicago stockyards, and a system that is not about to be changed by a pair of opportunistic collectors. In its way, the resistance to change in Morocco is at least half its charm.

What reigns in Spain

I find that in Barcelona cries of 'viva' are raised for Picasso and Gaudi—and an albino gorilla called 'Snowflake'.

Barcelona is a good-looking city. Modelled on Paris, it is a city where time has stood still. At the beginning of this century it was largely rebuilt in the style fashionable at the time, each wealthy family competing to build grander and flashier monuments to their success. The perfect patrons of architecture. General Franco, finding that Catalonia was the last bastion of Communist resistance in Spain, never forgave the region. As a result, there was no government investment in the area. Barcelona had few new buildings and consequently few old buildings were pulled down. The city, therefore, has the most remarkable collection of late-Victorian architecture.

Travellers leaving Barcelona airport by taxi on the way to the city centre will pass wide avenues lined with trees, and circumvent great roundabouts with sculptures or fountains at their hearts. Should they ask their taxi driver 'What is worth seeing in Barcelona?' he will not reply, 'You must look at Gaudi's buildings,' or 'Do not miss Las Torres de Avila . . .' The latter, incidentally, is no medieval castle, but a nightclub designed by two architects called Arrivas and Mariscal, set in the walls of a plaster castle which is itself part of the completely horrible imitation town built for the 1920 World Fair, and without charm of any sort. This nightclub, however, is remarkable; it is an example of contemporary design that demonstrates all the fantasy of Gaudi and Miró, a building fully in the tradition of this adventurous town. A town that, at the same time as it was constructing this horrible miniature Disneyland, was building Mies Van der Rohe's Barcelona Pavilion. Pulled down after the end of the World Fair, it was rebuilt just a few years ago from plans and a few photographs, which, of course, were taken in black and white. No one knows how accurately the original colours of the three marbles used have been reproduced, or if the red velvet curtain was quite that red. Nevertheless the result is remarkably beautiful. A pavilion or a sculpture that you can walk and sit in? Hard to tell. I doubt if it matters; as a building it enhances the life of all who see it.

How remarkable that Barcelona should have been rebuilding the work of one of the world's greatest architects at about the same time that public opinion was being mobilised—with great success—to stop the building of what was perhaps his masterpiece in the city of London. But Barcelona shows no fear of the new. Barcelona—careful of its past—is hell-bent on reaching the future.

Several great artists have museums exclusively to themselves. The Fundacio Miró, by the same architect as the Foundation Maeght in the south of France, is an exciting building with good pictures. The Palacio Berenguer d'Aguilar, the Picasso museum, is a boring building with sensational paintings. Between 1954 and 1960 Picasso engaged himself on a series of paintings, reworking subjects by Great Masters. Here there are several dozen works from the 'Las Meninas' series (the original by Velázquez). They are stunning.

But Barcelona is foremost a city of architecture, and the best known of her architects is Antonio Gaudi. Descended from generations of potters, Gaudi used ceramics in his work with an enthusiasm and a facility that could only come from such a background. His buildings are fantastic in concept and remarkable in detail: broken tiles reassembled; swirls of coloured mosaics; carefully carved wooden doors with exactly-cast bronze fittings. La Pedrera—a block of flats inspired by the strange rocks about an hour's drive from Barcelona—is a building that the Flintstones would feel at home in. And in one block in the Passeig de Gracia, there are three different houses: the Batello House by Gaudi (currently for sale), and the other two—Casa Lleo and Casa Amatller—by different architects, and each as remarkable as the other.

Gaudi's name is synonymous with Barcelona. Even at the age of 74 he was still working. When he was knocked down by a tramcar he was taken to be a pauper because of his clothes and, unrecognised, he was carried to the Hospital Sant Pau, a hospital built by his rival Dominech y Montaner. After three days he died, his greatest work—the Church of the Sagrada Familia—still unfinished. Exotic and frightening, the parts of this building by Gaudi's own hand are filled with majesty. Its great towers and the freshness of the Rosary doorway demonstrate a range of talent seldom seen in architecture of any other period. The parts built from his plans after he died are ponderous and uncertain. The building, still less than one-quarter built, continues. Perhaps with time those responsible will be able to catch the spirit of Antonio Gaudi.

But then time is the enemy of many great churches. The cathedral in Barcelona, in its third incarnation, was started in 1298; work was interrupted in 1422, and it was finally finished in 1887 when the main facade was built according to the plans that the French architect Mestre Carli had drawn up when he was commissioned by the city council in 1408.

'What is there to see?' our traveller asks the driver of his taxi.

Without hesitation he replies, 'You must see Snowflake.'

'Snowflake?' the traveller queries.

'Snowflake,' the driver repeats, 'at the zoo. He is the only albino gorilla in the world.'

Bravo

Chancing upon the work of artists and furniture makers galore in Barcelona, I unlock the artful secrets of the city.

Barcelona has been the workplace of a number of great artists—Picasso, Miró and Dali. Sadly, they are all dead. The architecture of the city ranges from Gaudi to Mies van der Rohe, whose pavilion built for the Germans at the 1992 Olympics was destroyed, and has now been rebuilt. The streets of Barcelona are filled with exciting buildings, the parks and squares with sculpture. The tradition of Barcelona as a city where patrons live and work is alive and flourishing.

Dining with an industrialist in his home, I sat opposite the most perfect small Miró I have ever seen—far, far better than anything in Barcelona's Miró Foundation. In the man's garden I came across a sculpture that seemed familiar. I couldn't place the sculptor's name, so after admiring the work I enquired who had made this 'thing'. I call it a 'thing' for although it had a title and was of immense beauty, it could not be described in words, at least not by any of which I am aware. My host replied with some surprise—did I not know the work of Xavier Corbero? Of course I did. I had seen pieces in London outside great office buildings, and I had even seen them in New York in smart apartments. I just didn't realise that they were by Xavier Corbero (who, I was informed, had the honour of being Spain's most important sculptor).

I visited Xavier Corbero and dined with him in his studio, a place of great antiquity and even greater beauty—the contrast between his highly-polished coloured stones and the brick and beam of centuries ago was a work of art in itself.

I discovered, as he spoke, that Corbero spent his youth in London. He trained at the Central College of Art and worked with Gerald Benny, the silversmith. Why, I asked, did he work with a silversmith? To learn how to hammer, he replied. Louis Osman, the architect and goldsmith, was also one of his teachers. Commissioned to make the investiture crown for Prince Charles when he was crowned Prince of Wales, Osman produced an amazing confection that, just before the ceremony, fell apart and had to be stuck together with Araldite. An omen, perhaps, of things to come! No wonder Corbero makes works of such precision after training with such wonderful—the disaster above apart—craftsmen. I admire his work, I loved his studio and the man himself is a delight.

Returning to the Arts Hotel where I was staying, I was confronted by two vast Corbero sculptures at the front door. The Arts Hotel has one of the world's best collections of contemporary Spanish art, including sixteen works by Corbero. No wonder I thought I had seen his work before! My apartment was spacious, and its furnishings unusual for a modern hotel as they were wonderfully designed. I enquired who they were by and was told Jaime Tresserra.

I visited his studio and tried his chairs, sat at his desks, reclined on his sofas, and opened and shut the drawers in his chests. This was only half of it, for almost all the pieces have their own secrets—fake bottoms, cupboards in the backs, and drawers that you would never have known were there. A lady watched as I explored and then started an expedition of exploration herself, finding hidden compartments where I never even dreamed they could exist.

So thorough was her search that it reminded me of the antique dealer who offered a well-known lady from New York a set of dining-room chairs—Sheraton chairs with their original upholstery. This lady turned them upside down, poked at them, pulled at them, examined each leg and then after examining each back set out on the whole exercise again—pulling and poking, pulling and pulling again. As this went on the London dealer became more and more exasperated. Finally his irritation overcame him. As the lady declared the chairs imperfect he confronted her (she was, I may say, a miracle of the plastic surgeon's art). 'Could you,' he said, 'have undergone such an examination as you have given these chairs and come away declared perfect?' The lady left; the chairs remained.

In Tresserra's studio, the search carried on, though the lady had no intention of making a purchase. She was just fascinated by the intricacy of the construction of the furniture—and so was I.

As I walked in the streets of Barcelona I though about Tresserra and his furniture with its secret places and I realised that his work perfectly mirrors the secret places of his city.

I looked over Jordan

. . . and what did I see? A miracle and added the Kingdom of Jordan to my collection of places.

Schoolboys of my generation were brought up on images of Arabia, of Lawrence, and of Glubb Pasha and desert soldiers with crossed bandoliers and flowing robes (for those of a higher turn of mind, the images came from the Bible). The land, crossed by Greeks and Romans, French and English, has left its imprint indelibly on our culture. Now Jordan has left its imprint on me as the most recent addition to my collection of places.

It is the home of Petra, 'rose-red city, half as old as Time', that remained undiscovered until the early nineteenth century when a Swiss explorer heard rumours of a hidden city and was allowed by the desert tribes through the narrow crevice that is the entrance to Petra. They let him stay only one day, but is was long enough for him to record the great tombs, the caves where people dwelt, the remains of the Roman forum, and the ruts cut by chariot wheels in the stone pavement (incidentally, the chariots drove on the left-hand side of the road).

This strange town was not built but carved from the rock by the Nabataean people in the first hundred years after the death of Christ. Rich through trade, they imported Greek and Roman architects to build their great monuments. Now the trade is in tourists, and on my first night I walked down the narrow defile that is still the entrance with thunder echoing round me, and saw the great building that they call the Treasury lit for moments by flashes of lightning.

How strange this relic of the long-gone Nabataeans seemed, for it is a monument to a people whose very name means to look outward, to accept innovation and change. In Petra traders exchanged the spices of the Far East for the furs of the north. Now they sell coloured sand, cleverly arranged in patterns and bottled. In spring Petra is carpeted by wild red tulips and later in the year with great clumps of tall white alliums.

Jordan, where being stuck in traffic on the busy, long, straight road to Aqaba means looking at scenery that has not changed for 2000 years. The ridges of the black Bedouin tents are like ripples in the ocean, and the shepherds still herd their flocks of camels, goats and sheep. And nowhere is the contrast between ancient and modern better expressed than in the town that surprised me most, for Jerash is regarded as the most complete Roman city outside Italy. Yet only one-third of it has been excavated; the rest is buried beneath a Palestinian refugee camp. Walking down a mile-long colonnade on a Friday I could hear the muezzin calling people to prayer across the valley. Each column of the colonnade was given to the city by a citizen whose name was inscribed upon it.

There is much to be learned in Jerash. In the Temple of Dionysus, for example, after it had become a Christian church, worshippers would bathe in great pools and once a year the priest would amaze the populace by re-creating the miracle of turning water into wine. Modern archaeologists have discovered a hidden pipe leading to the vats of wine, and the tap the priest turned to work his transformation. At the Temple of Artemis, where the tall columns are so finely balanced that they sway in the wind, larders have been found hidden deep in the earth where sacrificed animals were stored by gourmand priests for their own private consumption. And in the theatre, the acoustics are so perfect that a whisper can be heard clearly in the back row, and the stage could be flooded to become a swimming pool where perhaps a Roman Esther Williams swam at the direction of an early Busby Berkeley. One Roman was not impressed, however. When the Emperor Hadrian visited Jerash he looked around and suggested to the mayor that he ought to rebuild the town gates. Too small, said the emperor.

Jerash became part of Byzantium and its temples became churches, but its remains still exert an influence. The architecture is bold and unembarrassed by scale. It is architecture built for a certain future, making no cringing curtsies to the past.

Picking up the pieces

It was no puzzle why tourism and Greek culture just don't fit together.

The greatest jigsaw puzzle in the world lies at Akrotiri on the island of Santorini in the Cyclades. It consists of thousands of pieces of broken pottery. The man charged with putting together this vast puzzle is Professor Doumas—in one ancient cupboard alone his archaeologists found over four hundred pots.

The first human settlement at Akrotiri was in 3200 BC but the period that chiefly concerns Professor Doumas is the fifteenth century before Christ, when a volcano erupted and encased the town in lava. Unlike Pompeii, the town had been warned of its end by a series of earthquakes. The population fled, taking their treasure with them and leaving only pottery (most of it, from the point of view of fine art, quite boring) and the frescoes on their walls (in contrast, works of amazing quality). From these fragments the team has traced the history of these distant people: what they ate, how they lived, and the nature of their trade. Each piece of the puzzle will slowly be put together over the next hundred years. I saw a sheet of dusty plastic pulled back to reveal a fresco of incredible beauty, 3000 years old, reassembled from the scrapings of paint.

The Cycladic Islands, for the most part bare of all except the rudiments of agriculture, now have a booming tourist industry. One reason people come here could be a desire to observe the activities of the likes of Professor Doumas. It is true that they visit the archaeological sites in large numbers, but these islands hold something far more precious for the tourist—the chance to travel and yet feel securely at home. You can find a familiar accent in every square for the British tourist and a national tongue for the Germans, French and Italians; restaurants that call themselves pubs and sell meals for the unadventurous palate; and shops that make no demand on either the tourist's taste or wallet, selling goods that always look to be worth more than they cost. There are always the same shops on every island, the same goods for sale: goods that it is hard to imagine anyone wanting to buy or possibly needing. Cheap luxury this—the very stuff of tourism. And, most important of all for the tourist, there are more tourists—to jostle against and to drink with—offering the chance to make friendships that last a holiday. The stark beauty of the islands—with their white buildings picked out in blue, small churches and windmills—is just a stage set for this activity.

There seems to be a distance between the tourists and their surroundings, each hardly aware of the other. Only one island escaped tourism and that is the pilgrim site of Tinos, one of the most holy in the Orthodox Church. But tourists and pilgrims tend not to mix. Tourists put up the prices and pilgrims spoil the fun.

Across these much-fought-after ancient islands lies the skeleton of the Venetian conquest. For over four hundred years, Venice ruled here; leaving her lions over gateways, portraits of her doges and, in the square at Iraklion, a fountain of incomparable beauty. A Venetian may feel like the Japanese official who visited England at the beginning of the century and was taken to a stately home and shown their Japanese Garden. What did he think of it? 'We have nothing like this in Japan,' he replied. And so it is with the fountain in this square. A brass band plays tunes from *The Music Man* in the early evening and tourists and locals sit drinking coffee. The cafés advertise hamburgers, spaghetti and sauerkraut. Everywhere you find traces of Venice, though none of them as beautiful as the traces of ancient Greece in Venice.

In Delos, as in all the ruins elsewhere of these islands, it is not so much the beauty of the individual works of art that strikes you, because most have been destroyed or taken to museums; nor is it what was once there, for reconstructions, models and architectural perspectives of what once existed are rather dull. It is the presence of these places that has the impact: an invisible form of beauty hidden distant in the memory of the human race. It is its stirring that excites us. Ravaged by nature, torn apart by unappealing tourism, where myth begins and reality ends: such is the magic of these islands.

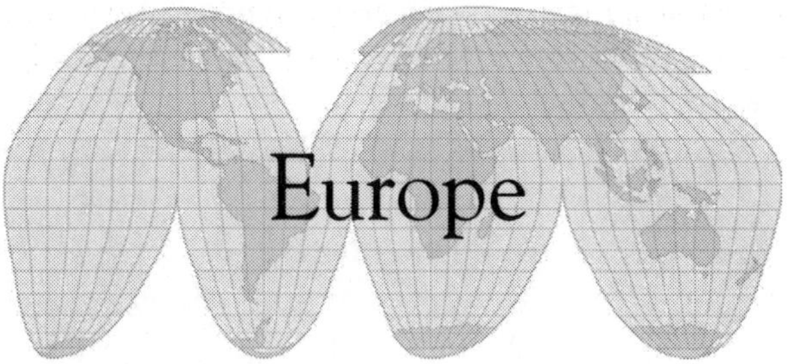

Europe

Hamburger relish

Retracing the daring steps of youth, in 1993 I discover a Hamburg that retains the art of sin, but beneath the gaiety and glitter walks with its own past.

A grave error would be made were I to suggest that Hamburg is a modern city; a new city, yes, for most of it was demolished by Allied bombing, but modern no—not in its layout or in its style, for Hamburg has been rebuilt much in the way it was before the Second World War. Never a truly beautiful city as Rome, London and Paris are, Hamburg is a provincial city and that is how it looks and how it is—built around two lakes, one large (the Aussenalster) and one small (the Binnenalster). It has some sort of beauty—the beauty that you might find in Geneva or Stockholm, but bear in mind that Stockholm has some distinguished buildings, and as far as I could see Hamburg has none.

I was young when I first visited Hamburg, and with the enthusiasm of youth I headed—as soon as I could respectably finish my work—to the St Pauli district. The joys (I found them so then) and the delights were in the Reeperbahn—a street near the port named after the ropemakers who once worked there. Perhaps it should have taken its name from the sailors and ladies who entertained them there, for they have abounded in that district for the last 150 years, while you cannot find a ropemaker to save your life.

On a recent visit I found that street and the alleys that surround it are just as seedy as they always were. The difference for me is that this time I realised how awfully shoddy and second-rate this district of cheap delight is. There is one difference in St Pauli from the days of my youth—a museum has opened at 69 Bernhard-Nocht-Strasse, just around the corner from that other long-running exhibition in the Herbertstrasse: ladies of a certain lack of virtue sitting in shop windows without having bothered to dress completely. The new museum, predictably I suppose, is the Hamburg Erotic Art Museum. It is not at all a shoddy affair. Housed in a converted warehouse, it contains much that can truly be called art—several very fine paintings by Allen Jones come to mind and a set of Japanese erotic prints is also well worth looking at—but for the rest it is the sort of art where so much imagination has been used by the artists that there is no need for those who would view their work to use any at all.

The day was cold, the people seemed glum, and the streets were decorated for Christmas—twinkling lights everywhere. The shopping district of Hamburg, these days a mass of interconnecting arcades, was busy, and the shops were filled with goods, but the population seemed to be looking not buying. The prices were high due in some part to the value of the deutschmark but also to the general condition of the country. In any event, the citizens of Hamburg did not seem intent on beating the Christmas rush. Many shops were selling clothes—boutiques stocking the famous brands. I was intrigued by one that sold only model ships and planes—most of them a couple of inches long; they must surely have in stock a model of every craft in the world. Then there were those selling craft-like goods—stock that has that home-made look about it manufactured in the factories of Mexico and the Philippines. These shops have about them a curious smell—a smell that is supposed to indicate that everything on the premises is made from environmentally conscious materials. It is a smell that will bring good luck and good health to your home and hide the fumes of cooking, a smell composed of candle wax, fir cones and stale potpourri—the most repellent smell in the world. And what is more you find these awful shops all over the world selling the same goods. I cannot resist going into them but the smell gives me hay fever.

On the streets, Hamburg has its share of beggars—Eastern European women sitting on the best sidewalks, their heads shrouded, bowed as if in shame or perhaps despair. Often they hold their babies, sitting hunched up as if trying to avoid notice yet desperate to attract the gift of a few coins. I dined at Peter Lemboke's restaurant where

Germans dine. It was packed—Mrs Lemboke made a table for me in her hall. I ate soured herrings and roast goose, and I noticed parties of German men dining together. But there was no joy in there, no exuberance nurtured by food and drink and the warmth of Peter Lemboke's restaurant.

I had walked at lunchtime among the Christmas stalls set up around St Petri's Church—stalls selling toys and Christmas goods and stalls selling drink and food. As I walked among the crowds gathered in this market I found them subdued—quiet and I suppose a little mystified. For these were the children who had set out after the Second World War on a new path. The past, too horrible to remember, was put from their minds by the work of building a future; their nation became wealthy and in time their nation was reunified. This was what they had dreamed of, but where was paradise? In a few short months all had changed—gone was the land of milk and honey. Their economy in which they had taken such pride no longer prospered. The marriage with East Germany that they longed for seemed in reality far less attractive than it once appeared and now a shadow of the forgotten past, a ghost they believed well laid, for a spectre had appeared at the feast: racism and violence. The Nazis are not just history; and the shadow of their violence—the burning of hostels, the harassing of foreigners and even murder—hangs over the normally exuberant city of Hamburg.

There's no place like Prague

Visiting the second city of the Hapsburgs, I discover a baroque fairytale place overflowing with caviar and souvenir stalls.

Prague is by repute a fairytale city, one of the most beautiful cities in the world—if not the most beautiful, or so it is said. The city has been held in two time warps. The first was in the time of the Austro-Hungarian Empire, when it was subservient to Vienna, though they were similar cities in a way: Vienna land-locked but astride the Danube, Prague situated on the River Vltava. That is where the similarity ended. Vienna was the capital of a great metropolis that set fashions in art and music for the world to imitate, and was home to emperors and empresses, their armies, their courts and all who surrounded them. Prague was forbidden by decree to demolish its city walls. Unable to grow, it found little opportunity to rebuild.

During the second of these time warps, Communism, the city barely developed. The old town, the palaces and the churches survived. Some attempts were made to restore them—attempts that extended as far as keeping the weather out, but money was mercifully short and thank goodness it still is. 'One of the most beautiful cities in the world'—it's hard to substantiate this claim. Prague is a fairytale city in the sense that Disneyland is a fairytale. Like Disneyland Prague has its crowds, and very impressive these crowds are—in fact they make the hordes that visit Venice seem a mere smattering of tourists. And just like Disneyland, the city of Prague is a vast retail premises with shops that sell the goods tourist like to buy—the craft-like products that you find from John o'Groats to San Francisco. As for clothes and other goods, there is little there to buy.

In Prague in 1993 it is in the streets that the selling is done—stall after stall in street after street—and these stalls you will find (that is, if you can fight your way through the tourists to get close enough to look at them) sell only four different items. First, there are Russian dolls, the swollen wooden dolls—sometimes as many as fourteen—that go inside each other: dolls painted as peasants, dolls painted as politicians. Then, of course, there are Red Army wristwatches, the watches of different ranks for different prices, and hats to go with them: fur hats with red enamel stars at their fronts or peaked caps with gold stars, their centres picked out in red enamel or, a great rarity, a fighter pilot's helmet. I was also offered his flying suit with all the attendant piping and buckles. And then there are the inevitable tins of caviar—I do not want to sound blasé about a produce as delicious as caviar, but the endless stalls with endless jars do leave you with the feeling that this product is not quite as exclusive as the head waiters in the world's better restaurants would have you believe. Caviar is very cheap these days in Prague. I ate a lot of it—some delicious, and some so salted it was almost inedible. To buy caviar from these stalls is to play Russian roulette—with salmonella poisoning taking the place of the single bullet in the revolver. Caviar has to be carefully kept or it becomes lethal.

To walk at night across the Charles Bridge that spans the Vltava river between the new and the old town is truly wonderful—despite the crowds who come to see the floodlit castle, the towers of the churches and the spires of the new town. It is all a bit like a stage set, the buildings mostly baroque, very like the gingerbread houses that you find in the windows of that famous Viennese coffee house, Demel. There seems to be something false about the whole place—a giant theatre built for the puppets that hang in many of Prague's shop windows. These puppets really are strange; they come in all sizes from an inch or two to several feet high. There are witches and devils, skeletons and evil spirits, but none with the beautiful smiles of the cherubs that gamble among the rococo swags and swirls of the city's churches. No, the faces of these small stringed figures come from a culture far older than that of Prague, a barbaric northern culture, a trace of which can be found in the National Museum, housed in the Lobkoic Palace, part of Prague Castle.

There, among a thousand and a half minor treasures of the Czech nation's past, is a remarkable object, an object that is truly a masterpiece—the head of a Celtic man from Msecke Zehrovice. Carved from limestone in the second century AD, this head has a broad nose, bulging eyes and a curling moustache; around its neck is a great torque, the symbol of a chieftain. It is one of the most important Celtic sculptures in the world. In the face of this Celtic man and the puppets is a great strength and beauty not found in Prague's baroque conceits.

Georgia on my mind

Skirting the Black Sea on a road trip to the Georgian capital of Tbilisi, I find that brave new post-Soviet commercialism hasn't managed to wipe out traditional sights and customs, or good solid country cooking.

On the shores of the Black Sea in north-east Turkey, the port of Trabzon rises into the hills, a tapestry of narrow streets and markets. It was to this city that Jason and the Argonauts came in search of the Golden Fleece.

For me, however, it was the starting point of my journey. I had intended to set out at first light, but found myself at 11.30 am taking tea with the spiritual leader of several million Sufi Muslims—in an office off the showrooms of a company selling copying machines.

Once on my way, I headed for Batumi in Georgia, a trip of about four hours along the shore of the Black Sea. I drove past hills covered in hazel groves, their nuts picked and laid out to dry like dark-brown carpets at the side of the road. Along this coast there is a wonderful air of dereliction, so potent that even the new buildings look second-hand. My driver pointed to three brick-and-glass tower blocks which looked as if they had been removed from a modern city and dumped on a promontory in the Black Sea. 'Brothels,' he explained. Once only the rich or politically favoured could afford to use these facilities. Now, he told me, with the region's new post-Soviet prosperity, business was brisk. The coaches parked in the forecourts seemed to confirm his words. Leaving behind these uneasy monuments, I felt as if I had lurched back in time when, stopping for coffee at a roadside stall, I had watched a man with a dancing bear and nearby a falconer who, without protective gauntlet, had displayed an unhooded bird.

Customs officials at the Georgian frontier now seem actually to welcome visitors to their beautiful country. The coast is hilly and almost tropical, vines grow around doorways, twisting through balconies, hanging down like streamers, their fruit full and ripe, and everywhere cattle wander along the roads, tolerated by drivers who seem to have little notion of driving on any particular side.

Batumi is a dignified town with wide streets, its grand buildings now tired and in need of repair. We arrived after four in the afternoon, just in time for lunch. In a smallish house-cum-restaurant I discovered the magnificent spectacle of a table laid for twenty with not an inch of tablecloth to be seen between dishes of smoked, boiled and fried fish, vegetables and meats—and this was only the first course. Georgian wine flowed, musicians appeared, toasts were drunk and still more food. At seven o'clock, after a tour of the town, I went back to my hotel—another token of new wealth—to change for dinner.

The next day, and three hours further north, my driver finally turned inland for Tbilisi. We drove across great plains dotted with the skeletons of abandoned industrial plants, through mountains and past deep ravines, stopping only by the roadside to buy fruit, nuts and kebabs. Then on through vineyards and small market towns, along tree-lined roads. Like an echo of the past, I caught a glimpse of a small, ancient church, a link with the beginnings of Christianity, silhouetted against the horizon.

Reduced circumstances

Doll's houses in seventeenth-century Holland were not mere childhood diversions. Their meticulously accurate interiors provide a matchless source of contemporary tastes and customs.

The canals in Amsterdam's historic centre are lined with beautiful houses, yet two of the most fascinating are to be found indoors, deep inside the Rijksmuseum. Turn right at Rembrandt's *The Night Watch* and you pass through a small doorway into a world of miniature perfection.

Here are two doll's houses, or, to be more accurate, doll's house interiors built inside large cabinets. The bigger is housed in a cabinet of oak veneered with tortoiseshell and inlaid with pewter. It was made for Petronella Oortman, a rich widow who married a silk merchant, Johannes Brandt, in 1686. Her doll's house was commissioned on their marriage and took fifteen years to complete. It cost between 20 000 and 30 000 guilders, which today would buy you a sizeable country house.

The skill lavished on these grown-up toys is amazing. Bed linen bears the monogram of the owners; their silver, glass and pottery match in style and quality that made by the great craftsmen of the day. The furniture has been faithfully reproduced from that in the homes of the owners. In the laundry there are wicker baskets, brooms and even a pincushion embroidered with its owner's initials. The larders have barrels marked 'wine' and 'beer', glass bottles and clay pots, and plates of food.

A painting of the Oortman doll's house by Jacob Appel, executed shortly after it was finished, shows that the rooms have altered little over the years. As a result, the doll's houses form an important source book of seventeenth-century Dutch household artefacts and social customs. In the cellar of the doll's house made for Petronella Dunols is a silver syringe used for cleaning windows. The full-scale version of this instrument would have pumped water from a bucket onto the tall windows fashionable at the time. Unlike Petronella Oortman, Petronella Dunols did not have her domestic implements made in brass or iron. She chose to buy them instead from the ready-made stock of the city's silversmiths, principally Wessel Jansen and Michiel Maenbeeck. Hence, the proportions of her doll's house implements are sometimes distorted, in contrast to Petronella Oortmans's near-perfect fixtures and fittings.

These two doll's houses give the feel of seventeenth-century life in a way that no full-scale museum display could. Watching the skaters on the frozen canals as I left the Rijksmuseum, I thought for a moment that nothing had changed in centuries. But, of course, it has, which is why we are so lucky that these doll's houses have survived as painstakingly crafted records of life in the past.

Home is where the art is

For the Austrian royal family, Schönbrunn Palace—Vienna's vast rococo showcase where the young Mozart performed—was above all a family home.

There are few, if any, palaces in the world as beautiful as Schönbrunn on the outskirts of Vienna. When built, the palace and its grounds were more extensive than the city itself and they are still larger than the state of Monaco. With 1441 rooms, of which 139 were kitchens, it housed and fed a court of about a thousand officials and functionaries.

On the face of it the palace seems gigantic, but that is not the feeling you get as you walk around. Instead it is not at all hard to understand how Marie Antoinette missed Schönbrunn when she moved to Versailles. Try as she might, Versailles defied her attempts (the building of the Petit Trianon and the Hameau) to create a feeling of homeliness like that of Schönbrunn, which has an intimacy that even 270 bombs, considerable rebuilding and all the bureaucracy of the Austrian Civil Service have failed to destroy.

As you walk in the Le Nôtre-style garden or stand in the bedroom of nineteenth-century Elizabeth of Austria you feel that this was a family home. Even though Elizabeth owned 250 pairs of gloves and thousands of dresses, kept in rooms hidden in the core of the palace and even though the Hapsburgs were a pretty grand family—and indeed still are—they were a family nevertheless.

The rooms are furnished austerely, but the bed that Emperor Franz Joseph slept in is still there, as is the screen that kept the draught from his shoulders as he sat at his desk—Franz Joseph was so obsessed by fresh air that he kept his study windows wide open. Portraits of Hapsburgs hang everywhere. The bombs did not do as much damage as might be imagined, for the Austrians were expecting them long before Allied bombers flew over Vienna, and the Germans had packed up not only the pictures and furniture, but also wall paintings, panelling and even parquet flooring. The crates containing Schönbrunn's fabric were dispatched to long-defunct mines until after the Second World War when, as if from a deep sleep, the furnishings were returned to the reconstructed shell of the palace, where they are today as if they had never been removed.

The Chinese room has painted panels of white figures on a blue background—their limbs picked out in fluorescent paint. In the dim light of candles of the figures glow, and as the flames flicker they seem to move. The room of seventeenth-century Indian miniatures is perhaps the finest rococo room in the world. With its panelling infilled by Indian miniatures it is a masterpiece and yet a tragedy; for the miniatures, cut to fit the room's ornate shapes, are among India's most important examples of miniaturist art, bought from the maharajah who collected them when he fell on hard times.

Off the ballroom are two black lacquer saloons; the one used by the Empress Maria Theresa has a secret stairway to her chancellor's apartment. She could entertain an important visitor in her salon and the court would never know that the chancellor had also been present. A table hidden in the parquet floor would rise at the touch of a button for maps to be laid out or for treaties to be signed. Then there is the room which gives no hint of its purpose except for plaster-cast musical instruments in each corner of the ceiling—horns, violas and trumpets. This must surely be the most famous of music rooms. Schubert and Schumann played here, and so did Brahms, Liszt, Beethoven and Strauss. What musical history was made in this room where the six-year-old Mozart, enthused by the applause at his playing, ran and jumped onto the Empress Maria Theresa's knee. The court watched in horror to see how she would react to this uninhibited display.

Now the musicians are gone and the death mask of Napoleon's only son, the Duke of Reichstadt, lies in a glass case. He lived and died here, and beside his childish face is a bird, now stuffed, that he is said to have played with in Schönbrunn's gardens. This palace was truly once a home, even if now it is a palace of ghosts.

Parisian tonic

Paris in springtime is for lovers, but for lovers of art, the winter months offer the most beauty.

Most people love Paris in the spring. Perhaps I am perverse, but I enjoy it most during the winter months. I love the way the greyness of the weather matches the stone of Paris's grand buildings, the pollarded avenues of plane trees and, most of all, the early evening when all the cafés and shops are lit up.

When in Paris, after having breakfast at the Deux Magots, and having read the English papers, I set off to find an exhibition. The last time I was there, I saw 'Picasso et le Portrait'. It put me in mind of the great Picasso exhibition of the early 1970s when 800 sculptures filled the Petit Palais and twice that number of paintings the Grand Palais. To my mind the exhibition completely refuted the opinions of those like Munnings, who in the 1950s was the president of the Royal Academy and still believed Picasso to be a fraud.

The exhibition of Picasso's portraits was stunning. There is, I feel, no better indication of the range of his technique. The portrait of Olga Kokhlova, *Olga avec Fauteuil*, of 1917, and *Portrait de le Femme de l'Artiste* of 1923, show his genius while being totally traditional in both composition and execution.

In the years before the turn of the century Picasso was working on a brilliant series of portraits of his mother. I once owned a charcoal drawing from this series, purchased from the long-defunct O'Hara Gallery for the princely sum of £1500, which Jacques O'Hara, being a kindly man, let me pay over a period of two years. That drawing, sold long ago, was the only work by Picasso that I have ever owned. Now, if I were given the choice of any Picasso's portraits, I would pass by his early work, ignore his blue and rose periods, leave hanging on their nails the immensely valuable cubist paintings and hurry home with *Jacqueline aux Fleurs* of 1954 tucked tightly under my arm.

Leaving the Grand Palais, I was put in mind of the days when Picasso was a common sight on the beach at Cannes, when he and his then wife Jacqueline Roque lunched at Felix's restaurant and Felix, a man the spitting image of a badger, fussed around the great painter. Seeing Picasso the customers would stiffen with excitement as he entered the restaurant. 'That is Picasso sitting over there,' those in the know would inform their friends. 'He is a fraud you know; he paints for money.'

Later, as I lunched at Le Voltaire on quai Voltaire, I reflected that, regardless of the season, a day in Paris is always a day to remember. It is a city that lifts the spirit and is good for the soul.

Money, money, money

Money makes the world go round but it can also be beautifully made, historically fascinating and strangely romantic.

Money has always interested me, ever since I was a small child and was given the coins my father had loose in his pockets when he returned from travelling abroad. But it was paper money that really excited me. Bank notes really meant something in the 1950s. You felt that if you turned up at the Bank of England and flourished a large white fiver it would certainly be exchanged for the amount of gold that the governor had promised when he signed it.

Shops that sell antique money seem to me places of mystery. For years I have been drawn to them although, apart from a few notes, there is rarely anything to be seen. I know, however, that carefully hidden in a safe or vault are bags of gold coins—one imagines Spanish doubloons, French Louis d'ors and English sovereigns—coins which, besides being made of the world's most desirable substance, also contain a history and geography lesson in their markings. It is strange that money—which most people consider tiresome if not downright vulgar—should, as it grows old, become so remarkably romantic.

If, like me, you are taken with the idea of money as a work of art rather than as the means of acquiring a work of art, hurry to Le Musée de la Monnaie at the Hotel de la Monnaie in Paris. The museum is housed within Jacques Denis Antoine's complex of immensely beautiful buildings dating from the sixteenth century. It is filled with the stuff of money making, such as giant seventeenth-century cast-iron coin-cutting presses. Supported by columns and decorated with classical figures, they are driven by long iron bars with balls at each end. As the bars swing to and fro, they drive down a metallic screw which in turn presses the small dies into the metal. Money making in centuries past must have been a time-consuming and physically exhausting job.

Alongside the museum's dies and printing blocks, the lead medal of 1512 designed by Durer and the commemorative medal of Richelieu stand out, making the attempts of modern engravers pale by comparison. Yet, though less historically important, my favourite piece remains a medal from the sixteenth century depicting an elephant.

The museum holds medals aplenty, among them a series of twelve medals by different craftsmen commemorating the exploits of Napoleon. There are small gold Celtic and Greek coins, large Roman silver coins, French coins and many others from around the world.

La Musée de la Monnaie is not large. You could see it all in a few minutes, or you could lose yourself for hours, for this museum contains a microcosm of France's history, her triumphs and her failures, her ambition and her achievements.

Paris unscrambled

After disappointment over breakfast, I have my appetite for Paris restored by the unexpected charms of the Musée Carnavalet.

My day started badly; it was mid-June and the Parisian weather was cold, windy and wet. It was not, however, the weather that had upset me—rather an experience that I had at breakfast.

Ordering scrambled eggs and bacon in the newest and most chic Parisian hotel, I picked up the *European* and began to read. After nearly 20 minutes, no eggs and bacon. On enquiring, I was told the eggs would take 30 minutes more. What on earth was the chef doing with these eggs? This was, after all, nine o'clock on a Friday morning, not an unusual hour to take breakfast.

'He is cleaning the kitchen,' I was informed.

'Impossible!' I exploded. 'This is ridiculous!'

'It is not my fault,' shrugged the waitress—a waitress of immense beauty.

A surly waiter is an abomination; a surly reply from a truly beautiful woman, whose eyes begin to fill with water, is a delight far greater than any scrambled egg. So I let the matter pass, unfolded my umbrella and set out for a museum that I had never heard of before, in search of an exhibition of Chaumet's jewellery.

It always comes as something of a shock when, having visited a city for many years, you come across a museum of whose existence you were completely unaware. Such a museum is Carnavalet, in the Marais *quartier* of Paris. My sense of humiliation at this discovery was somewhat heightened by the fact that the Musée Carnavalet is just around the corner from the Picasso Museum, where I am a frequent visitor. It would be impossible to walk past the Carnavalet without noticing the place, for the museum is situated in one of the most beautiful houses in the Marais, one of the few Renaissance mansions still standing in Paris. Its small courtyards are laid out as parterre gardens, with its arcades decorated with fragments of sculpture. Work started on this house in 1548, under the supervision of Nicolas Dupuis, a master mason. In 1660, the building was enlarged and modernised by François Mansart, the architect who gave his name to the mansard roofs so popular in Paris. It was a private house until 1866, when it was acquired by the city of Paris and converted into a museum by the architect Victor Parmentier. One of fifteen museums belonging to Paris that tell the tale of the city's history from first settlement to the present day, it is just the perfect size: a quick sprint around it takes in the Bronze Age, medieval Paris, and the styles of several kings. It was only when I finished with the kings that I discovered a first floor gallery that took me into the worlds of the French Revolution, Napoleon and the twentieth century. The twentieth century included the original interior of Fouquet's jewellery shop from the Rue du Parc Royal, designed by Alfons Mucha and constructed in 1900—as fine an example of an art nouveau interior as you could hope to find.

Intriguing, interesting and totally beautiful, this museum is what all small museums should be: a place that teaches you just enough to leave you with a desire to learn a lot more. It is only when visiting a museum such as this that the reality of Paris becomes apparent—the depth of French culture and vast hinterland of power and influence that makes this city the linchpin of the French nation. Its great palaces, its avenues of trees, its gardens, restaurants, hotels and famous shops—they owe their greatness not to modern ingenuity, but rather to their city's culture and history. I shall certainly make a point of visiting the other fourteen museums that chronicle Paris's past, and return another day—when the chef is not cleaning the kitchen—to be served scrambled eggs and bacon by the beautiful waitress.

Shirtless in the Tuileries

As a wanderer in Paris, I fail to acquire a shirt from Charvet and find a secret haunt of the truly un-shirted threatened by the tide of change sweeping down from the Louvre.

As the French prepared for their holidays in 1992 they were beset by lorry drivers who blocked all the motorways and farmers who set dead sheep alight—not to mention fishers causing trouble in the Channel. Everyone in France seems to be in a bad humour these days. The taxi drivers are pretty evil humoured as well; they have some private gripe against their government and are taking it out on the public.

Despite all this, France is still a wonderful place. I set off across the Place Vendôme in Paris to enjoy one of that city's great wonders—Charvet the shirt makers, the most elegant and orderly of shops. I intended to place an order for some shirts and purchase a few silk handkerchiefs—pure luxury, but what a way to start a day in Paris. But the general ill humour seemed to have struck this bastion of tradition too. They had a sale on, the lift was barricaded, and signs directed the crowds to the first floor, where the merchandise was heaped high enough to give each pile a certain instability. There were, however, no crowds, and few staff either for that matter. I found my way with some difficulty to the second floor, where they sell the shirts. This is a wonderful sight with bolts of cotton in a dozen qualities, and several hundred different patterns: stripes and checks, plain colours, and shades of each of these colours. There I found Joseph. Joseph comes from Egypt, and is a man of great charm and age. He was very helpful with the shirts. 'Show me your best quality of cotton if you please,' I asked. He did please, and produced a bolt of cotton of such quality that it was hard to tell from silk. 'Perhaps a dozen shirts,' I suggested, and then with some embarrassment I asked the price. Joseph, with equal embarrassment, told me. He gave me the strong impression that price is not an issue with the customers he serves. I wondered if he had indeed shown me silk, for all the things that amazed me in that shop—fabrics, cuffs and collars in a multitude of shapes, intricate designs for embroidery—by far the most amazing was the price of those shirts. I left humiliated, muttering excuses over my shoulder.

As I recrossed the Place Vendôme I noticed office space to let. As I walked in the Rue de Faubourg-St-Honoré, there were empty shops.

The recession seemed to be here as well. Nonetheless, Paris is still a city of wonders and one of these is the Louvre and the Tuileries gardens. Building goes on apace; I. M. Pei still works away, though underground, doubling the exhibition space of that great museum. Thank goodness no more pyramids pop up in courtyards—not at the moment anyway.

Work has just started on the gardens; the Jeu de Paume is restored and open as a gallery again, and the fenced-off lawns are green once more. Maillol's plump girls are now displayed on their pedestals surrounded by grass. The trees are still unruly; however, the avenues of pleached chestnuts and plane trees are no longer strictly pruned. Some trees have died and others have been allowed to grow too large, breaking a line that should have been as regimented as Napoleon's old guard; the gravel, or what is left of it, is dusty, the parterres gone. Still waiting for children are the entertainments; the Punch and Judy show is fast becoming derelict, and the children's ponies are standing bored and old, waiting for their small riders.

But the tide of change is sweeping down from the Louvre and will affect a secret garden in the most public of places—secret from all except those who walk on the embankment that borders the Seine. They can look down onto this patch of grass where tramps take their lunch, hidden by the builders' huts and tall shrubbery where convolvulus grows thick. An empty pond fills with their rubbish. In a few weeks, all this will be gone, the garden restored with swirling flower hedges and gravel paths, no accidents of nature allowed. Parterres and paths are beginning to materialise, and lawns are laid and watered. Earth-movers move earth, and gardeners plant plants. Gravel is spread; the assorted stone sculptures that arrived at different periods in these gardens are now all imprisoned in a wire compound, waiting for masons to restore them and their bases—the bases lined by size, and the figures caged in the solitary confinement of rough wooden crates. I stood watching all this activity, lost in admiration for the French and their civic responsibility, never wondering how it was allowed to get into this state in the first place, forgetting that they forgot to do it all before.

Where Nile meets Seine

Back in Paris, I applaud its citizens' confident pride, and their unabashed assumption of an imperial heritage Napoleon couldn't quite deliver.

There is no season that I do not enjoy in Paris: the freshness of spring, the emptiness of summer, the bustle of autumn, all are the same in that place—sheer bliss. The shops in central Paris seem to have shrugged off the recession, if indeed there were ever any real signs of that recession. The Parisian rises above such things. The people of Paris are triumphant; the mobs recently marched in the streets—well, the mob is part of their history. The mob is how Parisians show pleasure and displeasure with the politicians. The mob is their vehicle for expression. The desire to demonstrate runs in the blood of all Parisians. The French do not read newspapers—national circulations are derisory.

The cleaning of Paris continues apace with one exception: the area around Beaubourg gets dirtier by the hour. The sheer weight of people who now visit this remarkable development is clearly taking its toll. Its streets are stained by fast food. The curious thing about the architecture of glass and steel is that it looks either pristine or derelict; it does not age as well as that of stone and timber. The Beaubourg must be cleaned at once or buried. In the nearby Rue St Denis, the street is being repaved, the buildings to be used by the rag trade. It is the ladies of the night plying their trade, or rather in Paris the ladies of the lunch hour, who are not ageing well.

Nearby, the restaurant Chez Benoit is still the same. The food of Benoit is unmistakably French. His customers smoke cigars with style. There is no apology for the habit. Other customers do not object by waving the smoke from them with pathetic fluttering of the hands. There is no warning on the tables against smoking; in fact, Benoit positively encourages the habit. Two women at the table next to me were puffing away with obvious delight at the very best that Havana has to offer. The government may build aggressively modern buildings such as the Beaubourg in what was perhaps Paris's most traditional quarter, and even install a glass pyramid in the courtyard of the Louvre, and their citizens seem to love the government for it: but the government fails miserably when it tries try to stop them smoking.

Paris has been changing continually, and mostly for the better, ever since General de Gaulle decreed that the city should be cleaned—for who would want to be president of a nation whose capital had not had a lick of paint in centuries? Yet the feel of the place as you walk in its streets remains the same. The French people have also changed since the general came to power. Always a nation who cooked far better than the British, now they trade far better than us as well, with a larger share than ours of the world's markets. The extraordinary aspect of French pride is that it is not centred on their past. The French government has no fear of the new: it fills a courtyard of the Palais Royal with a contemporary sculpture, and the Arc de Triomphe has been replicated by a massive arch that is in reality an office building and stands a mile or so behind it. French pride has a confidence that believes France capable of producing architecture and thought far better than that of their past; the pride of most countries is the reverse. De Gaulle worked wonders for French pride and every president since has encouraged it to greater height. Tons of gold paint have been poured on France's public buildings. Its language is encouraged and its culture reinforced.

Their campaign for national pride knows no bounds. I was passing the Louvre when I noticed an exhibition called 'Egyptomania'. Intrigued, I entered only to find that the French were busy inventing an empire. Here was exhibited almost every aspect of France's connection with Egypt. Walking around this exhibition it was as if Nelson had lost the Battle of the Nile, Aboukir had been a French victory and Napoleon had established French rule in Cairo. This exhibition, which leaves Paris for Ottawa and Vienna, demonstrates wonderfully the obsession with Egypt by Europeans.

The objects and artefacts of Egypt fill not only the museums of Europe but also the squares and parks of Europe's cities. One ancient Egyptian obelisk stands in the Place de la Concorde on the spot where the French cut off the heads of their king and queen, twin of that which remains at Luxor, measuring its length on the ground and fatally split into three sections. Another, which first saw light of day at Heliopolis 3500 years ago and then graced Alexandria, is our own Cleopatra's Needle beside the Thames on the Embankment, where it is guarded by bronze lions. Its twin points to the skies above Central Park, New York.

'Egyptomania' includes examples of the Egyptian influence since Roman times, where it is found in sculpture through the centuries and in the twentieth-century jewellery of Cartier. There are some particularly good examples of late-nineteenth century Giuliano jewellery as well as Severs porcelain, clocks, furniture, glass and architecture. How strange that Egypt, a country not noted for its pride, should have had such an effect on France and the rest of Europe.

Not taking the mickey

Euro Disney is a blot of twentieth-century tack on the European landscape, or so I thought until I visited in 1994 and found it a surprisingly animating experience.

There is a strong likelihood of Euro Disney closing—its fate hangs in the balance, the victim of a high stakes game of bluff between backers and banks. The public of Europe are mostly indifferent, while those charged with handling Europe's cultural heritage are often positively contemptuous of whether Euro Disney stays or goes.

Euro Disney is Europe's only great manifestation of the need for entertainment that has dominated the second half of the twentieth century. The World's Fair of the late 1960s held in Brussels has gone; and all that remains of the Festival of Britain is scattered around the museums of the world or lurking in the shops and stalls of Portobello Road. Governments put preservation orders on disused power stations. But Euro Disney is likely to pass unmourned. There are clubs and journals that record the passing of the steam train, with museums set up to preserve the few remaining examples; collectors eagerly search for old fairground equipment and ephemera. Yet the greatest example of fairground art in Europe is likely to be broken up and distributed among the world's street markets, with only those who have lost money in the venture having any regret.

I hated the idea of Euro Disney; for twenty years I resisted all attempts to lure me to its American cousins. Then a year or so ago I was overcome by curiosity and visited this vast fairground outside Paris. I loved it so much I returned almost immediately. Clustered around a mock medieval castle stolen from the pages of *Les très riches heures du Duc de Berry* is a vast collection of conflicting architectural styles and national cultures. A sure recipe for disaster you might imagine—I did; far from that, I spent a night and a day there filled with delight.

First I hurried to a Southern Railway Station, whose attendants were dressed from the last century. I was directed to it by a lady attired in what must surely have been an army surplus uniform from Custer's Seventh Cavalry. I climbed aboard the train: 'clang clang' went the bell, stirring music played and we headed into a tunnel. Lightning flashed, stuffed animals stood in stuffed landscapes—of course, I was right about how banal this all was. As we drew away from the tunnel Paris was gone. France was gone. We were in the American Rockies. I knew because I travelled through them on a train some years ago. Below us was a lake with a paddle-steamer, beyond a township. The realism was staggering—I travelled through centuries on that train, and did not doubt any of it: I was terrified by the pirates of the Caribbean and lulled into a sensation of exuberant wellbeing by 'It's a small world'. I enjoyed it so much I went around the circuit three times.

I then lunched in the Key West Seafood Restaurant where the food and service were indistinguishable from those in America. I banged on the table with the wooden hammer for cracking crab claws. This is a tradition from the original restaurant at Key West: every time a fishing boat comes in a bell is rung, and every time that bell is rung all the customers hammer furiously—a quaint but contagious habit. Before long I was convinced that fishing boats were returning by the dozen across the plains of northern France. Euro Disney is not deceptive but it does seduce you into self-deception. Disney only hints at what might be; it is your own imagination that fills in the gaps and extends these fantasies. Euro Disney shows those who believe that they have no imagination the possibilities of their own minds. I wandered past stores selling Disney in every shape and form. I stood and watched Disney's characters—many of the great images of the twentieth century—cavort and play. All the while the music nudged my subconscious and I felt happy. I ate my dinner in a Western saloon. I slept in a hotel from New Mexico.

The next day I toured Euro Disney with a critical eye—surely the architecture was pure pastiche? Not at all. At first glance it seemed to come from the past; in fact, it comes from the future, using the ethnic traditions of America as a starting point. One thing was clear: the quality of the place, whether the landscaping or the building, the merchandise or the costumes—all were of the highest quality. The architectural detailing is magnificent, and the imagination of its designers incredible. If Euro Disney is closed and dismembered, within a hundred years some enterprising museum director will be raising money to buy bits of Disney Land in America and transport it to Europe, just as the Americans transported our medieval architecture. This museum director will point out to those from whom he seeks his funds that Europe has no record of one of the world's greatest social phenomena.

Côte of charms

Amongst the many delights of the south of France, I remember when you could still buy a Picasso for a tenner.

For most of last winter I had been hearing rumours of a new museum opposite Nice Airport. So it was, on a baking hot day in July 1999, that I set off and found, to my surprise, a cool museum of Asiatic art surrounded by gardens and built in the middle of a marble-edged tank of water. A pair of black swans floated towards me as I walked across a marble causeway to the circular building at its heart, which is quite beautiful—more like a temple than a museum.

Opened nine months ago, it is, however, a trifle short on objects to display. A bank of computers, a shop where most of the elegant goods seem not yet for sale, and a café with a large vending machine do not constitute a museum. (A room put aside for performing the tea ceremony seemed a good idea, but as I was the only person in the place it seemed presumptuous to ask for a ceremony for one.) The museum staff, while friendly in a way, adopted an attitude to their bureaucratic duties that you would not find in the Louvre. Even in the most unlikely spots, however, you will find something of beauty and, sure enough, here were three outstanding objects, all from Japan: an Edo sixteenth-century seated figure of a priest, carved in wood, an object of the greatest beauty; a sixth-century terracotta horse, 4 feet tall, again a wonderful object; and, in complete contrast, two chairs by Shiro Kuramata, a designer who died in 1991. The first, a perspex dining chair with roses floating in the perspex, I was familiar with; the second, a wire-mesh armchair, I had never seen before—it is a truly smart piece of Japanese design. Its title, however, I found a little strange. How an armchair should come to be called *How High the*

Moon I cannot imagine. It put me in mind of the old joke 'How high is a Chinaman?' and I giggled all alone in this marble temple. And that, of course, is what this museum really is: a marble temple. The department of Alpes-Maritimes, which runs this place, ought to remove the computers, the vending machines, the shop and the tea ceremonies—and indeed all the other exhibits—leaving only the wooden priest, the terracotta horse and the wire armchair. Then at least they would have a congenial place to visit on a hot day—a temple of art that has become a work of art in itself.

The morning's visit being considerably shorter than I expected, I was left with time on my hands, so I set off for Vallauris, home of a hundred potters, but famous for one: Picasso. The museums at the château are splendid; some of Picasso's work is housed in a Romanesque chapel, a place of considerable beauty partly decorated by Picasso. There are a number of fine paintings, plenty of drawings and, of course, Picasso's pottery. On the day I visited they were opening an exhibition of studies for *Man with Sheep* of 1943. This life-size sculpture stands in the town's square. Afterwards I visited Madoura, the pottery where Picasso worked. In the 1960s and 1970s, I used to buy Picasso's work here literally by the crateful. A plate, as I recall, was about £10; a large plate in an edition of 25, about £75; and a ceramic sculpture in a small edition, about £250. Sadly, I no longer have my haul of Picasso's ceramics. Not much has changed, except that what was once a pottery has now the feel of a shrine and the prices are now well into the thousands, perhaps even tens of thousands. It is wonderful how rising prices increase one's respect for the product.

Wandering about Vallauris in search of exciting pottery, I came across another museum, the Musée de la Poterie, which chronicles the pottery making of Vallauris. I had a bit of a shock when I came upon a lifelike waxwork of Picasso touching up a pot. Generally, however, the best objects in the museum were the domestic pots from the past and the wonderfully designed kitchenware. Looking at these old pots, I came to the conclusion that a lot of the old domestic crocks that we find in antique shops are not as old as we believe them to be, for the date of production of these simple but splendidly glazed bowls appears to have been 1955.

Going to chapel

I sing the praises of a winding valley behind the Côte d'Azur that is dotted with glorious chapels in a sleepy landscape untouched by tourism.

Behind the range of mountains that edges the Côte d'Azur there is a valley through which the River Roya runs. The scenery is much as it was along the coast 45 years ago. There is no view of the sea, of course, but to compensate there are also no blocks of flats or landscape smeared with houses. There are only trees and rocks and every once in a while a small town.

Driving along a tortuous road, the first town of any consequence I came across was Sospel. I approached across a small fifteenth-century bridge in the centre of which is a tower with a portal. The streets of Sospel are extremely narrow. I followed my way round them to the Chapelle Ste Croix, an oblong box of a building with a square tower at one end capped with what for all the world looks like an upside-down ice-cream cornet. The 1518 Chapelle Ste Croix is the headquarters of 'the white penitents'. Originally, five different groups of penitents each had their own church. There were the black penitents who were the nobility; the grey penitents who were the poor; blue penitents, youth; and red penitents, prominent people. Only the white penitents, the middle classes, seem to be active today.

From Sospel the road twists and turns all the way to Saorge, a village built on ledges in the mountainside. Again I found a country baroque cathedral and narrow streets, some of which have become tunnels as buildings have been built above them. Five minutes' walk along the mountainside from Saorge is the twelfth-century Chapelle Notre Dame Del Poggio, with its facade and tower built of rough stone; it was extended in the fifteenth century and has some fine frescoes around the altar. The chapel is part of a monastery and its gate is marked private, so seeing the frescoes is problematical—but the best part of the chapel is, anyway, its exterior. The air at Saorge is fresh, and the only noise is the rushing of the river way below the town.

In La Brigue, the only town of any size in the district, there is another baroque cathedral containing a handful of fine sixteenth-century paintings. It is strange that these once inaccessible churches managed to acquire pictures of such quality. Lunch at La Brigue is taken Chez Carla, at least by those who know the rules. Always book—Carla does not care for unexpected guests or for guests who turn up late. The food is delicious, and the bill modest.

About a mile and a quarter from Carla's place is the Chapelle Notre Dames des Fontaines. This small and simple chapel is a miracle. Its walls are covered in large square frescoes portraying the last days of Christ, the Crucifixion and the Resurrection. There is nothing else in the place apart from a few pews and the accoutrements around the altar. It stands beside a stream in a leafy valley with not another building in sight. This chapel is a place of true contemplation.

Candid in Cannes

Returning to the Côte d'Azur, I find Cannes has become a victim of its own still considerable charms.

The railway station at Beaulieu-sur-Mer has barely changed since my first visit in 1948. There are two taxi ranks instead of the horse and trap, and an automatic ticket vendor stands on the platform, but apart from that, everything is the same. This is not the case, however, with the town of Beaulieu—nor, for that matter, with the entire coastline between Monte Carlo and Cannes. Nowadays, there is barely a mountain ledge that does not support a block of flats. Houses stand on terraces where carnations once grew; the groves of olives and the woods of mimosa are long gone.

In May 1996, I took the train from Monte Carlo to Cannes. As we drew into Beaulieu, the memories came flooding back of that grey day in 1948 when I took the train ferry from Victoria Station, across the Channel and on to Paris, my sleep fragmented by excitement as the Blue Train raced towards the Côte d'Azur. I remembered the smell of smoke blown through the open window as we went into a tunnel, and the black specks of soot on the bed linen in the morning—but most of all, my surprise as the heavy blind on the window of my sleeping compartment cracked open to reveal a landscape of orange rock and huge cacti.

My electric train slides along its tracks past Beaulieu. The casino is the same, but the Bristol Hotel, derelict after the war, has been converted into smart apartments. Across the neck of Cap Ferrat, the train passes the pebbled beach that trims the bay of Villefranche, where early bathers are enjoying the first of the year's sunshine. The restaurants below the castle and the port are still there; waiters are putting out the checked tablecloths for lunch. I suppose the entertainers—the man on a bicycle who rode over motor cars, and the juggler-cum-comic who mimicked the passing tourists—are probably still there as well.

On we speed to Nice, a grand old railway station barely altered since my childhood. The racecourse at Cagnes-sur-Mer is green and fresh—I can remember racing there in the early 1960s. My father's horse won by several lengths, but was disqualified for bumping and boring. My mother was determined to protest, but the French trainers convinced her otherwise—it seemed that British horses were supposed to come second.

Antibes, Golfe Juan and Juan les Pins come and go. The restaurants on the beach that sell bouillabaisse and grilled lobster are opening up for the holiday rush. Then on to Cannes. The station is changed, its facade obscured by a new road system. I leave the train at Cannes and walk towards the Croisette. How different the town is! The casino has grown beyond recognition; the Majestic Hotel no longer has the majesty of past years. New hotels stand where once there were courtyards and dress shops. Shops selling gloves and hats have made way for apartment blocks. A conference centre crowds a fine mansion that used to stand isolated, surrounded only by palm trees.

Cannes is still a smart town: less British than it was, but smart nevertheless. When I first visited the Carlton Hotel in the early 1950s it offered a tired elegance, but today it is all gleam and glitter. The hotel had its own tennis courts but now these are gone, replaced by more apartments. Even the English church is now set among apartments. The very reason for coming to Cannes has been destroyed by the accommodation for those who come. Restaurants that have been there since I was a child have grown to a charmless size. The proprietors are dead, retired or living off their wealth gained during the boom.

I visit Felix's Restaurant, the second home of every Englishman staying in Cannes. Felix is dead; Jacques, his son, is off travelling. One waiter remembers me from the 1970s; all the rest are gone. Felix was among the greatest of proprietors. Once, I was eating lunch and he told me he was very unhappy: 'I have lost my best customer; he sat here every day.' I sympathised. 'That's not the point,' Felix replied. 'I took the evening off and my staff allowed this man to eat a whole bowl of hollandaise sauce. That would never have happened if I had been there; you can't afford to neglect your business.'

Escape artists

For 300 years, people miraculously saved from dire mishap have given commemorative pictures to Notre Dame de Laghet in the south of France.

The south of France has changed out of all recognition in the last 30 years. There is barely a piece of coastline without a building on it. The museums that house the work of Picasso, Matisse, Léger and Renoir are well known; the castles and chapels where their work is to be found have changed from places of pilgrimage to mere halts on a tourist itinerary. Even the dolls' museum of Monaco, which used to be a dusty place, is now smartened up and widely advertised. There can be few secrets left between Monte Carlo and St Tropez.

Yet there are still places with their own peculiar magic to be found. Deep in a wooded valley behind the mountain range that edges the Mediterranean is the village of Laghet, famous since the seventeenth century for its sanctuary of Notre Dame de Laghet and the statue of the Virgin housed there. In the mid-1600s miracles began to happen there. The poor, the sick, the distressed and those who had experienced miraculous escapes from danger visited the sanctuary in droves. Many left small paintings to commemorate the disasters from which they had been saved by the intervention of Laghet's Virgin.

By the end of the eighteenth century there were over four thousand of these paintings hanging in the church which had been rebuilt within a monastery occupied by the Carmelite Fathers. In 1792 Revolutionary troops passed through Laghet and burned the votive paintings, although the statue of the Virgin, luckily, was hidden by a local shepherd. The Revolution over, the chapel reopened, the Virgin was reinstated, the Carmelite Fathers returned and so did the pilgrims. Soon the baroque church was again filled with their paintings and they began to overflow into the surrounding cloisters.

I first came across Laghet in 1965, a period of my life when I had a wild enthusiasm for primitive painting. I remembered Laghet as having some remarkable examples, so this autumn I set out to test my memory. It was a sunny afternoon with a chill in the air as I took a taxi from Monte Carlo, up past La Turbie and then down narrow winding roads to the valley that holds the village of Laghet and its monastery.

There was a service in progress. A low chanting and the smell of incense filled the cloisters. Serried ranks of candles stood along the cloister walls, their flames without a flicker in the still air. The feeling of peace was intense as I walked through the cloisters and looked at the paintings.

It was more than 30 years since I had been here, and at first I was pleased I had made my journey. Here were primitive depictions of runaway horses, carriage accidents, train, car and motorcycle crashes, and relatives sitting at the bedside of the fatally ill. There were cars going over cliffs, hunting accidents and workmen falling from buildings.

They could not, however, be described as approaching art and when I left the church I was, I confess, disappointed with my memory. It was then that I spotted a nun sitting at a table, in front of her a small sign advertising a museum. One thousand of the best paintings, now under the protection of the 'Beaux Arts', are kept in this small museum.

What remarkable pictures they are. Mostly painted in the early nineteenth century, many depict the sea battles of the Napoleonic wars. One, brought to Laghet in 1804 by Captain Bavastre, records how his corsair escaped the attack of British men-of-war. The sails of the three vessels are lacy with holes made by cannon balls. I doubt if this picture is by Captain Bavastre. Rather, I believe it to have been commissioned by him because many of the maritime paintings here are by the same hand—an unknown painter who was clearly a genius. The offering of a family caught in a storm off the Gulf of Venice is another masterpiece.

Other pictures tell of accidents in mills, desperate situations with mules and, most delightful of all, a lady falling off a tall haystack, her arms and legs stretched out as if she were a beetle pinned to a board.

It was with some relief that I set off for home, faith in my memory restored. These paintings were truly as exciting today as when I found them all those years ago.

Fish out of water

I venture forth from my usual Monte Carlo haunts, and discover some curious marine artefacts in little-visited tracts of Monaco's oceanographic museum.

I spend a lot of my time in Monte Carlo and, as is the way of people who spend a great deal of time in a town, I have taken its secret places for granted. I tend to take the same walks and visit the same museums and churches. Monte Carlo, then, is not the first place I look for curious places and wonderful objects. Each day after my lunch at Rampoldi's, I pass the oceanographic museum. Aquariums aren't really my thing, so it wasn't until last week that I bothered to explore the museum's palatial rooms, built last century.

Upstairs, to my surprise, I found a most eclectic collection, displayed in two large galleries, of animals, fish and objects connected with the sea. There are, of course, fossils of fish in profusion, fish preserved in bottles, dozens and dozens of them, alongside stuffed fish and stuffed animals that eat fish. The star of the show is a giant lobster, about three feet long. I was terribly impressed with this specimen until I poked my head into the auditorium used for lectures. There I came across a pair of spider crabs from Japan, their legs as thick as fence posts and easily five feet long. I don't think I will ever go paddling again.

Spectacular though they are, it wasn't simply the exhibits that impressed me. Rather it is the way the museum sets out to demonstrate how humans and the creatures of the sea and coast interact. This interaction is of course a one-sided business, mostly involving humans killing sea creatures to benefit their own lifestyle. Here, a large stuffed gull sits proudly beside his mates, who have been made into a stole and a hat, both with the head and beak of the bird intact—a style highly fashionable in the 1930s. Displayed next to the gulls is a shark, then its skin, and then a pair of shark-skin shoes and a dozen other objects made of the same material.

Other exhibits teach a less dramatic lesson. There are objects made by sailors to pass lonely hours at sea—gifts for loved ones or trinkets sold to earn a penny or two—such as dolls, a model elephant and a box in the shape of a sitting hen, all made from seashells. There are shell and coral pendants and masks made by native Americans;

African shell belts, necklaces and headdresses; Indian miniatures painted on shell; shell marriage money from New Guinea; and religious shell carvings to safeguard sailors on dangerous oceans. There are even exhibits dating back to Roman and Egyptian times.

From the paraphernalia of whaling and deep-sea diving to the trade in tortoiseshell ornament, every conceivable use and abuse of the sea and its creatures is housed here. Unspoilt by the smart or the chic, this museum is a place truly worth discovering.

Train of thought

An impromptu trip by night train from Monaco to Venice gives me a twilight glimpse of sleeping towns, black mountains and, finally, Venice in all its morning glory.

Recently, on a whim, I decided to take the train from Monaco to Venice. Monaco station was a lonely place at nine o'clock at night and I had begun to doubt the existence of the train when, on time, a spanking new engine of monstrous size arrived pulling a motley collection of ancient rolling stock.

I climbed aboard and, with its corridors packed, the train began to speed past hillsides dotted with lights, and then emerged from long tunnels to trace the edge of the sea. After a town, where families dined at uncurtained windows and television flickered in gloomy sitting rooms, we stopped, as night trains do, in the middle of nowhere, for no good reason. After Menton, its station full of drunks, the next town had a brightly lit castle and church, and we could see boats and neon signs in the port. We pulled alongside another train filled with tired people, and caught them yawning and adjusting their clothes in preparation for sleep. Ventimiglia—the border with Italy—was full of bustling customs officials. At San Remo, a porter shouted unintelligible words as passengers ran for the train.

The couple in my compartment were young, she an American television executive, he her elegant Brazilian companion. Our old-fashioned compartment had red plush seats that converted into one giant bed. We slept in fits and starts—for the sake of propriety. The charming television executive and her devastatingly good-looking boyfriend slept with their heads to my toes. Through mountain tunnels, up winding tracks and over passes, our train travelled down onto the plains of Italy. Across the empty avenues of suburban Milan, the points of the terminus crunched and cracked beneath the train wheels. Milan's Porto Garibaldi Station was deathly quiet at four in the morning and not a soul passed along the brightly lit platform. At Brescia, a few Africans boarded the train with their bundles, going, I suppose, to sell handbags on the streets of Venice. Dawn broke at Vicenza and the sky became the palest blue with a streak of pink along the horizon. The landscape was filled with early morning shadows and silhouetted buildings. At 6.26 am, the station lights were still burning at Padua, as early-morning commuters boarded the train, half an hour from my journey's end. As we crossed the causeway over the lagoon, the sun was already shining brightly.

It had not been the most comfortable of journeys but I had enjoyed myself—and where else can you get such an experience, let alone be transported so far, for 307 French francs?

The United States

First bite at the Big Apple

I first visited New York as a small boy, travelling on board the Queen Elizabeth. *It was the first of many memorable trips.*

I first visited New York in 1956 travelling on the *Queen Elizabeth*—the old *Queen Elizabeth* that is. Travel for first-class passengers on this ship was a luxurious affair. Dinner jackets were worn every night except on the evening we left, and dinner for those who know about travel was taken in the Verandah Grill. Passengers booked their table at the same time as they booked their tickets, for tables were hard to obtain. The Grill was smaller than the restaurant and the food was believed to be better. Besides, it was *the* place to eat and it seemed to me as a small boy that all the grand people in their couture clothes and breathtaking jewellery ate little other than caviar.

Then there was a ship's photographer, determined to record every mouthful consumed. I travelled with my family. My mother hated the flash of cameras and took an intense dislike to this photographer. 'Please ask him not to photograph us,' she requested. My father became desperate, for the man was insistent with some reason, I suppose, for it was his job to take everyone's photograph and everyone except my mother was only too keen to have it taken. (This, I might say, was not the only respect in which my mother was unusual.) There seemed nothing that would stop the man; desperate measures were called for. 'Look—I'm not with my wife; I cannot be photographed,' shouted my father. This threw the photographer, and meant that my mother, father, grandmother and her aged female companion, my ten-year old younger brother, my older brother and an aunt who travelled with us were able to enjoy our dinner unphotographed for the next four days. My father, however, was pursued by the photographer, trying secretly to get a shot of this strange man who took his mistress travelling with such an entourage.

When we arrived at New York the port's tugboats were on strike, and many ships waited in the roads (the equivalent of a marine parking lot just outside a port). Waiting about for striking tugboat crews was not the kind of activity that the captain of the *Queen Elizabeth* engaged in. He docked his vast liner without their help in spite of the tides. His ship dwarfed the buildings on the wharf—and that was the first time I saw the skyline of New York. I have visited that city often since then and watched tall buildings fill out that skyline. Always it seems to get better. Now for the first time in my memory no cranes hang over the city and the traffic is not disrupted by building works.

As I wandered down Madison Avenue on my visit in 1994 I visited the great atriums of New York's towers. I went to the IBM building with its 30-foot (9-metre) high bamboos and Basement Art Gallery. What was once the AT&T office—and called the Chippendale Building because of its similarity to a giant grandfather clock—is now the Sony Building. Undergoing conversion at ground level, it will become a shrine to Sony goods and the gods of electronics. Two small traders who rent space in the buildings still hold out against these changes; building work goes on around them. At 380 Madison Avenue is what I suppose will be the last of these remarkable buildings, this one with a foyer designed by Alberto Pinto, famous for his work on hotels.

Other buildings have not changed since I first set foot in New York: the brownstone church on Madison and the streets that radiate off it with their brownstone houses—still largely residential, they stay the same. Then there are the apartment blocks of Fifth Avenue opposite Central Park; if they have changed you would be hard pressed to know it, for they are still the grandest apartments anywhere, looking out over the park side by side with the Pier and Sherry Netherland hotels. Across the square where the horsedrawn carriages wait is the Plaza Hotel. Nearby is the 21 Club where I ate on my first visit, and I still eat there. These are all names that New Yorkers have known for generations.

On 57th Street, a block or two away, is the new Four Seasons Hotel designed by I. M. Pei. Mussolini would have been proud of him—the public rooms are vast; marble and stone are used everywhere and the furniture has the shape and colour of the 1930s. It is less busy than Milan's Central Station and without a fascist iconography, but it has much the same feel about it.

Those who travel to New York must wonder why America chose Washington as its capital. The answer is simple—it comes to you as you walk in New York's streets, drink in its bars and eat in its restaurants. New York is not typical of America; New York is currently the capital of the world.

All is loft

SoHo, once the lofty home to New York's artists, has been invaded by commerce and all the mediocrities that go with it. I was saddened by this march of 'progress'.

Less than twenty years ago, New York's SoHo was an area of cheap and spacious accommodation. Its buildings' upper floors, called lofts, were turned into vast artists' studios, their lower floors into shops that could accommodate even the largest fragments of industrial archaeology. The area prospered, the cast-iron fronts of multistoried buildings were given a lick of paint and visually alert New Yorkers realised that these dinosaurs from the distant days of urban manufacturing had a beauty of their own.

Soon the galleries followed the artists, and then the cafés and restaurants followed the customers who were visiting the galleries. Shops opened—not only giant shops selling all the paraphernalia of decoration, but small shops selling rare magazines and gramophone records. SoHo had become an eccentric place for collectors who searched for the obscure but interesting. It was not about beauty, nor about ritz and glitz.

I remember dining during the period of SoHo's birth with Christo, the artist who specialises in wrapping up extremely large parcels with contents as disparate as a huge chunk of Australia's coastline and Berlin's Reichstag. Christo's wife was, I recall, a collector—a collector of jokes. I enjoyed my dinner and determined to send her a joke as a present.

This lady did not collect the kind of jokes that you can buy in joke shops, but the sort that one tells across a dinner table when the conversation flags. In the event I never did send a joke. I felt sure that joke collectors worth their salt would be certain to know any jokes that I could find, and I cannot think of anything more depressing than being a joke collector and receiving through the post a series of jokes that you have already heard.

Unlike other collectors, the joke collector cannot keep unwanted duplicates to swap—they must be torn up and thrown away. You can pass on to other collectors of the genre a rare joke that you already have, but in doing so you totally destroy the rarity of your joke. Nor can you show your collection. The moment another collector has seen one of your prized jokes, the cat is out of the bag—as everybody knows, a good joke spreads like wildfire. The collector of jokes seemed to me the ideal partner for a wrapper of parcels too large to take home.

SoHo boomed, but the art market died. Those dealers who still cling to their businesses in the hope that something might turn up have migrated to Chelsea, a suburb on New York's West Side where property is cheap. It is an inconvenient location, but with customers for avant-garde art as rare as hen's teeth, I suppose this will make little difference to the dealers' trade. In any case, the atmosphere that made SoHo attractive to such people is long gone.

Instead of the cafés where artists used to meet, SoHo has smart and, I may say, unreasonably expensive restaurants. As for refreshment, that can nowadays be acquired from the Tea Emporium, an establishment that serves a multitude of different teas to a clientele that drinks coffee. Even the Guggenheim Museum has opened a branch in SoHo, adding to a new form of pollution—the pollution of interesting areas by establishment institutions bringing with them people of conventional taste who buy goods in shops that sell tourist rubbish. The shops that once sold records now sell fashion—not the avant-garde fashion that was sold in SoHo a few years ago, but the fashion that is sold in shops all the way from Madison Avenue to Hong Kong.

Commerce has arrived in SoHo with a vengeance. Those who practise this new commerce do so with expertise; the inefficient and the interesting have been driven out by the cleverly managed and the downright boring. The graffiti is still on the buildings in SoHo, although it is changing from brilliant scribble to the carefully painted. The streets are cleaner, the people well-dressed and less eccentric.

The lofts have changed from artists' studios to grand apartments—one I visited had been fitted out to replicate a north Italian Renaissance palace.

SoHo has been ruined—as many other places have been ruined—by success. But at least the buildings remain.

No Mo' Boho SoHo

South of Houston in New York used to have a charm all of its own; now it shares the charms of every other major shopping district. It is still possible, however, to find a few exceptions.

On summer days, New York's SoHo is a splendid place to walk. Its tall, cast-iron buildings still boast the classic details of the nineteenth century. Its streets are wide, and its art galleries and restaurants numerous: all, it seems, is well in this unusual part of New York. The truth, however, is rather different, for SoHo is dying of shopping pollution. Thirty or so years ago, when SoHo was a place that offered large areas of cheap space, artists moved there and galleries followed, as did restaurants that catered for artists' tastes and antique shops that sold architectural elements garnered from demolition sites. On their premises fairground figures, made redundant by the new all-singing, all-dancing rides, became works of art. Outdated equipment from factories was sold to decorate smart new apartments where it became sculpture. Poets, painters, dealers and their hangers-on mixed in SoHo restaurants and the world came to look at them. Where the world goes, however, retailers follow.

Now SoHo boasts many fine shops. Banana Republic, Benetton, Country Road, Replay and Victoria's Secret are just a few of the major retailers that have taken vast premises in SoHo. Even Knoll has large premises selling universal modern furniture. The designer multiples are there as well: Dolce & Gabbana, Todd Oldham, Comme des Garçons and the rest, where once there were shops that sold the bizarre and the unique. There is nothing wrong with any of these new shops—but why would you go to SoHo to visit any of them when they all have premises in the more accessible part of town?

Each of these fashion multiples pays top dollar for premises that were formerly occupied by retailers of curiosities, who could barely pay SoHo rents when they were cheap. It is true that a retailer such as E. Buk Antiques, a dealer in antique scientific instruments, early outboard motors and other curiosities, has survived, and stores such as Tootsi Plohound, a shoe shop worth a visit for its name alone, have arrived to lighten the onslaught from shops whose twins are found in all the world's cities.

Among all this there is, however, a shop that has grown with SoHo. Though it has moved and modernised, it still feels like a treasure house. Sarajo, now at 130 Greene Street, has textiles and traditional clothing from all parts of the world. The place is as beautiful as the goods it sells. No one who visits can come away without a fleeting desire to become a collector. Its walls are lined with glass-fronted shelves piled with textiles. Each line of shelves accommodates textiles from a different region. This shop has all the attractions of a confectionery store.

As I was looking at this incredible stack of textiles one day, I heard a lady of a certain age announce, 'I have seen all this before, in the 1960s on the King's Road.' She hadn't, of course, because in those days textiles with the colours of the countries around the Caspian Sea weren't available in the West. It was the collapse of Communism and the opening up of closed countries in the Far East at the beginning of the 1990s that brought so many wonders onto the market. The lady, I believe, was referring to the hippie culture and the brightly coloured cloths of British and American manufacture, not the silks found in Sarajo that look like the paintings of Mark Rothko and predate them by a hundred years. It's shops like Sarajo, however, that still make it worthwhile for every serious collector to visit SoHo.

Bargain binge

The flea market of 26th Street is still the haunt of dealers in search of a bargain. Championing flea market values I never tire of rummaging through the street stalls of New York in search of undiscovered bargains.

Every Saturday in New York, around the junction of 26th St and Sixth Ave, there is a flea market. Unlike in London and Paris, where they are the home of upmarket specialist dealers, the markets of New

York are truly flea markets. A quick glance at the goods will confirm this. For, while it is unlikely that the used clothing actually has fleas, it is a downright certainty that any fabrics will contain moths. These markets—if you were to put your textile purchases in the deep freeze for a week or two—are happy hunting grounds for those who enjoy a bargain. The snag is that you need to sift through tons of clothing that, whatever the price, could never be considered bargains. To hunt for bargains you need stamina and a strong stomach.

The myth of bargain hunting would have it that you need to be there at first light, akin to hunting duck at dusk. It seems people imagine that bargains and ducks are only around at predefined times of day. Maybe this is the case with ducks, but not with bargains. And what of the clever dealers who speed through the markets at the crack of dawn? Surely these professionals will clean up, while the likes of us are still deciding which cereal to eat? If all the dealers in a city scoured its markets, they would still miss a few bargains. Dealers visit a few stalls regularly, and stallholders keep goods for them that they know they will buy. If bargain hunters camped out weeks in advance, they would not be able to buy these. Real bargains are hidden away in the rubbish.

Bargain hunters come in all shapes and sizes. Once, lunching with Paul Keating, then prime minister of Australia, I admired his collection of French Empire antiques, assembled with a brilliant, unerring eye.

'But what of the cost of all this?' I asked.

'Some people buy their antiques tame from well-known dealers; I catch them wild in street markets and junk shops.'

Imagine my surprise when I heard this, for I had found a great rarity in a most unexpected setting—a genuine, unaltered, unrestored bargain hunter.

It's in the blood, of course; some people are attracted to bargains, like the Bushmen of the Kalahari are to water. They (bargain hunters) will hunt until they find what they seek, and although it does not have to be a masterpiece, it does have to be a bargain. I have searched the flea markets of New York for marbles—the glass variety—political badges, beads and textiles. The flea markets are a productive source of second-hand ties. Imagine my excitement when I unearthed a bedraggled paisley-pattern tie. It cost only two dollars—what a bargain for it must, when ironed and cleaned, be worth *four* dollars. For me, however, it is priceless; I have never seen its like before.

Standing at a store one wet Saturday—wet Saturdays are best for bargain hunters, for most sane people give damp street markets a wide berth—I spotted two large bags made of homespun cloth, oatmeal in colour with a solid blue stripe. They had clearly been made for some domestic purpose in the nineteenth century. I picked up the first to look at; the stallholder picked up the other. I studied mine intently. With the bag he held, he started to wipe up spilt tea.

'Stop,' I shouted. 'I want to buy that bag.' The poor man could not have been more startled. 'How much are these bags?' I asked.

'Ten dollars each,' he replied.

'Hold on,' say I, 'you just used that one to wipe up tea.'

'Ten dollars for two, then,' he offered, and I accepted.

I was well pleased with my bags; the colour was only improved by a drop of tea. These were indeed bargains. Damp and cold, I returned to my hotel a truly happy man, for bargain hunting and collecting are two totally separate undertakings that give joy to different types of people. Sometimes, as in the case of my homespun bags, the two activities come together. My bags are both bargains and worth collecting.

Dem bones, dem bones . . .

Wandering around New York's vast Museum of Natural History I bone up on the countless skeletons and specimens both on show and behind the scenes—from the fiercest dinosaur to the millions of microscopic flies. Nowhere in the world are the museums as numerous or as good as in America.

The American Museum of Natural History in New York is a formidable building. It looks the way a great museum should look, with a large portico and flights of steps to its doorway. In front of it stands a statue of President Teddy Roosevelt on his horse. Roosevelt did not found the museum—that role was filled by Albert S. Bickmore. Nor for that matter did he lay the museum's foundation stone—that function was carried out by another president, Ulysses S. Grant. No, Teddy Roosevelt was one of that strange breed of men who like to kill animals, yet are intensely interested in their preservation, and he played an important part in the museum's history—indeed, a vital part. For when it opened in 1877 there was very little public interest and few people turned up for the ceremony, and by 1880 the museum set up to conserve and display animals long since extinct was on the verge of extinction itself. It was Teddy Roosevelt who saved the day: he acquired from the public purse a large sum of money to help them out. This is why he sits cast in bronze astride his horse on the steps. Somewhat of an embarrassment in this age of political correctness, but his presence cannot be escaped, whether it is the hall named after him, with its cavorting skeletons of dinosaurs, some of them 50 feet high, or as you walk among the stuffed elephants, past the windows behind which herds of stuffed oryx graze.

If you spend a day or even a week in this museum looking at the animals and the remarkable collection of artefacts, you will see but a fraction of what has been collected since the Roosevelt days: two million moths and butterflies, 8.5 million invertebrates, and more dinosaurs, birds, spiders, animals, fossils and whole skeletons than any other museum in the world. Over three million artefacts and specimens, and among all these is the skeleton of Barnum and Bailey's famous elephant, Jumbo. The museum is looked after by 200 scientists and their attendant technicians, porters and workers, guides, office staff and public relations officers. All this is housed in a building of 1.2 million square feet and all the time new specimens pour in.

The fish department alone has 120 barrels of fish waiting to be catalogued and taken into the collection. The scale of the whole operation is remarkable: five whole storeys of dinosaur bones—they call it the bone store—with rack upon rack of pieces of dinosaur. Dinosaur eggs not by the dozen but by the gross.

The history of the museum is stuffed with characters. Barnum Brown—or Mr Bones as he was called—dug up more dinosaurs than any other man who ever lived. At Hell Creek he found the huge carnivorous dinosaur, *Tyrannosaurus Rex*; this is not one of those gentle grass-eating animals that we read about, with small heads and big bodies, so stupid that they ate themselves to extinction. Mr Bones' dinosaur was a beast whose bite was poisonous—because of the rotting flesh left between its teeth. In the 1930s he discovered at Howe Ranch near the base of the Bighorn Mountains a dinosaurs' graveyard, and sent 4000 bones back to the museum in 144 cases weighing 35 tons. Then there was Roy Chapman Andrews. He started work at the museum scrubbing floors in the taxidermy departments;

fifteen years later, in 1922, he headed an expedition to he Gobi Desert looking for the missing link. He did not find it, but he did find the only *Baluchitherium* skull ever found. So rare was this skull that Andrews hired bandits to transport it around China, and then it was shipped back to America. Roy Chapman Andrews was the model for Indiana Jones.

Among all these wonders, I found the flies—two and a half million of them, case upon case, some so small they cannot be seen with the naked eye. I asked the curator which was his favourite, and without a moment's hesitation he replied, 'The New Guinea Antler fly, though I must say I am torn between the stagshorn and the elkhorn as to which variety I prefer.'

Newark numismatology

Coins are what count in New Jersey's industrial heart, where poor men can strike it rich and where I checked out the numismatic collection in the Newark Museum.

Nine miles from the centre of New York, across the formidable Hudson River, is Newark, the largest city in New Jersey. Be just a little careful when you ask a taxi driver to take you to Newark. Pronounced by a tongue unaccustomed to the American language, the name of that place can easily be confused with New York itself, leading, I suppose, to the inevitable response from the taxi driver that New York is a big place, so which part do you want to visit? (Taxi drivers, incidentally, in America's and indeed the world's greatest city have a considerable problem with the local language themselves. So the chances are that you will only be further confused by the taxi driver's question.) The streets were clear of traffic, and 20 minutes later I was in front of the Newark Museum. So efficiently had I been transported that I had the best part of an hour on my hands before the museum opened.

Newark is a large, rambling industrial city. Low factory buildings and vacant lots rub shoulders with shining new buildings. There is no doubt that if I had spent any length of time there, I would have fallen in love with this ungainly place. Newark has for me the most attractive quality of all: the possibility of improvement. In my mind's eye, as I walked the street, the vacant blocks became tall buildings surrounded by gardens, the derelict warehouses fashionable homes. Old buildings were restored and the clutter of tired commerce cleared from shop fronts.

It was lucky that the museum opened and I had to put my dreams to one side, or I would have moved to the place. The Newark Museum is not in itself exceptional. Its collections of American painting and sculpture, classical art and Asian art are all of considerable quality but are not outstanding. Its exhibits from the cultures of Africa, the Pacific and the Americas are well worth a visit, and its planetarium, mini zoo and coffee shop are a lot of fun. However, its collection of what is rather grandly called 'numismatics' is of international fame. Housed in a specially designed gallery, it is a shrine for those who collect money and other objects relating to finance. Newark has long had a reputation as a place 'where a poor man could strike it rich with hard work and the right kind of luck'. So it is not inappropriate that the city's museum should have a small shrine to the method by which its citizens measure success.

I enjoyed my day in Newark and its museum. The time flew and soon I found what I believed to be the exit. Once through the fire doors, I came upon a different world. It was as if I had been removed into a dream house of the nineteenth century; I stood in the hall of Ballantine House. Moving from room to room, I realised that this was not a series of room settings taken from houses long-demolished in the streets of Newark, but was, rather, a great Victorian mansion around which the museum had been built.

Ballantine House, built in 1885 (its refurbishment and restoration was completed in 1994), is a masterpiece. The only Victorian mansion open to the public in the district of New York, it houses the Newark Museum's collection of American silver, furniture and pottery as well as many other objects from the Victorian era. Strangely, it is not the old mansion's contents that are so striking—fine as they are—but the atmosphere of the place. To walk from a modern museum into a lost age so meticulously documented is a surreal experience. That Sunday morning, I stood alone in the Ballantine family's dining room. I walked their corridors, climbed their stairs and peeked into their bedroom. It was as if they were all out at church and I, a stranger, had wandered through their open door. This was once the home of a great industrial family, built by the children of a poor Scottish emigrant, a symbol of success, preserved as testimony to the American dream.

Manhattan transfer

An ill-timed New York snowstorm wreaks havoc on my holiday travel plans. Unable to find a way to Santa Fe, I spend the day grounded in Dallas.

Seldom had New York seen such a snowstorm; happily, it was publicised 48 hours in advance. Conscious of the New Year holiday, New Yorkers rushed to the city's three airports. I was among them. Some were quicker than others; I could not arrange a flight to Santa Fe, so I settled for passage to Dallas.

I last visited Dallas in the 1970s. The newly opened airport, then state-of-the-art, stood amidst rolling plains—not another building for miles. Dallas was a cluster of tall reflective buildings interlaced with malls, and the suburbs, almost walking distance from the centre, were avenues of trees edged with turn-of-the-century housing. What many would call junk shops—a source of delight to me—were there in plenty and, before long, I had acquired a half-life-size cast-iron figure of a groom, which had once served as a hitching post for horses. With difficulty the shopkeeper, the driver and myself loaded this trophy into a large black limousine.

'How can I get this to England?' I asked the driver.

'Leave it to me,' he replied. 'This little fellow will be in England before you are.' To my surprise he was right. I had expected it to suffer the same fate as a small carriage I bought in France which, I believe, is still somewhere on the French railway system. Delighted with my purchase and the helpful attitude of the driver I enquired where to take lunch.

The restaurant to which I was directed was distinctive in a Louis the Who sort of way; its decor sported centuries of French style with stray touches of Dallas chic. I warmed to the place, however, when I found Château Latour 1949 on the wine list. A quantity was poured for me to taste—it was superb. Then the waiter dropped the bottle. 'Don't worry,' said I, 'just fetch another bottle,' only to be told this was the last one. I found myself apologising to the waiter out of a misplaced sense of guilt.

As I travelled, I wondered how Dallas had changed. The once-pristine airport was in a state of trashy confusion. At last I was advised on the Santa Fe flights: 'They are all overbooked.' Perhaps fate would dictate a New Year in Dallas. 'There is, however, a seat on the 7.14 flight.' I set out for the airport hotel, and was soon in bed with an alarm call to catch the 7.14 flight; up at 5 am I was delivered to the airport, only to find that the flight was for 7.14 pm. My day was to be spent in Dallas after all.

Well . . . first breakfast, and I tried to reconcile the wonderful menu with the inappropriate raw vegetables on display. I confess, I cannot resist listening to conversations; perhaps it is the reason I enjoy eating alone. Two men well past middle age were deep in discussion. Bush, Gore and the presidential election? Taxation? I could not quite catch their words. They were, however, clearly discussing a tragedy, with sucking of teeth and glum looks. Then it came. 'Just who *are* the new people who have the rights to the Indian motorcycle?' They were discussing the fate of an American bike—a subject for more important than mere presidents—and while the conversation was largely unintelligible to me, their words clearly came from the heart.

As I despaired of breakfast, the tannoy system announced an unexpected Santa Fe flight. Like a greyhound from its trap, I sprinted for the bus and boarded that flight, my day in Dallas cancelled. Television later revealed the full chaos of that day, and the folly of public-holiday travel became obvious; in fact, the public holiday is a folly in itself. The notion of everyone taking the same day off is ridiculous; why not allot all workers a number of days as holiday and let them take them as they will? Then, the load spread, we can all travel in comfort and the vagaries of the weather will not wreak disaster on our holidays.

L. A. Lore

After New York, Los Angeles is the place for collectors. Los Angeles, home of supermarket-sized pet stores and the nearby 'Roman' villa of the Getty Collection, left me reeling.

Los Angeles is not a town, not a city and not really a district—it is a world complete in itself, a world of near total fantasy. The people who live here are like actors in a play as they walk the streets, sit in the restaurants and go about their work, seemingly conscious of an unseen audience who watch—or perhaps they just act for each other. The citizens of Los Angeles dress for their roles as well and take some care in their choice of clothes, whether they buy them in the expensive shops of Rodeo Drive (there is one boutique in that street where you have to make an appointment just to gain entrance) or in the second-hand stores of Melrose Avenue, where young people crowd on a Sunday—literally crowd—to search through racks of second-hand clothes. These have become so popular in Los Angeles that manufacturers are now reproducing them, for the supply of the truly second-hand comes nowhere near to meeting the demand.

Los Angeles is a place of extremes: the marina at Marina del Rey is the largest in the world—most of the boats in it seldom put to sea. The largest street, Figueroa Street, stretches for 26 miles. Everything in Los Angeles is done to excess. The health clubs are wall to wall, and the pet-supply shops are as supermarkets would be in any other town. Indeed, 60 million people in America own cats, and while there are no figures for the feline population of Los Angeles, you can be sure that it is far and away above the average. I found one large store that sells only light bulbs—I had no idea that there were so many different kinds. Another shop I visited specialised in full-size dinosaurs—skeletons, I hasten to add, for it would not have surprised me one little bit to find them advertised as pets in the local paper. The car is supreme in Los Angeles, and one Toyota dealer alone—he has the name of Longo—sells 19 000 of these cars in a year. Like most cities Los Angeles has its ethnic quarters: but while it is not unusual to find a Chinatown or even a Tokyo Town in Los Angeles, you will also find a Korean Town, a Little Saigon and even a Little India.

It is an extraordinary place and most extraordinary of all is not Charlie Chaplin's old studios on La Brea near Sunset, nor the great production companies' studios, nor the Chinese Theatre (which is really a cinema), nor Disneyland. No, by far the strangest place to visit in the whole of Los Angeles is the Getty Museum. This museum perched in a valley overlooking the sea at Malibu is, so I'm told, the exact replica of a Roman villa formerly at Herculaneum—the Villa dei Papyri—built in California. There is nothing particularly odd about this, except that this vastly expensive structure filled with culture is cheek by jowl with a mass of other villas built in the styles of the twentieth century—built for the pleasure of people who wished to live near the seaside. You can, in reality, only visit the museum by car—there are a whole posse of security men who direct vehicles up and down the narrow drive. The first question they ask is whether you have booked your parking space. Without such a booking, unless you are driven, you will be turned away. The garage is truly impressive, a great cavern underneath the whole undertaking. It is not the least bit Roman—pure functional twentieth-century America. Up a fire stair and, blow me, there you are back in Herculaneum. Then there is the bookshop and rather tacky restaurant with its machines and plastic tables that fill a garden designed for Roman ladies to take their pleasure in. Up another fire stair is a different world again. You could be walking through the galleries of the Wallace Collection what with the Louis XVI furniture and even a Goya. It really is a place of the most remarkable contrasts—even for California, this is pushing it a bit.

Then there are the antiquities, including both wonderful sculpture and pieces that give grounds for wondering whether they were worth the freight to get them there. All this is housed in a series of rooms of which even the larger ones are small, while the smaller rooms are so small that entrance is forbidden. Upstairs is French furniture and superb-quality china, and paintings that span the history of art—or at least span its easier periods. Outstanding among them is Van Gogh's *Blue Irises*. As a private collection, this place is wonderful, but as a museum, presumptuous. Why for goodness sake do the directors of great museums the world over shudder at the very name of the Getty—if these people keep at it for a hundred years there still will be no comparison with their collections. The guidebook, *Masterpieces in the Getty Collection*, proudly announces that many of the best things in the collection have been acquired since Mr Getty's death. There is no feeling among the pieces that they were collected with an unerring eye for quality. Nor is there the quirkiness that makes a collector's accumulation so interesting. This museum has money to buy what it will, but what it needs it cannot buy—for Mr Getty is dead.

If the boot fits

On the trail of the perfect fit I went to Los Angeles, land of the cowboy boot, where I encountered ostrich, kangaroo and ruby-encrusted versions—and returned with sore feet.

The cowboy boot started in Texas as civilisation came to that part of America and cars took over from horses. The boot remained, and so

Texans learned to drive cars in high-heeled boots. But what was convenient in the stirrup proved awkward on the pedal of an automobile. As the state became richer, the boots became fancier. Now, in Texas, when you are introduced they will only look at your hat and your boots: your social status will be judged by these two accoutrements. In time the cowboys moved to Hollywood—the ones with the guns and horses that is—and they, of course, took their boots with them.

Now in Los Angeles there is barely a street that does not boast a shop selling cowboy boots. These shops, unlike normal shoe shops, do not have a range of footwear. If you sell cowboy boots you sell only cowboy boots; for the retailer of these exotic items there is no question of wearing anything else. Ready-made boots cost from $500, handmade from $1500, and full alligator boots from $8000. Alligator boots are inconvenient things to own, for if you travel you will spend a good deal of your time explaining to customs officers just why you are wearing a large chunk of CITES-listed reptile (CITES is the convention for international trading in endangered species). You can argue that you did not kill it, and you can argue that it has been dead for a hundred years—it will do no more than prolong the discussion when you have just got off a long flight. Avoid boots made of endangered species like the plague. So when offered exotic boots by a salesperson, say no, and ask for fancy instead. The range is extraordinary—from boots with oil-drilling rigs up their sides (your own if you have oil wells, someone else's if you don't) to cactus and barbed-wire designs. These boots are likely to be made of calf skin inlaid with kangaroo hide. If you want fancy toes, ostrich is the hide to choose—your boots will then have small pimples all over them. Ostrich skin does not, however, come cheaply—a pair of breeding ostriches can cost £25 000.

It is obvious as you visit these shops and see the rows and rows of boots, all in different colours, materials and styles, that before long these remarkable objects will be collected. Indeed, they are already being collected: there is a thriving market in second-hand boots. Aficionados of the Western boot will tell you that it is a great mistake to buy a new pair, far better to get a pair that has already been worn in: 15 per cent of handmade boots are returned to the makers with the words, 'These do not fit'. The makers will tell you that this is because the people who return them are unused to wearing cowboy boots, which are made for riding, not walking. Be that as it may, a good second-hand pair is probably a better bet anyway; boots are made to outlast people, and you can sometimes go through a dozen new soles with little sign of wear to the boot itself. The problem, of course, is that second-hand boots fetch higher prices than brand new ones—even if they have been custom-made to fit you.

One smart pair I came across was made of cream leather inlaid with rhinestones. The salesperson told me that they had been used in the movies in the 1950s; he was unsure by whom, but a star no less. I could have them for $5000.

'But they don't fit me.' (I have the oddest feet, nearly as wide as they are long.)

'I thought that you were a collector.'

'So I am.'

'Well these are a collectors' item.'

'Well who did they belong to?' By way of answer he reduced the price to $3500.

A remarkable pair called The El Ray The III boots took three months to make. Of black alligator (not for travellers), inlaid with 24-carat gold and encrusted with 384 diamonds and rubies, they were made in 1951 and cost $5000. They have twice been stolen and are now said to be worth over $30 000. When exhibited they come with their own armed guard. These boots are, I suppose, the top end of the range. But you can still put together, without, it seems, too much trouble, a remarkable collection of boots carrying the symbols of the States, other people's favourite horses, swooping eagles or just plain initials. For that matter you can pass idle hours tramping round the boot stores of LA looking for a pair of boots that, soft with use, fit your feet exactly and, as I did, find only that your feet get so sore you can barely walk on them. I went back to my hotel for a long bath. However, the next day, inspired by Tyler Beard's great book *The Cowboy Boot* and his words 'cowboy boots give you an attitude—they can be euphoric', I was out again searching for those boots that will perfectly fit my feet. I am afraid I still am.

Aloha L.A.

Denim has faded and ties have slipped, but Los Angeles' second-hand clothes scene can still offer a nice line in classic Hawaiian shirts. I tried some for size.

The vintage clothes industry in Los Angeles has undergone certain changes in the past year: the home-grown fad for torn jeans and denim jackets has abated—anyway, the Japanese have sucked the market dry of rare early denim clothes—and the fashion for flashy shirts and ties is over.

Many of the small businesses dealing in these goods have closed, while others have moved away. On Melrose Avenue, Time and Time Again—a shop that once boasted the most splendid selection of ties—now deals almost exclusively in second-hand wedding dresses (there are plenty of these in LA).

Only the large stores around Melrose—American Rag, Yellowstone and Wasteland—now survive, but there is little chance of finding a minor masterpiece. Head instead straight for 901 South Broadway, in the heart of the garment district. You may, upon arrival, wonder why I recommend this address, for the building seems to be unlet and ready for demolition. But on the mezzanine floor you will find the Sally Ball Art Studio and Vintage Textile Library. This vast space is filled with racks of textiles and bundles of what, at first glance, seem to be old rags.

On the same large scale as her establishment, Sally is the friendliest of people, and she has a vast knowledge of twentieth-century textiles. It was Hawaiian shirts that I sought when I visited her studio. She swayed between the rows of textiles, issuing orders to her staff, and soon there was a pile of shirts lying on the table in front of me.

The most sought-after Hawaiian shirts came into production in 1924 when the DuPont company began manufacturing rayon, an ideal fabric for printing. For years, they were immensely popular and sold in dozens of patterns and colours. Dating them is made easier by the fact that the DuPont factory burned down in the early 1950s—the manufacture of rayon was decreed to be dangerous and ceased.

The finest of these Hawaiian shirts have a single image on the back; they now fetch thousands of dollars. Next in importance are those with patterned borders and, finally, those with an all-over pattern. Sally's collection is a delight, but only half as delightful as it is to sit and talk to her as she tosses in the names of Hawaiian-shirt-sporting celebrities from the past.

It was Hollywood that made Hawaiian shirts famous: Bing Crosby wore them; Paulette Goddard and Ida Lupino posed in them; Betty Grable wore a Hawaiian swimsuit; Elvis sang in a Hawaiian shirt; and Montgomery Clift died in one at the end of *From Here to Eternity*. As I listened to Sally, I remembered the first time I visited Hawaii, in 1958. Little did I realise as I sat in the foyer of the Royal Hawaiian Hotel, sipping an exotic concoction, that the passing tourists were wearing what would decades later become millions of dollars' worth of Hawaiian shirts.

Invitations to die for

I regret being a VIP in LA, where the parties can seriously damage your health.

Once, at a barbecue in Australia where the sand mingled with the food, and the beer had run out, I met a Greek.

'There's another party going on not far from here. Let's go on there,' said a sweaty-shirted hero of the Australian beaches.

The Greek replied: 'Even if it's ten times more enjoyable than this one, I still do not want to go.'

Standing in a vibrating queue for a party given by a British gin manufacturer in a Los Angeles film studio, I knew just how that Greek felt. For a start, my invitation had 'This invitation does not guarantee admittance' printed on it. Luckily—or unluckily, as it turned out—I was a VIP, plucked from the queue by a PR lady and inserted in a rugger scrum. In time, insulted by at least three security men who could not understand my English, I made it past the barrier. (Why people promoting products allow security men to insult their guests—whose goodwill, presumably, they are trying to obtain—I shall never know.) Once inside, I found the food had run out, but there was plenty of gin and crowds of people, most of them looking slightly down-at-heel. The best dressed guests were the transvestites. The party was to promote a handful of British designers—among them Liza Bruce, who had the good sense to miss the whole affair.

At the hub of this seething mass of humanity was an altar where barmen distributed gin. Around it were the stalls of the various companies involved; behind, a giant set of bookshelves some 50 feet high. On each shelf a buxom model danced in a lackadaisical manner. I was unimpressed by their gyrations, but it came to me, in a blinding flash, that big girls really can wear Liza Bruce's bathing suits. As Bruce is a designer well known for her clean-cut, slim look, this came as a surprise. In possession of a new fact about a brilliant designer, I decided to leave. Getting out of this party, however, was harder than getting in—there were queues everywhere for everything.

Liza Bruce's new shop in Los Angeles is stunning. It has been decorated by Nicholas Alvis Vega, Bruce's husband. Simple as can be, it is painted in short horizontal stripes of colour: deep reds, aubergine, mauve, purple and dark blues. The furnishings—tall skeletal tables, squat brass chinoiserie chairs—are also designed by Nicholas Alvis Vega; the clothes form such an important part of the decor that it seems a shame to take them from the racks.

Across the road is the shop of Jenny Armit, another British designer, who stocks furniture by Mark Brazier-Jones and hand-painted fabrics by Celia Birtwell, along with the work of a dozen or so other top designers. There is something wonderfully cool and different about this shop. In a street where everything second-hand is considered marvellous, and where the most ridiculous old tat is sold for serious prices, Jenny Armit's shop is a delight.

But it is, I suppose, its obsession with nostalgia that makes LA such an extraordinary city. Where else would you find a Museum of Death? This is to be found on Hollywood Boulevard, in a 1920s drugstore. The contents are generally pretty awful; a letter from Son of Sam, describing how to kill a fat lady while enjoying a meatball sandwich, is downright creepy. Ripley's Believe It or Not Museum, also in Hollywood, is not much better—you come out of that one with hair, teeth, nails and toes curling like mad. Nor is the Museum of the Weird a place to go, if it's a good night's sleep that you require.

Stranger than all of these, however, are the four-storey-high hoardings that enclose areas in the middle of palm-lined avenues. 'What are those?' I asked my taxi driver.

'They are working on oil wells,' he replied.

Coming next December: the Vatican

In search of the offbeat in Los Angeles, I find the Vatican, albeit in miniature, is relocating round the corner from a second-hand clothes store for the rich and famous.

Los Angeles is a strange place. Driving down La Brea in a search of things curious, I came across a gallery which advertised the following artists: Monet, Wiggins, Manet, Gauguin, Geofferies, Renoir, Savage, Matisse and Picasso. I do not know who Wiggins, Geofferies and Savage are—or were—but despite their grand promotion business appears to have been bad. The gallery had closed. I then caught wind of a museum dedicated to the banana, sadly also closed.

Undaunted I soon came across the Museum of Miniatures. Its entrance did not inspire high hopes, so imagine my surprise when within its first gallery I came face to face with the Doge's Palace, reduced to a mere 10 feet by 5 feet. Its back was open, and inside, the rooms had been reproduced, as far as I could tell, perfectly. Each piece of furniture is in place, each painted ceiling true to life. Then there was Hampton Court, Versailles and the White House, each facade exact, open at the back for visitors to see into every room. The museum also contains tiny motor cars, boats, aeroplanes and furniture—rooms of it. There are shops stocked with goods, panoramas of the Wild West and nineteenth-century England, Dixie mansions and European castles. The most extraordinary exhibit of all, however, is a village, built among the branches of a giant tree. As I left, I noticed a poster which shouted 'Coming next December: the Vatican'.

My exploration then took me to Lily's, a large second-hand clothes store. Lily's is run by Rita, who stocks 5000 items of *haute couture*, nearly 100 000 other dresses and 400 000 accessories. To test the scope of her renowned collection I asked if she had any dresses by Rudi Gernreich. 'Oh, about 500,' Rita replied. 'We deal in dresses from the 1800s to the 1970s,' she explained. As others lay down wine, so Rita is laying down fashions of the 1980s and 1990s, but they are not yet for sale. Naively, I suggested that she must spend a great deal of time in Europe, searching out dresses. Not a bit of it. Apparently, 90 per cent of all European *haute couture* goes to America including a large number of dresses by Europe's most interesting new designers. Who wears these dresses? 'The rich and famous,' says Rita. Any interesting dress worn at the Oscars ceremony usually comes from Lily's.

That evening I met a baby-faced lady in her early eighties. She told me she had been married to a famous trumpet player, had been the mistress of a well-known disc jockey and had spent the night with a significant member of our royal family. How many of her dresses, I wondered, had found their way to Lily's? And how many palaces in the Museum of Miniatures had she been invited to?

LA day-dreamer

Going into a pleasant reverie about one of my favourite cities, I constructed this perfect day in LA, complete with Gaudiesque towers, a bumper breakfast and Gene Autry.

I was in no hurry to visit Los Angeles for the first time. I had heard only evil reports of the place: the smog; the riots; the traffic; and the people—well, the ubiquitous 'they' told me that the people were truly awful. They don't drink, don't smoke and even disapprove of those who wear perfume. They barely eat (just lettuce and carrots), they are obsessed with exercise (they jog all the time) and worst of all they go to bed early. How different I found the place. To me it was all a little like the south of France except the traffic is handled better. I love the weather, I love looking at the people and I love the place. And I keep going back and back.

On my last visit I set out to construct the perfect day. The best days begin with breakfast—and I don't mean coffee and a croissant in a hotel room. In downtown LA there is a place that understands what it should be like: The Pantry. It serves breakfast 24 hours a day, seven days a week—and so it should. The Pantry stands preserved among giant glass towers—a relic of the 1930s, with its swing doors with flywire, its brown interior with formica tables and green linoleum. The waiters show no hesitation—a brief good morning and a brief pause for your order. My waiter ordered for me, for my dithering could have wasted his time. Eggs scrambled, two or four? 'Two,' say I. Bacon crisp, hash brown potatoes? I nodded. Hot cakes—a stack? Well, why not—in any case he was no longer there to argue with. 'Coffee?' a voice asked, and my cup was filled. The Pantry is situated somewhere between the police department and the Town Hall. Tourists don't go there. Why should they? The place is the haunt of off-duty police officers and the on-duty mayor who is collecting the votes of the police officers and artisans who eat their breakfast there. A remnant from the age of Rockwell—patronised by Norman Rockwell's people.

Half an hour from downtown LA is Watts, famous for its riots when it should be famous for its towers. The towers are no corporate or civic undertaking, rather the work of Simon Rodia, known as Sam, and built on some open land. They are Gaudiesque structures built of broken crockery and other odds and ends, and seem at first the work of a demented magpie. Then as I wandered among them I realised that these strange buildings are but a maquette for a masterpiece—and the man who built them, who all thought to be mad, a genius. Sam took 33 years to complete this work, and then he just walked away, leaving the authorities with the problem of what to do with the towers. Happily they decided to keep them—in an ideal world they would be rebuilt 300 feet high in the centre of a city.

For lunch, I went to Rodeo Drive, the most chic street in town—actually just off Rodeo Drive to The Ivy. I sat in its garden and watched the passing cars. The other customers watched me. The Ivy's garden is as like an English cottage garden as one in Somerset. It has no ivy, but every other plant, from hollyhock to delphinium, and all in flower. A garden complete with hay fever. I sneezed and sneezed and the diners watched in sheer horror—germs everywhere. The true charm of LA lies in the fact that it is one of the world's most sophisticated cities, yet still totally provincial—its streets tree-lined, its housing suburban, all as peaceful as can be. Yet the city has a remarkable record for violence—the place is an illusion.

Among America's other great illusions is the cowboy. Gene Autry, a singing cowboy, made a great deal of money out of this illusion, though his greatest hit was 'Rudolf the Red-Nosed Reindeer'. His collection of art and artefacts from the Wild (and Hollywood) West is in the Gene Autry Heritage Museum. Since a child I have loved Westerns. What bliss—I would spend my afternoon there among Annie Oakley's gilded pistol, the Lone Ranger's spurs, not to mention his mask and red scarf, the guns and pistols of Teddy Roosevelt and the official Colt firearms collection. To spend time in this museum and to wander among the stuff of fact and fiction is to begin to understand America.

Where to dine? Well, first I repaired to the bar of the Peninsular Hotel for a dry martini. 'Straight up?' asked the bartender. He is a man who understands Martinis. I asked him where I should go to eat.

'A new place, Ciao Bella on Melrose.'

'Wonderful, can I use your telephone to make a reservation?'

'I am sorry sir, but we lost the telephone at lunchtime—a man made off with it,' he said, pointing at the empty portable phone stand.

Ciao Bella is an Italian restaurant—pizzas and fun. The chef, from Milan, cooks Italian food the way Americans like it, and the Italian proprietor Mario Cesario is from just across Melrose Avenue where he runs Formula Uno, a second-hand clothing store of considerable distinction. The food is good, the customers are beautiful and Mario a generous and entertaining host. 'I am worked off my feet, I cannot keep up,' he states. When a place is fashionable in LA it is really fashionable. He took from his pocket a bundle of business cards printed with the names and addresses of women, each one annotated in Mario's own hand. 'Look at this, and I have only been open three weeks. How can I make time to see all these girls?' Such are the problems that beset restaurateurs in Los Angeles.

The great escapism

Suffering from an overdose of reality, I broke loose in Los Angeles and immersed myself (almost literally) in the vivid fantasies of Universal Studios' back lot.

During 1992 it was almost impossible to pick up a newspaper and find good news in it, while to switch on the television or the wireless was to be told only tales of gloom, whether the subject was the monarchy, the church or the state of our nation. Shops seemed almost perpetually in a state of sale time; the tourists kept a tight grip on their purses; the auction rooms announced triumphs, but they had a hollow ring to them; antique dealers failed; and even the great dress houses were feeling the pinch. How on earth could one get away from it all? Well, I hit upon the solution while visiting Los Angeles, a city where reality has very largely become make-believe. I spent the day at Universal Studios—a place where reality has never existed, where make-believe is more believable than any reality you may come across and, I may say, where there is very little to be depressed about when it has just made the runaway bestseller *Jurassic Park.*

I set out after a hearty breakfast. For those who have never visited the worlds of make-believe that emanate from California, take my tip and eat beforehand lest hunger persuades you to indulge in a bite to eat while there; the results of such a meal are terribly real. I arrived at 7.30 am, and already the park (which had opened at 7 am) was busy. I followed the crowd through the theme park, which is as good or bad as most theme parks, and I suppose if you are interested in how to perform a gunfight on the hour every hour, or how to fall from a rooftop apparently shot (covered in red paint), then you will enjoy this place. Conan the Destroyer calls up dragons to slay; the characters from *Miami Vice* go through a nerve-chilling routine of their most exciting stunts; and *Star Trek* is a masterpiece of modern technology only bettered by *Back to The Future* 'the ride'—its advertisement warns you to 'prepare to scream through the future', and in part it is right for almost everyone who goes on this ride screams most of the time.

There is little escapism in this park, however, with its heaving, squealing and screaming mass of humanity. Move quickly on and descend by the giant escalator several hundred feet (an experience that makes the best that London Transport and its Underground system have to offer seem tame by comparison) to Universal's actual studios, to a world of magic that has given us *The Hunchback of Notre Dame*—and Paris is still there; *Spartacus*—Rome is still there; and *The Sting*—New York is still there. Board a tram and tour this world where the unbelievable happens and leaves you untouched to head for the next event. The tour of Universal's back lot is really something; it has, apart from everything else, the most incredible collection of buildings, and a textbook of nineteenth-century architectural styles beautifully built in wood, chicken wire and plaster—accurate in every detail. The guide, a personable young lady with a considerable sense of humour, announced that we were travelling up New York Street—and indeed, it looked for all the world just like parts of New York where the nineteenth century has survived. She added, 'Actually it can become a street in any of the world's cities'. I was about to ask how, but she anticipated me. 'We change the signs, the colours and a few of the shapes—the street however stays the same, it just *seems* different.'

Top hats and tales

The Wild West has fascinated me since boyhood. Always a cowboy fan I take a trip down the Wild West's memory lane in Santa Fe, before setting off on the trail of the most handsome cowboy hat.

The notice on the wall of the adobe building came as no surprise to me. It told the story of how Billy the Kid had been incarcerated there—how he had escaped and finally how he was treacherously shot by Pat Garrett, a man he believed to be his friend. The building was in Santa Fe, New Mexico, a city where the governor's palace was built at the time the Pilgrim Fathers landed on America's east coast, a town that boasts the oldest street in the United States. I was truly in the Wild West, now tamed and manicured to popular taste.

As a man who since boyhood has loved everything to do with cowboys, a visit to Santa Fe is my idea of complete bliss. The horses are long gone from the streets but their equipment is still sold in Santa Fe's shops. Indians sit in the shade of the arcaded streets and sell their silver and turquoise jewellery. The cafés serve breakfasts of massive omelettes smothered in chilli peppers. Chillies play a large part in the culture of Santa Fe. Wherever there is a beam, necklaces of red peppers hang from it. The scent of red chilli is on every breeze that cools the town.

All of this I suppose is totally predictable and as far as I am concerned completely perfect. My surprise came as I stepped away from the bronze plaque that told the tale of Billy the Kid and I looked into the window of the shop next door. It was filled with Father Christmases. I could not resist going inside. The store was long and narrow, and the shelves that lined it piled high with Father Christmases: Father Christmas with a lariat and six guns, Father Christmas as an Indian chief and Father Christmas riding a Bucking Bronco. There was in that shop no aspect of life in the Wild West that Father Christmas was not participating in; what is more, where he was neither cowboy nor Indian, the poor man was in his normal role, with and without his reindeer. He came in all shapes and sizes from an inch or two to twice life-size, and what is more he came in all varieties of materials from gingerbread to plastic, and from chocolate to pressed paper, tin or wood. There were white Father Christmases and black Father Christmases; in fact, there was a Father Christmas to cater for every taste.

Out in the streets of Santa Fe again, I was once more in the world of fancy jeans and leather jackets with exaggerated fringes. I have long since given up my search for cowboy boots. I have corns and I cannot take the pain. But cowboy hats, that is another matter. I am a complete sucker for an eccentric hat. I seldom wear the things but they make a fine frieze around my bathrooms. For the seeker of hats Santa Fe is just the place. In my search I disregarded all further shops selling Father Christmas—and I may say there were more than enough of them. I then disregarded all commercial hat shops. I was after a hat of character. My search was not easy. I bought a peasant hat for $3 and wore it for a morning.

The problem in Santa Fe is not that it is hard to find a shop that sells a cowboy hat, but rather that every shop sells them. In time I found my way to an establishment called Back to the Ranch. It dealt in second-hand cowboy hats. To be fair it sold boots as well, but I explained to the lady who seemed to be in charge why I don't wear cowboy boots. She, a third-generation cobbler, was tolerant but puzzled and showed me her second-hand hats. Tall ones, short ones, shiny ones and battered ones. She sold hats of personality but she did not have one to suit me. This lady explained to me that in Texas a cowboy employed on a ranch would wear a hat battered to bits—in fact, the more battered the better. The owner of the ranch's hat must be pristine and fancy. As each hat was rejected, I seemed harder to please. 'Do you know Milton Johnson?' she asked. 'You'll find him at the Montecristi hat works'. And indeed I did. In his shop Milton had hats in a hundred shapes. The options—the Tom Mix, a hat that when I tried it on it covered my entire head, the Tear Drop, the Plantation and the Gambler, not to mention the Whistle, the Trail-blazer, the Gentleman Jim and the Troublemaker, complete with Rattlesnake band that rattles when you shake your head. Milton has hats in many qualities and prices that range from $100 to $10 000. Milton doesn't just sell hats to customers (and he sells thousands a year), he sells hats that suit and fit his customers. Milton measures and applies steam to the raw shape and it becomes a hat. He fits, presses and twists and it becomes your hat. Milton showed me an Extra Fino Select. I asked the price. '$7000,' I was informed. 'This one is $12 000 dollars. Look at the slight colouring of certain straws, see how they swirl among the pattern, and feel the smoothness of the weave—no joins—its tightness.' I expected to be shocked by this figure but, as Milton explained the points of quality to this hat, it seemed the most natural thing in the world that he should ask such a price.

Praising Arizona

I spent happy days being misdirected by the locals in Tucson, Arizona.

In Tucson the cacti grow higher than the houses or so it seems. The giant cacti, however, are not the only aspect of Tucson that is noteworthy, for the city is also home to the world's largest aeroplane graveyard.

There is no centre to Tucson; even the business district is not really a centre, but more a collection of tall buildings among underpasses and flyovers. Despite these disadvantages it is an attractive place, where desert and commerce meet in the friendliest of manners. As for passing the time there, the problem is easily solved as it takes—owing to the complexity of the traffic system—at least four times as long to find the simplest destination as one might reasonably expect. Five thousand aeroplanes all parked together should not have passed unnoticed, but in Tucson this is not the case. 'Aeroplane graveyard? Never heard of it' or 'Yes, I know just where that is' were the responses that I received when I enquired after this remarkable place. Three times I was sent to the airport, on each occasion by a different route. 'No. It's not the airport that I want, but the aeroplane graveyard.' The number of 'Don't knows' grew, but still a small handful of locals knew exactly where it was—they sent me hotfoot to the Aviation Museum, which I suppose could be mistaken for the aeroplane graveyard.

The Pima Air and Space Museum, to give it its correct title, is a splendid place. One of its many delights is that it flies a different exotic aeroplane over Tucson each day. It also arranges guided tours of a missile complex, including the silo; better still, it has guided tours of the aeroplane graveyard. As it had taken me most of the day to find the museum, however, I was too late for these tours.

Surely, I thought, 5000 aeroplanes parked together must be out of town, in the desert. How wrong could I be. Just outside the museum, as I mounted a flyover, I spotted the tail fins of a multitude of aeroplanes, and it was not the airport. Parked in serried ranks, civil and military, dating from the early 1950s to the present day, they make an impressive sight, well worth a day's driving around Tucson to find.

A place of serenity, in a town that has a pace so slow it has almost stopped, is Paul Shepard's shop at 3026 E. Broadway. Shepard sells ethnography, among which is a range of Navajo weavings. An interesting shop run by an interesting man, it has the great advantage of being situated above a café that makes the best cappuccino in town.

If you can miss 5000 aeroplanes, I suppose you can miss anything—certainly this was the case with the gentleman who passed for a concierge at my hotel. My suspicions should have been alerted by his efforts to book me into a restaurant he recommended for lunch—when I arrived, thirsty, hot and ready to eat, it was closed, as it always was at lunchtime.

'Where does the gem show take place?' I asked him.

'Never heard of it,' he replied. Sixteen thousand dealers have stands at this show and thousands more visit it over a three-week period. Since he was in the hotel business, you would imagine that he might just have noticed it.

The Gem and Mineral Show was terrific; it takes place in February at over 40 locations, not including fringe dealers. There is nothing curious or unusual that you cannot buy. Fossils come in 50-gallon oil drums, minerals by the crateful, cabochon emeralds hang by the row and diamonds are in a heavily guarded security area. As for Venetian beads, this show is the mecca for collectors.

On Sunday, I asked the concierge at my hotel the way to church. After a considerable amount of religious banter, he directed me—to a church of the wrong denomination.

Tourist syndrome

Tombstone was a disappointment but I was glad that I went there.

Enthusiasts of Wild West films will be disappointed with at least one aspect of Tombstone. Set in the wildest part of Arizona, only a hard gallop from the Mexican border, this town has become an icon of Hollywood Westerns. So often admirers of this genre have watched the population trudge uphill behind a horse-drawn hearse to bury the victim of a gunfight. How surprising to find that in fact one trudges downhill from the town to the famous graveyard of Boot Hill. It's logical, really: why pull a dead man uphill when you can more easily let his corpse freewheel downhill?

Tombstone today is a poor excuse for a Disneyland: a historic facade hiding a cheapjack souvenir reality. But then, things were never as they seemed in Tombstone. The gunfight at the OK Corral, that moment celebrated in Western history, was a one-sided affair, for the Clantons and their supporters were unarmed when Doc Holliday and the Earps riddled them with bullets; the nearest gun was on a nearby horse's saddle. The whole episode—no more than a gangland massacre—took place outside the studio of C.S. Fly, the photographer who recorded so many scenes from the Wild West. Sadly for Fly, technology was not up to photographing gunfights, and he could hardly ask the participants to pose for pictures. As always in gang wars the murder was not one-sided: Virgil Earp was shot from the second-storey window of the Bucket of Blood saloon, soon renamed the Old Café and now the Longhorn Restaurant.

Across the street is Big Nose Kate's saloon. Here they have caught the essence of the past, for today's period-costumed waitresses seem as tired and ugly as those of the 1880s, when Kate served whisky and more besides to Doc Holliday. Gift shops with gifts you would be pushed to say thank you for, cafés, restaurants and bars, each more scruffy than the last. A run-down funfair, the place is a cruel joke. Indeed, the name 'Tombstone' *was* a joke. The prospector who founded the place used to leave the safety of a nearby fort to chance his luck with the hostile Indians in search of gold.

'What are you looking for?' the soldiers who guarded the fort asked him.

'Stones,' the prospector replied.

'The only stone you'll find will be your headstone,' the soldiers retorted.

When he found not gold but silver, he named the town that sprang up Tombstone; the joke was on the military.

The land around Tombstone is as wild as the Indians who lived there; it's not hard to imagine Geronimo creeping up on you. The scrub is dry, the rivers are mostly dry, and the air is dry; deep gullies and high ridges run across the desert like oversized furrows in a ploughed field. The scrub is old and thorny, and the landscape various shades of brown with trimmings of black, dressed for a funeral; and here the Indians died, not defeated in battle but diseased and starved into submission. In the distance all around the town are mountains rising from the high plains, their surfaces cut into jagged crags. Beside the single road is found the occasional half-hearted attempt at agriculture—a land of milk and honey this place is not. No, this is a landscape that, had Dante seen it, would surely have found pride of place in his *Inferno*. The miles and miles of desolation are relieved only by open-cast mining that kills beyond redemption the wild beauty of the place, rendering the wilderness so tame and thoughtless that there is no point to it at all.

Geronimo was right: these men who came from the east meant no good to his land or his people. What a place this could have been were it not for pylons, mining and random structures built seemingly without purpose.

On the Santa Fe trail

Those addicted to boot fairs who fall prey to temptation should dodge the city of Santa Fe at all costs.

In the last five years the population of Santa Fe has tripled. A visitor today, however, would be unaware of this. The low adobe buildings still hide in folds of the landscape, and many more of them remain concealed by the rugged beauty of New Mexico's high plains. The mountains still rise from behind the cathedral at the end of Santa Fe's main street; the mesa, still visible from the town square, stretches out beyond its other end. In August the weather is hot but not oppressive; at 7000 feet above sea level the evenings are never stuffy. In the winter people come to Santa Fe to ski. The weather—bright sunshine, seldom unbearably cold—makes it for once easy to see why people settled in this place.

To imagine those settlers arriving down the old Santa Fe trail . . . the delight that mountain men must have felt as they reached the tail of the Rocky Mountains and looked down on the thriving metropolis of Santa Fe, after a long, lonely year of trapping for fur in the mountains. For Santa Fe was in those long-off days a metropolis; the town boasts the oldest street in the United States. Santa Fe is, by the standards of North America, an old place, and it still feels that way;

stuffed with history, regardless of the efforts of Banana Republic, Gap and numerous other high-street traders who try to immerse the town in a wave of shopping pollution.

This August the mountain men and women came to town again, and they had a meeting, much as they might have done 200 years ago. In the gardens of the old governor's palace they set up stalls selling the produce of their hands and the artefacts of their history. For me it was a great delight, as I have always been much taken with bowie knives and buffalo guns, neither of them practical objects to collect these days. The mountain men and women, indeed, were worth collecting themselves; dressed for the part that they played—each accoutrement, hat, boot, belt and buckle carefully researched for authenticity—these were no ordinary high-street people. Abnormally tall or thin, short or fat, they are a race apart. One evening they roasted a buffalo, played mountain music and danced the night away. Myself, I sat at the opera, set in hills beyond Santa Fe, and watched one of the best productions of *Rigoletto* I have seen in years. The air was as soft as the velvet night; the new moon seemed to light the world.

Santa Fe is a junk-shop junkie's paradise. There are dozens of them—junk shops and junkies—from those that buy and sell the most expensive junk to those whose life revolves around a bargain: some old table, second-hand at best, with a leg missing for a dollar or two.

The definitive market is the Indian market that takes place a month or so after the Spanish market, remarkable in itself. Halfway through August the centre of Santa Fe becomes a hive of activity—it is always active but the level of activity reached by the Indian market is truly amazing. Over a thousand stalls are erected, selling handmade goods, basketry, beadwork, carvings, dolls, drums, flutes, gourds, jewellery, masks, moccasins, pottery, paintings and drawings. The Indian nations truly meet at Santa Fe: Comanche, Zuni, Hopi, Navajo, Apache, Tlingit, Chippewa, Haida, Arapaho, Sioux and Paiute; and they come with the traditional and innovative goods that they make. More remarkable by far than these objects, however, are the different faces of all these tribes; images from a thousand Westerns tumbled through my mind as I walked among the stalls with their colourfully dressed proprietors. Collectors wake before dawn and—literally on occasion—fight for the work of the best known artists. The market lasts for two days and then the stalls vanish, along with the Indians. The municipal cleaners set to work tidying up the town.

Tourists fill the gaps left by the departing tribes, and life in Santa Fe goes on much as it always has.

Stake and chips

Even the architecture in Las Vegas is a huge gamble. I found my taste for kitsch overindulged by theme park hotels and restaurants. Las Vegas is a place apart, and there is nowhere like it in the rest of the world.

The road from Los Angeles to Las Vegas climbs sharply through the mountains that border the city up to a high plain which it crosses on its way. From there it stretches across the desert with its sagebrush and cacti, surrounded by mountains that have the look of sand heaps, through small townships with such romantic names as Calico, Searchlight, Shoehorn and Needles—often the hottest place in the United States.

After about five hours' driving, the road comes to the Nevada border and the landscape changes from a desert with shacks and abandoned vehicles to a desert with multistorey buildings and car parks. These buildings are but a foretaste of Las Vegas—extraordinary in their way but only an hors-d'oeuvre for the full-blooded meal that is but 28 miles further on.

In fact, Las Vegas must be the most extraordinary place on earth—a complex road system with giant hotels dotted in its midst. For the rest, it is all parking lots and caravans. Each of the hotels is a mini-Disneyland. The Luxor, for example—not, I write with feeling, a name derived from a shortening of the word 'luxury', rather named after the place in Egypt—is built in the form of a pyramid and entered through equally large sphinxes, with an obelisk for its signpost and an Egyptian theme to its decor. Nearby is The Excalibur, with a medieval theme and an Italian restaurant called, I suppose almost inevitably, The Lance a Lotta Pasta. That, I'm afraid, was only the beginning. I also found King Arthur's Restaurant with two advertised shows 'knightly'.

These horrors carry on one after another: The Mirage, with its white tigers kept in a white cage, with white rocks, white palm trees and a jungle in the foyer—actually a mass of coloured plastic flowers;

Treasure Island situated where else but Buccaneer Boulevard; Aladdin that looks just like a vast Indian restaurant; and The Barbary, an unimpressive building by day, and by night covered in coloured lights to make it look like a paddle-steamer going full steam ahead, making, I suppose for the Mississippi. Anchored firmly in Las Vegas, a fine example of pure Las Vegas taste, nearby Hannah's Hotel is built to look like the steamer by day which The Barbary impersonates by night. The only hotel that pretends to be an architectural thought is the MGM: a vast green and black geometric pile clad in shiny glass—you enter the MGM through the mouth of a giant lion.

The hotel complexes of Las Vegas are pure unashamed vulgarity. Subtlety does not exist in Las Vegas—not even by accident has anything beautiful been built there. It makes Euro Disney seem the height of sophistication, and so it is in comparison with the tawdry show put on in the Nevada desert. The desert, incidentally, is the best thing about the place; you look out of your bedroom window at a view away from the synthetic mountain of the strip, past the parking lots and across the Nevada desert to a range of empty mountains—for Las Vegas is ringed by mountains, and this is perhaps why the place feels so strange. In the distance is the harsh and beautiful reality of nature. Down the inclinator, which is what they call an elevator in a pyramid, is self-indulgent humanity at its worst—all you can eat for $9 a head, and rows and rows of one-armed bandits.

Las Vegas has changed: built as a town where the rich could gamble in privacy, it has become a tourist city where the masses play the fruit machines. Listen to the names of the past—Jerry Lee Lewis, Paul Anka and the Everly Brothers. Eat at Hamburger Hamlet or Prime Rib. It costs $5.95 at Aladdin, or at The Sands, breakfast is $3.99, lunch $4.99 and dinner $6.99. When the tourists are not fully engaged eating, drinking, watching shows or waiting to be allowed to do these things, they pull the arms of one-armed bandits or wander aimlessly among them clutching paper buckets filled with coins—giving real meaning to the old phrase 'buckets of money'—frustrated by the queues, disorientated by moving from Arabia to Hawaii to Ancient Rome in a short walk. Tired beyond belief by carpets so soft that walking on them is like walking through sand, exhausted by the flashing lights, battered by non-stop sound of the basest possible kind mixed with the crash and seductive tinkle of the gambling machines, the wretched tourist dips into that paper bucket and tries to get rid of those coins as quickly as possible. For Las Vegas is not about entertainment, holidays and sun—Las Vegas is only about gambling.

Amazing Graceland

Memphis, Tennessee, is remarkable for many things, but none impressed me so much as the extraordinary decor of Graceland, the home of Elvis Presley, local boy made good.

Travelling by taxi from the airport that serves Memphis to my hotel in the city's centre, I fell into conversation with the cab driver. Among many other questions, I asked him what sort of food his city was famous for. Without hesitation he replied, 'Bar-B-cue.' What, I enquired, did the good people of Memphis barbecue? The driver answered with one word, 'Ribs.'

I let our conversation lapse as we drove along the bank of the Mississippi River. I judged that this was neither the time nor the place and particularly not the man to engage in a discussion of how the founding fathers perceived a similarity between their river, the Mississippi, and Egypt's River Nile; both rivers they believed were the providers of plenty, and having come to that conclusion they called their city Memphis. True, at one time the Mississippi, like the River Nile, provided great wealth to those living along her banks. Civil war, however, removed much of it, and such wealth as returned left again with the assassination of Dr Martin Luther King in 1968.

For six years after that traumatic event the most famous hotel in town, the Peabody Hotel, remained closed. Now, in 1994, the Memphis mayor and corporation are doing all they can to bring both people and business to Memphis. The city skyline is still like a mouth of rotting teeth. Some buildings are missing; some are just closed. None are new. Memphis is a rare thing indeed—a city without cranes.

The motel where Dr Martin Luther King was assassinated has been restored and preserved, a fine example of 1950s motel architecture. The room where King slept has been left as he left it, the bed unmade, and the breakfast half-eaten. Memphis has taken its history head on. There are no apologies for the past in Memphis, no attempt to hide it or to hide from it. A visit to the Civil Rights Museum, which fills an extension to the motel, is a moving experience.

Not far from Beale Street, famous for the Beale Street Blues, is the Sun Studios where Elvis Presley made his first recordings. I doubt if that place has changed much since Elvis left it for RCA. It still operates as a recording studio, and the café beneath still sells coffee to would-be stars and the few who have made it.

Memphis's greatest tourist attraction, however, is Graceland, the house that Elvis Presley bought for his mother on the outskirts of the city. Remarkable for its modest size, Graceland is worth a visit if you find yourself in Memphis; and you should go to Memphis, if only to see Graceland, for the house is the most remarkable example of 1950s kitsch anywhere in the world. No museum has anything like it: the living room with its peacocks in stained glass, the white carpet and white upholstered furniture, the fireplace's mirrored surround and the gilt sunburst clock over it; the lamps, the tables and the ornaments—all are wonderful. Even the TV is a collector's piece. There are gold curtains, and blue curtains with gold trim to match, and gold curtains with blue trim in the dining room across the hall. A mirrored staircase shows a thousand images as you descend to the TV room in the basement—in fact, so many mirrors they are impossible to count as they reflect each other, and in each is an image from one of three TV sets which used to play simultaneously. Mirrored tables, mirrored pedestals—no wonder the poor guy went a little strange. Even the small square cushions have small round mirrors set in them. A mirrored bar and then the grandest jukebox in the world and cases of records to go with it, and so it all went on.

Thank goodness the house was small. I was relieved to return to the vast comforts of the Peabody Hotel, a pile built just after the turn of the century, with every cornice a yard deep and every frieze a multitude of curlicues. A hotel where majolica and marble embrace and gilded bronze is fixed to every surface, and where you sink into a giant armchair in the air-conditioned cool of the foyer that could double as a railway station. A hotel where at the flick of a finger a mint julep is in your hand, where the notice on the door of your room warns that death and violence walk the streets of Memphis and that you should not linger as you walk or for that matter open the door of your hotel room to strangers, and where staff must show their passes.

This, however, is the dark side of Memphis. Its history is tortured, but its music close to magic, its climate sweltering in summer, its atmosphere mysterious and its attractions eccentric, and none more eccentric than the ducks that twice a day parade to martial music in the foyer of the Peabody Hotel—ducks that live in a palace on the hotel's roof. But that is another tale.

The Cone zone

Letting the train take the strain, I visited Baltimore and discovered a city getting to grips with its problems, the joys of the Cone Collection . . . and a string of other delights.

Penn Station was almost deserted at six o'clock in the morning. A lone policeman moved from one sleeping figure to another, administering a prod with his night stick and, occasionally, a few words as well as he sent the homeless back onto the New York streets. The weather was chilly and wet. Winter had started to set in. People began to appear out of a dozen or so holes, holes that led to the trains. The station stalls and bookshops opened and soon the place was a seething horde of humanity.

I caught the 06.50 metro liner to Baltimore, club class, and pretty grand it was. I sat in a seat that reclined and reached for my safety belt. I couldn't get away from the idea that I had boarded an aeroplane and it was about to take off. The carriages themselves did nothing to persuade me otherwise. They were long and sleek, made of shiny aluminium, with rows of seating either side of an aisle. A steward offered magazines or newspapers and handed me a breakfast menu.

I was going to Baltimore by train because I fancied seeing the countryside on the way. However, like the sailor in the musical comedy 'who joined the navy to see the world, and what did he see? He saw the sea', I saw not countryside but suburbia, miles and miles of it. Sometimes I saw houses, but mostly wasteland, swamp and ancient industry interspersed with smart new office parks—all the way to Baltimore.

The railway enters Baltimore between rows and rows of terraced houses that look like chicken coops and are about the same size. Baltimore has a population of mixed descent of about a million. Most are poor. The town, however, is tackling poverty and its attendant crime. The inner harbour, formerly derelict docks, has been developed, and old buildings preserved. Fells Point, an area popular with the youth of the town, feels like a film set. The rest of these former docks boast the usual new hotels and museums. There is a new museum to celebrate Christopher Columbus, and what I suppose is the inevitable maritime museum, an aquarium, a shopping centre and warehouses converted into luxury apartments.

Nearby is Baltimore Street, mysteriously described by my taxi driver as a street where the girlies are, a street of strip shows, although it wouldn't offend you if you came across it in Edinburgh—a city Baltimore strongly resembles with its fine churches, elegant squares, tall monuments and rows of terraces famous for their marble steps. Baltimore has its fair share of museums and fine buildings, which are well supported by the city's wealthy citizens. If you need a reason to visit Baltimore, then it is to be found in the Baltimore Museum of Art. The Cone Collection has three thousand or so paintings, drawings, sculptures, fabrics—silks and lace—ancient and primitive works of art and a large collection of jewellery.

The Cone sisters—Dr Claribel and Miss Etta—were all that is best in American collectors. They visited Europe at the turn of the century and became friendly with Henri Matisse who introduced them to Picasso. Their collection of twentieth-century paintings is stunning. I could not find a poor picture or a lazy sculpture in the whole collection. The room devoted to Matisse, to my mind, gave a better feel for the painter than the blockbusting Matisse exhibition put on by the Metropolitan Museum of Art in the early nineties. The sisters bought at least one of Matisse's paintings every year for 40 years and a quantity of his drawings and sculptures. The paintings are not all large, but they are all brilliant. Picasso's painting of 1902, *Woman with Bangs*, is small but has a drama that would fill a canvas many feet its size. Cézanne's landscape and view of Mont Ste-Victoire is as you would expect. The one for me is Matisse's *Reclining Nude*, a painting of a large red naked woman lying on a blue check tablecloth.

The Cone sisters were not Baltimore's only collectors. Houssmers Restaurant boasts 'Masterpieces in Art and Dining'. I am clear about the German cuisine—it was wonderful; as for the art, well there was lots of it, mostly from the last century, in barn-sized rooms, several with paintings hung edge to edge in all directions and cabinets filled with china and glass, silver and ivories. Among all this, hidden in a stairwell, is what must be the world's biggest ball of string. It is nearly ten feet high and growing as the binding from the restaurant's daily laundry is added to it. Baltimore is a city that shows its delights slowly.

Bargain hunting in the Bay

The wild East Shore of Chesapeake Bay has a pioneering feel to it, though the most enterprising visitors these day tend to be antique dealers.

Chesapeake Bay is a large stretch of water on the east coast of America, an inland sea whose waters run through canals to the Great Lakes from its mouth on the coast of Maryland. The longest bridge–tunnel in the world crosses Chesapeake Bay and all the other bridges are vast in their scale. You cross the bay hundreds of feet in the air as huge cargo ships pass below you. The land on the far side from Washington is called the East Shore. It is a land of rivers and wild fowl, perhaps the most beautiful part of America. It is not hard as you look out over timber fencing, past eighteenth-century houses to a backwater with its banks clothed in forest to imagine the woodland filled with hostile painted savages.

The town of St Michaels is still much as it was in 1812 when British ships shelled what they believed was the town. The townspeople, warned of the ships' approach, put out all the lights of St Michaels and erected an array of lanterns on different-height poles about a mile away. The British passed over the town and bombarded the lanterns before passing on to attack Washington and burn the White House. St Michaels is a lonely place, with only cars, trucks and motorboats shouting that the twentieth century is here. Despite these accoutrements of modern living the place still has the feel of the pioneer about it.

There is nothing bucolic about the East Shore's farms or anything permanent about its 200-year-old buildings plucked from England, their proportions slightly distorted in the transplanting, in a way that gives their architecture an extra vigour. The most modest doorway has a grandeur that you would not find in its ancestor from Kent or Hampshire. The East Shore is a place of hunters, men and women who sit in hides and wait for wild birds to come, fishers who pull in the crab pots from these waters and sailors who navigate the wide spaces of the bay and know how cunningly to use its winds.

To this place came one day the London art dealer Daniel Katz. He had been told of a great prize that lay hidden there. He did not know exactly what it was, but being a man of incurable curiosity he had no option but to seek it out. The weather was cold, and by the time he reached the East Shore, the sleet that had hit his car for most of the journey had turned to snow. Katz hurried into the house where he believed all would be revealed. The owner, a collector with rather more enthusiasm than taste, showed Katz his collection. The man had an unerring eye for the mediocre. Katz had travelled hours to visit him.

'Where is this thing I have come to see?' he asked.

'In the garden,' replied the man.

By now the storm was heavier. They walked into a landscape much as I have described, a garden set between broad rivers with forest at its banks, and then to the bottom of the garden.

'Well, where is it?' asked Katz.

'You're standing on it,' the man replied. Katz looked down at the large brown slab of stone on which he was standing. The man continued, 'It's a meteorite.'

All Katz could reply was 'Oh.'

'Michael Jackson is very interested in buying it,' said the man. Katz recovered his composure although still somewhat shaken. He had had a long and tiring journey and Katz deals not in meteorites, but fine art. In any case the thing was vast and obviously extremely heavy. 'Michael Jackson will pay 5 million dollars for this.'

Katz by this time realised that he was involved in the sort of situation dealers hope to encounter only in a nightmare. He set about disengaging himself from the man and his meteorite. The weather was cold and the journey he was about to undertake long so Katz, always a thoughtful man, asked if he could use the man's cloakroom.

As Katz stood and washed his hands, reflecting on his misfortune at having been lured to the back of beyond on a fool's errand, he noticed a terracotta figure on the shelf above the basin. A figure of a river god, nine inches high and fourteen-and-a-half inches long, a figure of immense quality. Now Katz has a real eye for quality—his discoveries of fine objects in dull places are legendary. Katz dried his hands and began to negotiate, and in an hour or so bought the river god for a small price. He sold the figure, which was by the French eighteenth-century sculptor Jean-Jacques Caffieri, for £85 000. In the world of the collector and his cousin the dealer, no errand is a fool's errand.

Defenceless castle

The castle that William Randolph Hearst built is a Californian dream turned nightmare. I found its mad mix of styles unappealing. Nowhere in California is there anything quite like this castle.

High above the coastline at San Simeon in California is an outcrop of rock called La Cuesta Encantada (The Enchanted Hill). It was here that William Randolph Hearst built his great palace, now called Hearst Castle by the local people. This folly cost Hearst most of his fortune: he was $169 million in debt by the end of 1929, a figure that would today be equivalent to over $3 billion—and his castle was only half built. Folly it may have been for Hearst, but for the locals living in San Simeon, Hearst Castle has become a nice little earner. Tourists flock to the place.

As tourists leave the place along the savage coastline with its bent pines and rocks carved by an unforgiving sea, it is easy to imagine them turning to one another and saying: 'I have seen nothing like it in all my life.' Love Hearst Castle or hate Hearst Castle, you have to admit it is dramatically different from anything else you have ever come across.

Hearst's architect, Julia Morgan, when questioned later about her influences replied, 'The style that influenced my work at Hearst Castle is a simple one and it is called pleasing my client.' (Morgan, a graduate from the College of Engineering at California University in 1894 went on to study architecture at the Ecole des Beaux-Arts in Paris and designed more than 700 buildings.)

Work at Hearst Castle started well enough. The idea was to build the structure in reinforced concrete and plant Hearst's amazing collection of architectural fragments on to it. The problem was that Hearst could never really make up his mind as to what style to build in. The main building hovers somewhere between thirteenth-century Venice and sixteenth-century Spain. The swimming pool is pure Hollywood. There can hardly be an order of architecture that has not been used in the construction of its surrounding colonnade. The pediment over the rather grand pool-house is a jumble of Roman carvings. Hearst's real problem was that he knew what ought to be good but failed miserably when it came to sifting the genuine from the pastiche. I suppose much of what he bought in Italy stayed there, and poor copies arrived at San Simeon.

Hearst set about building this folly with an enthusiasm last seen when Waddesdon was built and Rothschild moved mature trees, and shifted large quantities of earth to build hills that didn't exist and removed ones that did. Such was Rothschild's energy that the Prime Minister Disraeli felt moved to say of the world's creation: 'If the Good Lord had been helped by Rothschild it never would have taken him seven days.'

So it was with Hearst. The imagination and energy of the man were immense and worthy of admiration. It is just that the result is a total disaster. Hearst Castle does not even have the style of an amusement park or the vulgarity of a Victorian palace. There is no form or reason to the place, or even an attractive lunacy. Nothing looks right or even wrong enough to look right.

Perhaps the missing element is the man himself telling you that some awful fragment of marble was really an important part of the Parthenon. There is no sense as you walk around this vast pile that anyone of consequence ever lived there and the truth of the matter is that Hearst barely did.

The Castle is like a disused film set, without the spinner of fantastic tales. Just concrete and stone, empty, irrelevant, filled today with gawping tourists longing to see a magnificence that does not exist. A total of 7000 tourists a day are bundled into buses for the five-mile drive from the tourist centre to the Castle, de-bussed and briefed: 'Do not touch anything except the iron handrails; do not lean against pots or statues, and under no circumstances stroke them. Do not smoke, do not eat, do not drink and do ask lots of questions. Do not dawdle, do not lag behind, and do not wander off to look at anything that is not on the route of the tour. My job is to show you the Castle, and I am trained to explain matters to you. You will ask the questions.'

No one did. They wandered like zombies past the municipal tennis court, through the indoor Moorish-style swimming pool, past beds of municipal flowers, up unfinished concrete steps and wondered at the Castle's concrete walls. 'These windows come from Venice,' we were instructed. I dared not disagree. I suspect that they were sold by Venetians, which is a rather different matter. It was with some relief that we headed for the wine cellar and looked at the collection of empty bottles. Due to a local ordinance the state of California is not allowed to own alcohol; so the Hearst family has inherited the cellar's contents and drink them as they will, faithfully returning the empty bottles to the castle. I had heard much of this castle and I longed to admire it. However, when I left I did not even hate the place.

Shirts and scandals

There's never a dull moment for me in Chicago, where the architecture overwhelms, the shopper's every desire is no sooner voiced than satisfied, and the gossip runs free.

Chicago is a beautiful city; that, however, was not always the case. Twenty-five years ago it was the centre of civic unrest and urban decay. Now the place is an architectural museum, each high-quality building carefully placed and at ease with its surroundings. Derelict buildings have been restored, converted or pulled down and turned into parking lots. Trees have been planted, shading the pavements alongside the wide streets.

The architecture varies from the Nickerson House, grey stone with an arts-and-crafts interior, to the buildings of Mies van der Rohe, Skidmore, Owings & Merrill and Frank Lloyd Wright. Minimalist glass towers sit beside the mock-Gothic fantasies of the early twentieth century—skyscrapers King Arthur could have held meetings of his Round Table in and felt at home. Tall buildings and street musicians, bars with jazz and restaurants with steaks as big as your thigh.

Affluence has come like a wave in the last ten years. Michigan Avenue is advertised as a mile of luxury shops, and the area between Wells and Franklin Streets a mass of shops and galleries selling way-out clothing and home furnishings. Banana Republic is always one of my favourite shops—somewhere I can buy a pure linen shirt that fits my ungainly shape for $29 must surely be a favourite place. There is, however, a limit to the number of shirts a man can buy and as I am inextricably drawn to this shop. I was relieved to find that its Chicago branch has a home furnishings section with all the latest produce of

India: embroidered bed linen and elegant glassware that fills your hand. American pottery has its place there as well: generous bowls glazed in white, beige, mustard and the palest green.

Next door is the Pottery Barn, with more American pottery, and a block further up Michigan Avenue is a branch of Crate & Barrel, with yet more. It ranges from the reproductions of utilitarian designs of the Depression to jugs, plates and bowls in the colours of the African Bush. In Chicago, I found everything from reproductions of nineteenth-century dairy buckets to individually turned plates, each piece a work of art.

At the Museum of Contemporary Art, however, I did not find works of art, at least not many of them. They are to be found in a modest Terra Museum of American Art, which has a brilliant exhibition of work by artists living in Chicago. The Museum of Contemporary Art, however, has just revealed a considerable scandal. A former chairman charged with raising $55 million in fact raised $95 million. In a fit of generosity, he promised $5 million to the development fund, but never delivered. His successor and the trustees sued him for the money, which on the face of it seems a bit churlish considering they had $40 million more than expected as a result of his efforts. But his name was on a plaque, he had been entertained and thanked—he must pay. In the end the poor fellow died and his son settled the case by giving the museum two paintings. It was a hot day when I viewed one of them, but, that apart, had I been offered a choice of the painting or a cold beer, I would without hesitation have chosen the latter. As a reason for not delivering the promised money, the recalcitrant donor said that he disagreed with how the director was spending the museum's funds.

Walking around the museum, I found that I had considerable sympathy with that view. In fact, raising the extra $40 million may well have done the museum no real favour, because the place is simply a triumph of architecture over art. The building is architecturally a welcome addition to Chicago, but for so much building there is little space to exhibit art. In the most unpromising settings, however, great gems are sometimes found. So it is with the Museum of Contemporary Art. One small room—in fact, more of a landing than a room—held a collection of eleven mobiles by Calder, along with a 1920s wood carving and a 1940s bronze, complete with its delicate hanging objects. This room is a place of great beauty. Other than that, the best thing about the Museum of Contemporary Art in Chicago is its stunning view of the lake.

The treats of San Francisco

My eyes got misty over the fate of an old friend in foggy San Francisco, but I was delighted by the bay city's rolling waves.

Arriving in San Francisco by air was spectacular; not for the view, but rather for the lack of one. Nothing could be seen until the aircraft had touched down and groped its way to the terminal. By mid-morning, fog had given way to rain and fog.

'Will this weather clear?' I asked.

'Who knows?' was the reply. 'In San Francisco we could have sunshine at any moment.' The taxi driver was an optimist.

But San Francisco is not just a city with a pretty view. There is plenty to enjoy, regardless of the weather: the San Francisco shopping centre, which has the only spiral escalator in America, for instance; or the Frank Lloyd Wright building in Maiden Lane, now the home of the Xanadu Gallery which sells folk art. The rain was a positive advantage in this spectacular building. 'Watch out for the bucket,' a helpful assistant warned me. 'All Frank Lloyd Wright buildings leak; until today we thought that ours was the exception.' But there it was, a considerable leak spurting rain into a yellow plastic bucket.

The next day, bored with the weather's games, I set off for Carmel and the John Picard Trade Bead Museum. The journey from San Francisco takes three hours and involves driving through some of the most beautiful valleys in America. The museum, the creation of Ruth and John Picard, sits in the almost Japanese setting of Berkeley Drive, Carmel Valley, and houses the world's greatest collection of trade beads. These beads, used in trading with Africa, date from the fifteenth century through to more recent times. Many of the most beautiful of them were made in Venice. Wonderfully displayed in countless rows, their thousands of different designs and colours make each one a miniature work of art.

The drive back to town was along the coast, with the ocean on one side and fields of artichokes on the other. On the way, my driver took a phone call—there was, he said, a big surf at the Mavericks; the quicksilver men were riding the mountainous 20- to 30-foot waves. This only happens a few times a year, and when it does surfing enthusiasts will drop everything and head for Half Moon Bay. Not wanting to be dropped, I followed my driver. When we arrived, the *cognoscenti* were of the opinion that the fog had ruined the great event. I disagreed: the fog, and the uncertainty that it brought, only made it all the more exciting. I don't know much about the finer points of surfing, but the waves were terrific.

It is 35 years since I first visited San Francisco. In that time the place has changed a lot; there are, however, parts of any growing city that should stay much the same: the restaurants in the Bay area, for instance, where they serve avocados the size of small footballs and prawns that could double as boomerangs. Even Trader Vics is not much changed since my first visit.

My favourite restaurant in San Francisco, Jack's, is one of a half-dozen in the world that I would make a special pilgrimage to visit. A restaurant where you stand at a bar by the door and drink Bloody Marys until a table becomes vacant; a restaurant that is always full to the gunwales from 11 am to 3 pm; a simple, stark restaurant with white tablecloths and waiters in black; a restaurant without a shred of decor in the whole place, serving perfect food in the simplest manner, straight from cooker to plate—no frills. But not any more. This near-perfect restaurant has, in truth, been destroyed by a new owner's desire to improve the unimprovable. The prices have gone up, and the magic of the place has gone forever, lost under heavy plasterwork and extravagant gilding. The spirit of the place has gone, rubbed out as easily as are San Francisco's fogs by a hot sun. The fog, however, will return; Jack's restaurant is gone forever.

A Bargain Box

Fakes progress

When it comes to the art of deception, truth lies in the eye of the beholder.

The fear that lurks behind the first major purchase of any collector must always be, is the masterpiece genuine? He draws his reassurance from the dealer he buys it from, the look of the dealer, the position of his shop, the confidence with which he expounds on the history and background of the piece, and the books that he produces to show similar pieces. The more experienced collector backs his own judgement and sometimes becomes the greatest of experts. The most interesting collectors choose by eye. Is it the right shape? Is it aesthetically interesting? Is it beautiful? Is it ancient? This is the way to collect. But if you are impressed by professional expertise, go at once to the Victoria and Albert Museum, where there is a whole gallery of fakes bought by some of the world's greatest experts. And if that gallery does not strike horror into your breast, then go to the British Museum, for it is baring its soul with a fascinating exhibition of fakes that have been unmasked over the years, including a mermaid that I would give my eyeteeth for. It must be a fake, for mermaids do not exist, or do they?

Of course, not all fakes are bad. In the British Museum's exhibition there is a carved panel, a nineteenth-century fake but, by chance, the fakers used a fifteenth-century altar panel, long lost, to make their fake. The painting on the back of the panel is of far more importance than the carving on the front would have been, even if it had been genuine. Then there are fakes collected because they are fakes. 'Billies' and 'Charlies' for instance. These are objects supposed to be ancient—knives, medals, dishes and the like—cast in lead by Billy and Charlie, two nineteenth-century mudlarks. Their technique was to be seen arguing about a newly found piece until they engaged the attention of a pedestrian crossing London Bridge. They explained that they could not agree on the ownership of a medal they had found and could not split it, as Solomon might have wished, for each half would be worthless. So the solution was for the pedestrian to purchase the medal from them and they could easily split the money. And for years they deceived even the most learned scholars in the land, until they started to come up with objects dated 250 years before Christ.

Some fakes are made just for devilment. I remember a dealer in guns, Pip Roberts, now regrettably dead, who was shadowed in the salerooms by someone who, if you called him an amateur, it would be an unjust slur on that fine status. If you called him a dealer, you would have to apologise to everyone who had ever sold an object in their lives. In any event, when Pip Roberts raised his hand to bid, this man always went one bid more. He lived for some years off the expertise of my friend. In time, Roberts decided to teach him a lesson. Buying a Spanish gun of good quality for £50, for this was in the early 1960s, he inlaid it with silver and gilded the barrel, polished and carved it until it seemed like a masterpiece. Putting it in the salerooms, he waited for the auction and bid on it, bid and bid, casting glances of fury at his enemy. He was Italian, so you can imagine his antics as he bid, still higher. Suddenly he stopped. His enemy owned the gun at a very high price. It was a matter of minutes before everyone in the room knew the real story.

More recently, a man from the Middle East visited the showroom of a famous West End dealer to offer him a cuneiform tablet. As usual, the dealer asked him to leave it and he would show it to a museum. The man agreed. The museum was over the moon with excitement. The tablet was inscribed with a rare and complicated script. It would take a month to decipher, but it was well worth doing, for the tablet seemed of great interest. Part of the first line said 'Nebuchadnezzar King'. The man from the Middle East returned and the dealer explained the delay.

'This is unacceptable,' came the reply. 'I have to return home tomorrow; I am afraid that I must take either my piece or the money.' The man asked a high price for the tablet.

'I'll pay,' said the dealer. The month passed and the museum rang.

'Rather funny, really,' they said.

'What do you mean—funny?'

'Well, there is a whole poem.' I will not quote it all, but it will give you the gist of the thing if I say the poem is well known and it begins with 'Nebuchadnezzar King of the Jews' and ends with the twentieth-century words 'the evening news'.

Some fakes are not fakes or, rather, they may not be fakes. At the moment, in the streets of Venice, there is a rash of men from North Africa selling luggage, supposedly fake, by the likes of Louis Vuitton and Gucci. Some Venetians believe these bags to be fakes while some believe they are genuine bags, stolen from the factories and being sold as fakes. In the end does it really matter much? If the object gives you pleasure, and if it is an object of beauty, this is what counts. If it happens to be a truly great object and genuine as well, so much the better.

When shabby means chic

I discuss why, when it comes to gardens, buildings and works of art, age cannot whither, nor custom stale.

To many of us the romance of the slightly derelict landscape, or the once grand but now decaying house, has a strong attraction. Seeing this, decorators and dealers have promoted the crashed look, with carpets short on colour and long on holes, newly 'distressed' furniture and walls painted to imitate the effect of decades of tobacco smoke or crumbling plaster. The broken statue becomes an object of beauty, although if it is to be an art object, the break must be in the right place. It is a look with a little dust, but no dirt.

Objects look better when they acquire a patina, and the same is true of houses (even of people). But this is perhaps most true of gardens. The best are unkempt but never neglected. Bosky gardens celebrate the art of extraction. The principle is, if it looks wrong, pull it out. No clever placement of plants, just the luck of nature aided by the gardener. Time is caught still, and the stone roller and the broken wheelbarrow are seen as if through a cobweb. The plants and trees seem rebellious and unconfined, with a life of their own.

Neither is such a garden the domain of the lazy. It is another stage set arranged with care to look careless. The right type of weed has to be carefully chosen—and not too many of them—and wild dog roses planted so they seem to dance with old roses the size and shape of ball gowns. This is not so much the perfect garden as the secret garden, best in early morning or at dusk. Bright sunlight is not unknown, but seems to come only in patches—staining the stonework. Just as in a house the paint must peel but the timber never rot, there can be moss in the gravel but never weeds in the lawn. Incidentally, this reminds me of a British ambassador to Japan some time past, who knew about lawns with no weeds, and instructed his Japanese gardener to pull them all out. In fact, he instructed him several times with little result. Finally, he said: 'I shall be away on leave for six weeks and if the lawn is not weeded by my return I shall be most displeased.' It was. True to Japanese tradition, the gardener had pulled out all the grass and left only daisies.

Buildings are the same. The tired look is the fashion. I am prepared to bet that the vast majority that greatly admires our medieval cathedrals would cry out with anguish at the suggestion that we should restore them to their original colours—garish colours, painted not only inside but all over the outside walls as well. Public taste, while claiming to admire past centuries and despise the look of our own age, does not, in fact, much like things to be presented as they really were. A fine example of this was to be seen at the Frans Hals exhibition at the Royal Academy. The show was worth seeing for the pictures, but I was most interested in the frames: old gold, new gold, frames encrusted with smoke, frames stroked by time till they become a gentle yellow and frames burnished bright for the customer. Each prefers a different style.

This tired look was not always the fashion, however. A London picture restorer recently expressed surprise at the change in fashion in his trade—though why, for heaven's sake, eludes me. Fashions in every other trade change. It seems that quite a few years ago a dealer bought a picture of a dog—a tired picture way past its best.

'Brighten this up for me,' he had said.

'But this is way past its best,' said the restorer.

'Rubbish—a touch of red here, a bright blue curtain . . . Put some life into it.'

The painting came back to life in the marketplace bright in its new coat, and was sold several times before the price began to lag a little. Fashion was changing. By now a dealer would be thinking that there was probably something under all that junk. It might be by a good hand, perhaps even a great one. The picture was returned to the restorer.

'Clean this off—let's go back to the original,' said the dealer.

'But there's only a fragment there.'

'Exactly—just what I want!'

So the painting of the dog became tasteful in muted colours, leaving much to the imagination, and is once again perambulating around the art market, its price restored as well.

Heartbroken and stockbroken

Eyes and ears open for the dealers' occupational hazard—the sight and sound of precious objects slipping from a butter-fingered grasp.

Sometimes you can be too careful. I recently returned from Italy with two rare and extremely interesting glasses made by Venini in the 1930s which I had nursed and protected from the ravages of Alitalia. I arrived at my shop and with the utmost of care unwrapped the first: there it was perfect—perfect even to its original label. Gently, I placed it in the middle of my table and with caution unwrapped the next—again it was perfect, at least until it jumped from my hands, falling directly onto the first bowl. Both were destroyed and I was left looking at a small heap of coloured glass. I am afraid this is an occupational hazard when you deal in glass.

One dealer of my acquaintance refused to allow his staff to touch glass after four o'clock in the afternoon on the basis that they were too tired by that time. This was really quite surprising as he seldom had a glass out of his hand after twelve in the morning and, as far as I can remember, never dropped anything.

Breakages can sometimes be turned to a dealer's advantage—or so one Kensington dealer believed. He had just sold a majolica plate for a fabulous sum to a German client and taken his cheque. He was passing the time of day while his female assistant wrapped the plate in the office, when he heard what can only be described as an ominous crunch. He quickly entered the office and there she stood, pieces of plate around her. 'Foolish child,' he said and she began to apologise. 'Wrap it up,' he said quickly, 'and give it to the customer.' He returned to the shop and continued his conversation with the German. After a long wait, during which time the German was getting a little impatient, the girl appeared carrying the parcel. The dealer handed this over and somehow contrived as he opened the door that the German dropped the parcel. 'What a shame, probably broken,' he said. 'No chance of a refund, what a shame.' The German was speechless, and the girl was somewhat agitated. 'Unpack the parcel; let's have a look,' hectored the dealer. To nobody's surprise the plate was broken into a dozen pieces. But, unfortunately, the girl had wrapped each broken piece individually.

Stories of broken glass abound. A tall flute, engraved with naked women by Maria Tesselschade Visscher, survived a trip across the Atlantic but was destroyed when it was being placed in its custom-made cabinet. Unfortunately, the luckless keeper of glass in that museum did not realise that the shelves had been made too close to each other. As he took care that the top got in all right the foot of the glass struck the lower shelf.

But my favourite glass story is of the famous London dealer Christopher Sheppard who, having travelled to Basle to buy a very rare glass, found himself a little short of money, so he rode on the tram. Carefully, he placed the glass on the seat beside him but within moments a large lady sat on it. Horrified he turned to protest: 'Ya,' she said, and 'Ya' was all he seemed to be able to get out of her. After which he got up and left the tram, the broken glass and the Swiss lady who seemed totally unaware of the mayhem she had wreaked.

As I said before, breakages are an occupational hazard of a dealer in glass. But imagine my surprise as I watched a customer examine a silver bowl—third century BC, Greek and quite beautiful—the centre shaped like the fullest of breasts. Suddenly, exactly where the nipple had been, appeared his finger—right through the middle of my silver bowl.

Arms and the man

Weapons and armour might seem strange things to collect.

When is a gun not a gun? When it is an oil pipeline, if the stories in the press about the Iraqi super gun are to be believed. In sheer size alone it seems to be without precedent, with its barrel, over a yard across, that bolts together in sections. But no, history has known one such gun. In the nineteenth century a large mortar was needed for the siege of Sebastopol and a civil engineer called Robert Mallet designed it. The gun was 11 feet long and weighed 42 tons. It fired a shell one yard in diameter weighing one-and-a-quarter tons and holding 480 pounds of explosive. This, it was thought, would be powerful enough to penetrate the fortress the Russians had erected in the Crimea. The gun was so heavy that Mallet designed it in four or five pieces, none of which weighed more than 12 tons. When in position it was to be bolted together. It was very similar to the Iraqi gun.

Mallet's first design was finished in 1854. Lord Palmerston ordered two of these guns at £4900 each from More and Company, which were completed in 1857. When they were tested on Woolwich Marshes, a few shells were fired with success. The greatest range achieved was 2759 yards, but in the end, needless to say, the guns blew up and the venture was abandoned.

All my life, I have been interested in arms and armour. I think perhaps as a small boy that it was the romance of the knight in armour and the excitement of the Wild West that attracted my attention. Later, perhaps, it was the beauty of their potential that I loved. In any event, I believe that these weapons of war, now obsolete and long retired, have a functional beauty—a sculptured quality.

Guns are strange things to collect. But if you put at the back of your mind the purpose for which they are made, they do have a great beauty and, as antiques go, they are cheap.

In my youth the dealers in arms and armour were a pretty strange lot. But they all had one thing in common: their kindness to me as a boy. Most are not long dead: the eccentric Mr Donald; Percy German, the butcher in Edgware Road who, when offered a collection of arms and armour—20 000 items at one shilling each—bought it and changed professions to become one of the great dealers; Robin Braid Taylor, always short of money, one of the most entertaining men I have ever met, always keen to buy, always on for a gamble; Fairclough, a jolly man like the proverbial farmer; Pip Roberts, an ex-waiter from the Savoy, whose shop in St Martin's Lane was a great centre for the buying and selling of almost anything but who had a demon eye for a good gun; and Keith Neal, the grandest of them all, with one of the most remarkable collections in the world.

While still very young, I was invited fishing by an elderly friend of my father and stayed the night at his house before setting out. That evening he gave a dinner party and, young as I was, I attended. I sat and listened to the talk, silent until the lady opposite me leant across the table and, in a voice to catch the conversation, asked me what my hobbies were. I suppose that she expected the reply cricket, football and trainspotting. None of these things, I am afraid, interested me, so I replied arms and armour. In shocked tones she repeated my words and added, 'When I think of boredom, armour comes immediately to mind. Armour is totally synonymous with boredom.' I wish I could remember that lady's name, for I would like, now that time has passed and I am better able to debate, to talk to her about armour and the awful boredom of dinner parties before a day's fishing or shooting.

As the years have passed, armour has become a real fascination. Its changes and development seem to parallel history, and its whole *raison d'être* the vagaries of the human psyche—all those protective instincts that forbid us from truly showing our emotions, that hold us from love and hate, that stiffen all our actions and constrict our lives so that we live bottled up, disguised and hidden from our fellows.

Of arms and the woman I sing

An epic tale beginning with the clothes of war and ending on vestments more suited to amour.

For heaven's sake, why would anyone collect a bracelet made of the thighs of flies or a cloak worn by an Indian chief? The Tradescants, father and son, were such men, and they exhibited these items for profit on the south bank of the Thames, not far from Lambeth Palace. The cloak once belonged to Powhatan, father of Pocahontas, the famous Indian princess. This cloak, later acquired by Ashmole, is now in the Ashmolean Museum, along with a collection of what now appear to be exotic shoes collected at the same time. The bracelet of flies' thighs has disappeared—a delicate but remarkable thing, it must surely have disintegrated with the passage of time. It was, however, a remarkable curiosity in the sixteenth century. Imagine the Tradescants' barker calling out 'Roll up to see the miraculous bracelet of flies' thighs!'—a tongue twister if ever there was one.

In any event, I only write about these items to illustrate that even at an early date collectors were interested in clothes and personal adornment. Captain Cook brought back shiploads of clothes worn by 'primitive' peoples. The textiles in Charles I's collection, when it was sold by Cromwell's government, fetched ten times the prices achieved for the paintings of Titian and Tintoretto. Pitt Rivers accumulated quantities of unusual clothes from many different countries, and until the beginning of the last century armour—the clothes of war—was much collected. In fact, the highest price ever paid for a work of art at auction before 1914 was for a suit of armour. The great museums of the world have vast collections of clothes and textiles, and anyone who has ever stopped at a newspaper stand will know that dozens of magazines are published on how we dress.

The collecting of clothes is a long-established business, not likely to be abandoned because of a change in the fashion of collecting. What is more, museum directors are beginning to realise that the public love clothes—in particular, other people's. The Vivienne Westwood shoes that brought Naomi Campbell to grief on the catwalk are the most popular item in the Victoria and Albert Museum. It is, therefore, no great surprise that the Museum of London decided to put on an exhibition of Vivienne Westwood's clothes. The clothes in this exhibition all come from the collection of Romilly McAlpine—here I declare an interest, for she was my wife. About 50 items are on show; Romilly McAlpine's collection has in it about 150 items by Westwood, which form less than 10 per cent of her collection. The show, designed by Tim Hatley, is—and I am without prejudice in this matter—brilliant. Luxury and quality radiate from every inch of the set. These clothes, exhibited in this way, demonstrate the expert eye of the collector. For me, and I am by nature a hard critic, the taste is as close to perfection as you will get in a small collection.

Leslie Waddington, the veteran Cork Street dealer, remarked, 'I never thought of clothes as works of art before.' They are works of art in the same way as a suit of armour is considered a work of art. In an age where arms and armour are unpopular, they have been replaced by silks and tweeds, necklaces and bracelets. The baroque concoctions of Negroli, the world's greatest armourer in the sixteenth century, are replaced by the designs of Vivienne Westwood. If this notion seems a trifle fey, the catalogue still exists of a collection shown some twenty years ago where the dresses of Capucci were shown together with armour. A brief look at this catalogue makes the point exactly.

Decorating trophies

The problem of pub and hotel decor—first prize goes to three obsessive collectors, one of whom fills his hotels with Lord Nelson memorabilia.

Proprietors of hotels and restaurants all have different ideas as to what kind of decor will bring in customers—the proprietors of pubs for that matter have strong views too. As a theatrical friend of mine once said: 'You have to give the customers something to make them cross the road.' What most owners of eating and drinking establishments provide does just that for me—but in the opposite direction. Every once in a while you come across a proprietor who has succeeded in getting the decor of their premises exactly right.

The Old Mill, a pub at Dipley in Hampshire, was run by one of these. Not a grand public house with oak furniture and horse brasses, this was a one-room pub. The door from the road entered into that one room. It was a small room and the bar ran the length of one side of it. Behind the bar stood Mrs Crate; small like the room, she could scarcely be seen over the top of it. On the shelves behind stood her collection, a row of spongeware mugs, blue and white with tobacco stains shaped like trees in the glaze. Some of these mugs had been used in her pub a hundred years ago for drinking beer, while others had been collected as they were discarded by the other proprietors who changed to glass tankards. In the middle of this display was an old photograph of the yard behind the mill where, on Sundays, a game was played that involved throwing small cast-iron discs. There were several of these discs on the shelf, but the pride of Mrs Crate's collection were half-a-dozen extremely ancient bottles of Newcastle Brown

Ale, each bottle garlanded with plastic flowers. The whole display was never dusted. Sadly, Mrs Crate is now dead, her pub sold and her collection dispersed.

In London there was another such place, different, but a place that with its contents had the imprint of its owner's personality—the Cavendish Hotel. This was the old Cavendish Hotel that stood in Jermyn Street on the site where now a new hotel stands. I never met Rosa Lewis, who was the owner of that first Cavendish Hotel, but I did visit her premises after she died and before it was pulled down. Rosa Lewis made a speciality of providing what she loved to call 'nice clean young girls' for the English gentry or visiting Americans. She also made a penny or two by selling antiques to the rich Americans while they were either intoxicated by liquor or the charms of the 'nice clean young girls'. Maybe, she acquired these antiques from the English in lieu of cash for the services of the nice girls. In any event, her hotel was filled from basement to attic with antiques. I remember, as the hotel stood almost empty ready for the demolishers' hammers, there remained just one object, an object so large that no one knew how it had got there in the first place, and certainly none of the Americans who had bought and paid for this object had ever been able to arrange to have it removed. It was an archway, a large stone archway. The building was pulled down around it and at last this archway was free. The archway came originally from Dorchester House, the mansion that once stood where the Dorchester Hotel now stands. Why Rosa Lewis bought it remains a mystery. There must surely have been more manageable objects available to deal in. That she never paid for it remains a fact, but that was the nature of the woman.

By chance I was travelling in Sweden and I visited Stockholm. I found myself booked into a hotel with the unpromising name of Victory. I expected a clean and soulless hotel, the sort designed to cure tourists of the tiresome habit of wanting to travel—how wrong I was. The Victory is indeed part of a chain—a chain of hotels owned by Gunnar Bengtsson, a true collector in the mould of Mrs Crate and Mrs Lewis. His other two hotels are called The Lord Nelson and The Lady Hamilton. This man is obsessed with Nelson. He collects everything that has even the loosest association with that admiral, or is Mr Bengtsson just a collector and Nelson a vehicle he uses to satisfy that need? Mr Bengtsson sought out a very large collection of ship paintings of the late nineteenth and early twentieth centuries. Not content with this, he found photographs of the captains who commanded the ships. His three hotels are filled—literally—with collections: boxes, pipes, toys, Swedish furniture and anything nautical, from ships in bottles to bottles of wine that come from ships. Gunnar Bengtsson is still alive and still collecting. He recently bought Nelson's home, Trafalgar House, in Wiltshire. Many other proprietors try to furnish their hotels with antiques but few know how to succeed because the hotels only pretend to have antiques—as so many antiques only pretend to be antiques.

Artist turns the tables

Artists used to pay their restaurant bills with paintings. At the Pharmacy, Damien Hirst's latest attack on good taste, the restaurant pays the artist.

In my childhood I often visited the Colombe d'Or at Saint Paul de Vence. In those days it was a simple restaurant, the walls of which were hung with the paintings of Picasso, Chagall, Matisse and Braque. At that time they were pictures of no great value. Today they are considered masterpieces, and most of them are long gone. As a small boy I watched Picasso and Matisse eat their lunch, which, I was told, they paid for with the paintings that hung around the restaurant. Today, the tables are turned. Instead of swapping pictures for food, young artists are becoming proprietors, or at least shareholders, in restaurants.

So, along with almost every other contributor to a magazine of quality, I made my way to the Pharmacy, the latest example of this phenomenon.

The restaurant is part-owned and decorated by one of the bad boys of art, Damien Hirst. Hirst has a penchant for suspending dead animals in formaldehyde, often slicing them in half with such precision that in any other age he would have been a butcher. For some years the public greeted his activities with horror. Had they been to the museum at St Bartholomew's Hospital, however, they would have discovered that it is stuffed full of Damien Hirsts.

No matter, the butterfly paintings littering the Pharmacy are gentle things, despite the way Hirst made them. Butterflies are released into a confined space and in time they land on freshly painted canvases. Dying, they leave yet another Hirst masterpiece. Thank goodness there are only dead butterflies in this place. Lunch beside a dead sheep might put one off the braised lamb.

It would be wrong to suggest in any way that the Pharmacy is just a PR trick. Despite deceiving the public into thinking that it is a chemist's shop, it really is a restaurant and the customers flock there in droves. Fascinating people, these customers, notable for their immensely boring clothes and faces. I had, knowing of Hirst's reputation as a wild man, expected to find the place populated with young men and women with Mohican haircuts performing the delicate trick of eating steak with rings through their tongues. Not a bit of it: ties are the norm for men; the women are fashionably dressed in Donna Karan and Jil Sander. They are mostly in their early thirties, and they tuck into their floating islands with gusto, their appetites quite unimpaired by the terrible death of the butterflies that surround them.

My lunch went reasonably well, despite the fact that the blessed youths around me had eaten all the floating islands and I had to make do with a banana, chopped and wrapped in a pancake. If I were a food critic, I might write that the whole confection was tepid, the sort of stodge you need when you have drunk too much. The menu I might describe as California meets Cool Britannia, only the tastes of both have been lost somewhere mid-Atlantic.

The moment of horror for me, however, was when I went to the lavatory. Its urinal—a trough owing more to a pigsty than a hospital—is decorated with a collage of surgical rubbish, perhaps from the waste bin of an operating theatre. I am allergic to doctors; show me a syringe and I pass out. The place smelt like an operating theatre, too, though whether this was intentional or merely owing to the fact that both places use the same disinfectant, I do not know. Back at my table, I sat subdued and studied the drug-label wallpaper. If it gives you a migraine, fear not: the cure is surely in there somewhere.

The restaurant is dominated by Hirst's work. It reminds me of the barn where Kurt Schwitters, another artist who shocked his contemporaries, decorated the walls before starving to death, still determined to paint pictures nobody wanted. He is long dead, and his work now sells at high prices. Perhaps he should have opened a restaurant?

Art à la carte

Pictures that hang on restaurant walls can whet or dampen an appetite—the scene in 1991.

There is hardly a restaurant or hotel in the world that does not have a picture or two in it, and the habit of placing paintings in commercial buildings has been growing for the last 25 years. The great skyscrapers of the world's capital cities have sculpture in profusion (often very good sculpture), and their foyers have large paintings by contemporary artists; these are large because their foyers are large. Indeed, that is the way artists have preferred to paint in the last three decades—producing pictures far too big for most domestic premises. The bulk of these paintings and sculptures are of good quality. You even find the works of masters of the twentieth century—Rothko, Henry Moore and Calder.

Hotels are a disaster area for works of art—in London at least—from the merely bad, at the Hilton and the Royal Garden Hotels, to the totally disastrous at the Connaught. Who chooses these paintings is a matter of some fascination to me. I would love to meet that person if only to ask why such awful works are hung there. The Dorchester, The Ritz and Claridges make do with gold paint—there is no real attempt to introduce works of art. Have these proprietors no eye for art? I suppose the question answers itself when one visits their hotels, and the answer is a resounding NO.

Mark Birley, on the other hand, the proprietor of three of London's best restaurants, has an extremely good eye for paintings. But then he should, being the son of a considerable portrait painter. Annabel's has an interesting selection of pictures ranging from Matthew Smith to Munnings. Mark's Club has a collection of Victorian paintings, and Harry's Bar a selection of posters and an enormous collection of original cartoons by Peterano. The taste in all these places is extremely personal—and extremely good. But if you wish to eat *and* look at pictures, the only place to eat is the Garrick Club, which has the world's largest collection of theatrical paintings. Several of these are by Zoffany; some are good and all of them interesting. As for the food—well, the members of the Garrick Club go there for the conviviality of their fellow members and their guests; looking at the pictures takes your mind off the food.

The National Gallery and the Tate Gallery are both places where you can eat and look at paintings. Both galleries are stuffed full of masterpieces, but their restaurants are another thing. The Tate Gallery has a mural by Rex Whistler. The National Gallery in its fine new extension has a large mural by Paula Rego; this is not the sort of work of art that sticks in your mind—far better to miss lunch and spend the time walking round their galleries looking at the paintings and sculptures. In the Tate Gallery there is one room of paintings that were once destined to be hung in a restaurant; the paintings are by Rothko, and they were painted for New York's Four Seasons restaurant. Why they were not hung there is obvious when you stand with them in the Tate—their quiet beauty is overpowering. Painted towards the end of Rothko's life, they have a deep sadness about them. Objects of the greatest quality, they are not at all the sort of works that would go well with the clatter of cutlery and the clink of bottles, let alone the idle chatter of fashionable New York as it consumes its food. These are silent and reflective pictures suited to where they are hung. Why anyone has to eat in a museum at all is a mystery to me. It would be far better to get rid of all these restaurants in our public galleries—to give up catering and show more pictures, which after all, is what they are there for.

There has always lurked in the minds of those who would open restaurants an idea that hanging pictures will attract clients who believe that they will be able to watch the artists whose work hangs there eat. This occasionally works. The Neal Street Restaurant has the work of Hockney and Richard Smith—but then they had the good fortune to have Kasmin, the remarkable West End art dealer, as a shareholder. They are currently hanging a large painting of a mushroom by Sidney Nolan, which is there, I think, because Antonio Carluccio likes Nolan's work, and both he and Nolan like mushrooms. The Ivy Restaurant has work by Howard Hodgkin and Allen Jones—and the artists themselves can be seen there.

These restaurants and their paintings are all very well in their way, but they cannot compete with the Colombe d'Or in Saint Paul de Vence—a restaurant that collected art 40 years ago. Whether or not the likes of Picasso paid for their food with paintings I do not know, but I can remember in the early 1950s sitting on the terrace of that restaurant and looking down over the then beautiful valley—at terraces of olive trees and the occasional row of vines. White doves sat in the lemon trees, and I watched as Chagall and Picasso sat with their friends and ate their lunch—in those days lamb or chicken cooked on a spit and served with salad. The paintings still hang in the Colombe d'Or—Picasso and Chagall are gone. Now the valley is crammed with holiday homes, the pictures are worth very much more and the food is much worse.

Nunc est bibendum

A masterpiece of the winemaker's art is as worthy an object of praise and enjoyment as any painting or sculpture.

Sotheby's recently gave a dinner party for many of the leading wine writers. The meal was extraordinary, and so it should have been, for it was cooked by Michel Roux of le Gavroche. The wine defied belief. Let me record the list: champagne Krug 1982 followed by Haut Brion 1961 en magnum; Margaux 1953 en magnum; Latour 1952 en jeroboam (I asked the excellent gentleman from Château Latour why he chose this vintage, and he replied that Château Latour was most famous not just for great wines in great years, but for making good wines in bad years); Mouton Rothschild 1949 en magnum; and Lafite Rothschild 1945 en jeroboam. All this finished off with Yquem 1970. Some of them may see the like again, but I doubt that I ever will.

In the midst of all this—the dinner was held in Sotheby's main saleroom in Bond Street—stood the sculpture of the *Dancing Faun* by Adriaen de Vries, unsold at that time but known to be of great value. Some weeks later it fetched £6.8 million, or about the price of a good-sized Jasper Johns. This comparison between the Renaissance and the twentieth century seems to me to demonstrate what a bargain it was. In any event, the old couple from Surrey in whose garden it had stood for 30 years cannot have been displeased with the price—nor indeed the Chancellor of the Exchequer, who no doubt will have his cut. The King of Sweden, Carl Gustav, owner of 31 bronzes by de Vries, should be pretty pleased too. They decorate the garden of his palace at Drottningholm.

The old couple's windfall reminds me of a story which, I am told, emanates from the luncheon room at Malletts and was told by Frances Egerton, which means it must be true. In any event, a titled family sent three pictures to the auction rooms and they were sold one Thursday in the early 1970s—lots 161, 162 and 163. The estimates were £10 000 for the three lots, split equally. The next day the wife rang the saleroom and was given the results.

'Lot 161,' said the girl in Sotheby's, '£150 000.' There was a crash followed by silence, 'Hello; hello,' said the girl.

Then a strange voice at the other end said, 'Hello.'

'Who are you?' said the girl.

'I am Lord Whatever,' said the voice.

'But I was speaking to your wife.'

'I know,' said Lord Whatever, 'but she has just passed out. Can you give me the figures?'

'Lot 161,' said the girl, '£150 000' and then blurted out, 'Lot 162, £300 000.' There was a louder crash at the other end of the line.

'Hello; hello,' said the girl.

'Hello; hello,' a strange voice replied.

'Who are you?' asked the girl.

'I am the gardener. Her Ladyship passed out and now I am afraid his Lordship has passed out as well.'

'Do you want the results of the sale?' said the girl.

'No, I think I had better call the doctor instead,' replied the gardener.

This just shows there is no such thing as an absolute value, a point wine illustrates as well as anything else. Christie's also recently asked me to drink some of its fine vintages, and since I was in a wine mood I waxed lyrical about the merits of wine. I remarked that I had seen a bottle of Cheval Blanc 1949, a superb wine, for £600. The lady on my left attacked my enthusiasm for this bargain: 'What extravagance.'

'But,' say I, 'we have just seen a beautiful Cézanne due to fetch £10 million. If you were to buy that painting it would cost you about £5000 a day in interest; you could buy a lot of wine for that.'

'Rubbish,' she replied, 'you drink your wine and it's gone. I still have my Cézanne.' Rather weakly, I suggested she must have worked out a way to take it with her when she had gone.

But the truth of the matter is that there are many types of collecting, and two are the collecting of the tangible and the intangible. Each, I suppose, is legitimate; each is for quite a different sort of person. Of course, there are collectors who understand neither one nor the other.

Blooming good riddance

Farewell haughty-culture. Let us rejoice that the tyrannous 1980s fad for 'clever' flower decoration is at an end, replaced now by simple arrangements of flowers—and cacti.

Right through the 1970s and 1980s flower arranging grew in extravagance, finally reaching a peak with the creation of trees out of seashells, great arrangements of fruits, coloured mosses made into swags and bows, and montages that covered the walls made of disused garden implements. These implements had been heaped in a shed and were of no account until taken out and carefully arranged in London apartments—a sort of dubious salute to a rustic world long gone and now inhabited by electric hedge trimmers and the like. Now—the beginning of the 1990s—is the time for a change.

Flower arranging had, people believed in those booming years of the 1980s, an honest, simple beauty. They talked of the integrity of the materials: nothing handmade, or, if made by hand, it was formed out of clay or wood. The fashion was for bunches of flowers, but only one sort of flower, and preferably a simple country flower tied with raffia, pushed into a crude pot or industrial glass vessel as though no thought had gone into this casual arrangement, when the truth was that an immense amount of thought *had* gone into it. They used five times too many flowers in a vase bought at five times the right price. These were rich years and flowers were one of their more attractive aspects. Old wooden seed trays, the rougher the better, were planted with rows of the most elegant of tulips ready to flower simultaneously. Those years of plenty created, in flower arranging, a sort of fake poverty.

A change has come. The bills of florists who thrived during that prosperous period are now being carefully checked. It is time for a new style in floral decoration: no more clever arrangements of mosses. No more clay pots wrapped in raw linen. No more acid jars filled with great bouquets. Economy is the word these days, and flowers will be chosen with care. No florist will be allowed to pass on blooms at the end of their careers. Today's customer for flowers wants them firmly in bud. Now it is one branch of lilies that is put in a vase, along with the leaves of *Magnolia grandiflora* or some other long-lasting evergreen, and very likely the stalk of lilies will only be changed when the last flower has dropped.

Today the vases need to be different. Flowerpots are back in the garden, seed boxes have become tinder, and don't bother with raffia. Attics have been raided and the vases that some great-aunt brought back from Murano in Italy, the ones that once seemed so awful, have been brought out. If they are not good enough for Sotheby's or Christie's, then they are just right for flower arrangements: for the small vases, posies made up of all sorts of odds and ends, and as one odd or end dies it is replaced with another; for large vases use foliage—long-lasting foliage.

Thought is being given to the flowers themselves now the extravagance of the past is, for the moment, gone. Because flowers are being used singly or in small bunches, there is a need for stronger, brighter, harder colours. Gerberas, for many years a sort of joke flower (their petals were used on hats)—flowers that really look like flowers—these are the flowers for today. Roses should not be the delicate pastel shades of the old-fashioned rose, but the hard, vibrant colours and Mr McGready's roses of the 1950s.

More care has to be taken with the choice of these flowers. The sloppiness of the old-fashioned rose, where you could pick a basketful and no single colour clashed with any other, those days are gone. The roses of the 1950s need careful thought: a few to a vase and plenty of foliage. In recession people turn to plants that really last, not gardenias and orchids that need expensive hot houses, but cacti. These exotic plants come in thousands of varieties. The large ones form horticultural sculptures in a room; they withstand the central heating and benefit from a forgetful attendant. If you tire of them, shuffle them around the house. Bonsai look wonderful as well, but they are plants for the enthusiast. When you become hooked on tinkering with your collection of bonsai, holidays are lost. Leave these valuable little trees in the hands of someone else? Never! Arrangements of flowers? Not in the house of a bonsai lover—there is never any room.

Houses are changing to suit their owner's way of life. The last two years have been years of change and disturbance, from Berlin to Abu Dhabi. These are years of reassessment: the year to clear out rubbish, jettison the unwanted and decide what you really need. That piece of junk bought for so much in Chelsea at the end of 1989 looks just like a piece of junk. Take it to the saleroom and find that it is worth about as much as it looks. Houses will be clearer, decor harder and sparser, and the arranging of flowers will follow that pattern.

To boldly grow

I trek to Chelsea for the annual flower show and, despite finding the event much changed, conclude it's still the only place to be for horticultural enterprise.

Chelsea Flower Show may have a fine new wrapping, but its contents are still remarkably familiar. Inside the New Tent, which is ten times more elegant and a good deal more convenient than its predecessor, is found the palette that gardeners use to express their art—or lack of it, as the case may be. There are banks of lilies, peonies, irises, tulips, old-fashioned roses and shaped box—all wonderful to behold, but much the same as last year or, indeed, many years past.

Later, reflecting on the gardens from the security of one of London's finer shopping streets with not a plant in sight, the conclusion I came to is that Chelsea is the poorer for the passing of McGready and his roses, with those wonderful side whiskers and vulgar colours. Today it's all too delicate: too much clipped box and elegant topiary. In a way, however, the growers of orchids have taken over from the propagator of vulgar roses—blooms that once filled a coffee cup now overflow a soup plate. These orchid growers are definitely the odd ones out at the smarter, more elegant, tasteful Chelsea Flower Show.

Outside, a row or two of gardens the size of a dozen bedsheets show just what can be done with the blooms inside the tent. Sadly, the demonstrations that the garden designers give of this do not amount to a row of beans on an urban allotment beside the Great Western Railway track; the tribute to Le Nôtre must have made the poor fellow vomit in his grave. A more prissy, trite, over-stuffed offering would be hard to imagine. When a designer needs to introduce a large mirror to a knot garden, it's time to take up the ideas of Palladio and let fields rush to the walls of buildings. And that is what Her Majesty's Prison Service has done with its splendid wild garden—a serious garden with a wistful look of freedom, held captive in the metal, plastic, plaster and terracotta of Chelsea Flower Show. A place to lay on your back in the sun and to suck on a stalk of grass—not at all the place to think of jokes about thyme and borage.

But Chelsea is not really about gardens; it is a phenomenon of 'The English Summer'. It heralds the season where those of suburban

England who have never shown any interest in design or cooking are suddenly gripped with the idea that they can cook on a barbecue and design gardens. They tour the show armed with plant lists and catalogues looking for all the world like veteran gardeners. Then, for a month or two, they will brave wind, sleet and rain as they mow, plant and burn meat on barbecues.

In the end Chelsea Flower Show gets to us all. I loved the painted terracottas on Jane Hogben's stand. There I saw life-size terracotta gardeners looking as gardeners are meant to look: strong, reliable and intelligent. I bought a pair for my new garden in Italy. Chelsea Flower Show is, however, not just an entertainment; it is there to sell the stuff and produce of its industry, and this it does wonderfully.

Buy laws

The collector's desire to buy can be so overwhelming, that all sense of whether the purchase is good, very good or indifferent is lost.

For a collector there is nothing more exciting than hearing of a dealer who has a shop in a distant place—a dealer whose stock is reported as interesting and might contain some great treasure. Well, perhaps not quite a treasure but definitely an object or two worth collecting. The journey to the town where this dealer, known only to a select few, resides is filled with expectation, and almost inevitably the dealer's shop is closed when you arrive. A notice will say 'back in five minutes' or 'gone to lunch'. It really matters very little for the minutes pass like hours. The collector peers through the dealer's dirty window at dusty stock, and then paces the pavement imagining masterpieces. He holds his hand to the plate glass better to see the contents of the shop and believes he spies a masterpiece or half a masterpiece (the rest being hidden by an old curtain) lurking at the back of the shop.

The tension becomes unbearable and then the proprietor arrives. He fumbles in his pockets for his keys and, finding them, takes an interminable time turning the keys in innumerable locks. The collector is into the shop like a rabbit into its burrow and what does he find? Very little. The collector searches and searches, but nothing strikes the eye. The place is filled with banal rubbish. There is no object of imagination to be found there. Still the collector searches, for although the lack of quality of this dealer's stock is obvious to anyone with an eye in his head, the collector who has travelled a long way is blind to this fact. Now in every shop, regardless of how bad the proprietor's stock may be, there is always something that is better than the rest. On this something the collector's eyes alight. By comparison with the rest, this object seems like a masterpiece and the collector, not wanting to come so far to no purpose, buys the object.

I have a friend, Ralph Parr, a dealer in guns, who found himself in just this situation. My friend is no amateur, but a serious expert, practised in all the wiles of the antique arms and armour trade. A man with an iron will and certain eye, he still fell victim to the collector's urge to acquire. He travelled far and finding nothing bought a flintlock pistol. On his return home the purchase preyed on his mind. Was it a fake or merely a poor example of its genre? After driving for two hours, he stopped his car and tossed the pistol over a hedge. He had come to the decision that he didn't want to have such an object in his stock. He didn't care whether it was fake or just second rate.

Many readers will believe that they are immune to the dangers I have described. I recommend a small test for them. This is not a visit to a shop with awful stock, but rather a visit to a tomb which is the work of many masters and took 500 years to complete. Among the tomb's carvings are three by Michelangelo. It is far from simple to spot them among the work of Niccolo dell'Arca, Girolamo Goltellini, Jacopo Roseto, Giovanni Battista Boudarol, Alfonso Lombardi, Nicola Pisano, Capo Arnolfo di Cambio and Fra Guglielmo de Pisa. The tomb of St Dominic is housed in a stunning baroque chapel whose walls are lined with niches containing sculptures of the virtues by Giovanni Battista Tedeschi. The chapel is in the Basilica Santuario di San Domenico in Bologna.

As if this puzzle was not enough to test even an expert on Italian art, across the aisle is the Cappella del Rosario, around whose altar are fifteen panels, five telling the story of the Misteri dell Gioia, five the Misteri del Dolore and five more the Misteri della Gloria. These panels are by a number of artists: Ludovico Carracci, Bartolomeo Cesi, Dionigi Calvaert and Guido Reni. All seem to be of similar quality and—I suppose because they are the same size and hard to see—appear to be by one hand. There is a further puzzle. Which of the two organs high on either side of the chapel is the one on which

Mozart played when he studied in Bologna and which is just an imitation? I certainly couldn't tell and I have never found out.

Changing of the avant-garde

Over recent decades opinions of avant-garde have swung from revulsion to admiration. I suspect my views have gone the other way as I view the Apocalypse *show in search of revelation.*

In the early 1960s I collected paintings and sculptures, and collected them with a wild enthusiasm. The quantities in which I bought them were almost on a scale equal to the famous collectors of today's avant-garde artists. The difference, of course, lay in the fact that today avant-garde art is the fashion—in 1960 it was reviled. A stuffed fish by Damian Hirst would today arouse admiration in a visitor to the home where it is housed. In the early 1960s a painting that I owned by Allen Jones—a lady stepping onto a set of plastic steps while wearing a tight rubber jumpsuit—was regarded as pornographic rubbish by my guests. Not only regarded as pornographic rubbish, but described as such at my lunch table. An important sculpture by Philip King was jokingly called a tube of toothpaste by a guest who neither understood the nature of sculpture nor that of humour. Rothko's paintings (I had seven of them) were dismissed as daubs; and the far from avant-garde Alfred Wallis, a Cornish primitive of whose work I had over 200 examples, was treated as a complete joke. Twentieth-century artists were all con tricksters and I the owner of a thousand or so con tricks. The work of Bill Turnbull, the most mild mannered of painters and a brilliant, innovative artist, was treated to a terrible anger. Works by Turnbull that I sent to the Tate Gallery were defaced by visitors to the exhibition.

The mood among wealthy educated people was one of intense dislike for contemporary painting, even Matisse. I owned several of his sculptures and two decoupages were beyond the pale. Picasso was and always had been a suspect figure. Alfred Munnings, President of the Royal Academy, on hearing that Picasso was coming to London, announced at an Academy dinner: 'If Picasso sets foot in England I shall kick his bottom.' When told of this, Picasso asked, 'Who's this Munnings?', a question that few outside of the hunting and shooting fraternity of England could answer.

Then it all changed. The Royal Academy decided to get with it. The Saatchi Collection was shown to encourage collectors of contemporary art. In truth, however, they needed little encouraging, for the social imperative was at work. Art and artists had clambered up the social stepladder—those who spurned my collection were now collecting like mad. No work is too grotesque, too large or too awful to fill houses and gardens—each work is a feather in a social cap. Judgement is no longer among the criteria for choice. Fame is the name of the game. These socialites collect with all the fervour of the newly converted. The end of the nineteenth century is with us again—the battle of the acceptance of contemporary art is over, and the consequences of the victory awful. For me the joy has gone out of collecting the young painters and sculptors. There is no battle to be fought; it's all so obvious these days. Leave the door of your cleaning cupboard open and a guest will admire your Tracey Emin. From passionate collector of the avant-garde to dedicated reactionary in 40 years is the story of my counter-cyclical life, and I don't care for any of it.

With these thoughts in mind I visited the latest offering of the Royal Academy, open-minded and determined to be proved wrong in my reactionary views on the work of today's heroes and heroines. There was a queue to enter the exhibition—this must be good. It takes a little time to climb through a trapdoor into a cellar, hence a queue. This cellar was just like those that infested Chelsea in the early 1960s, one that was endemic in London's East End at that date—what a clever thought, a cellar. Exhausted by the scramble into this work of art that blocks the exhibition entrance, I pondered on it. In truth it was very like an old cellar, but the smell was wrong—a smell only of people, not at all the smell of a cellar.

On to the next room—truly wonderful. Forget the unfortunate figure of the Pope bowled over by a boulder and ignore the heap of broken glass. Look at the beauty of this newly painted room, usually cluttered with works of art, seldom seen before in its near-naked state: its scale, its shape, the gilt tracery and the complex cornices. The place is brilliant. Then on to turgid exhibit after exhibit. Take a rest in the realistic bus shelter—a disappointment; the bus never comes. One after another of these imaginary masterpieces, and then the Academy's bookshop, what a relief. And these great new works, what of them? Vacuous, totally vacuous.

Conclusion

Once again I have disposed of 'a collection' or rather the stock of my antique shop. The market at the moment is not favourable for dealing in antiques and I intended to reduce the scale of my operations to suit that market. With a few exceptions, all my stock sold and to my great delight Sotheby's had over 450 clients bid in the sale. I am pleased that old bones and curious stones appeal to people other than myself. Had no one cared for natural curiosities it would not have stopped me from buying them in the first place, for I have never been a collector who followed fashions or, for that matter, a collector who made fashion. I have bought works of art—both natural and handmade—that appealed to me. I have bought objects for no better reason than that I thought their shape to be beautiful, or paintings for their colour and composition.

I have taken as much pleasure from watching the sun go down over the northern coast of Western Australia, where it seemed for a moment or two that all the world was on fire, as I have from the painting by George Stubbs of the Baron de Roebuck on his rearing horse with his galloping dog at his side. I have woken and, in the early morning light, looked at that painting, which once hung on the wall opposite the bottom of my bed, seeing not the work of Stubbs but the influence of Giorgione.

Apart from the convenience of having a particular work in my house, I care not one jot for ownership. I am a nomad, both in my taste and in my habit, drawing what I will from a painting or a place and then moving on. Never feeling the distress of departure, only the excitement of arrival: not restless but blessed, or cursed, with incurable curiosity.